MECHANICS-
MERCANTILE
LIBRARY.

Arthur F. Mathews '06

# SELLING THE DREAM

# SELLING
# THE DREAM

## Why Advertising Is Good Business

JOHN HOOD

Westport, Connecticut
London

**Library of Congress Cataloging-in-Publication Data**

Hood, John M. (John McDonald), 1966–
    Selling the dream : why advertising is good business / John Hood.
        p.   cm.
    Includes bibliographical references and index.
    ISBN 0–275–98435–4 (alk. paper)
    1. Advertising—Social aspects.   I. Title.
    HF5821.H637 2005
    659.1'042—dc22          2005018656

British Library Cataloguing in Publication Data is available.

Library of Congress Catalog Card Number: 2005018656
ISBN: 0–275–98435–4

First published in 2005

Praeger Publishers, 88 Post Road West, Westport, CT 06881
An imprint of Greenwood Publishing Group, Inc.
www.praeger.com

Printed in the United States of America

The paper used in this book complies with the
Permanent Paper Standard issued by the National
Information Standards Organization (Z39.48–1984).

10  9  8  7  6  5  4  3  2  1

To the Little Conqueror (Charles Alexander Hood) and the Little General (Andrew Jackson Hood), whose salesmanship and entrepreneurial instincts may prove exceedingly valuable in a future advertising career—even though they rarely succeed in delaying their bedtimes.

# Contents

# Preface

Writing a book, any book, is a major investment of time. Writing a book about a subject outside the scope of one's daily work—while seeking to perform that daily work effectively—is a great challenge, to say the least. That I was able to complete *Selling the Dream* is a testament to the valuable assistance of many people, including coworkers, colleagues, friends, and family members, who helped me juggle my various roles and projects during 2004 and early 2005.

*Selling the Dream* was based on an idea I had many years ago, after the publication of my first book, *The Heroic Enterprise: Business and the Common Good*. Having just studied and written on the subject of corporate social responsibility, I realized that while some business activities were poorly understood, and in some cases demonized, by academia, the news media, and the general public, the bum-rap award clearly belonged to sales. Creative tasks such as invention and innovation are exciting. Financial wizardry is impressive, sometimes mind-boggling. Managerial or organizational talent is instructive. But what about the marketing process is worth celebration? Isn't it all about form over function, about artifice instead of authenticity, about the pitch rather than the product?

I do not think so, as you will soon discover.

Some of the research I did for *The Heroic Enterprise* and a subsequent book (*Investor Politics*) about the intersection of personal investing and political economy turned out to be useful in laying the groundwork for my argument in this present volume. But for the most part, I needed to "go back to school" to refresh my memory and fill in the blanks on a host of related issues. A partial listing would include the ancient and medieval history of journalism and advertising, retailing innovations in the nineteenth and twentieth centuries, the birth of independent newspapers, prominent schools of criticism of advertising, the economics of information, the evolution of the current marketing mix, what theologians and ethicists have to say about the commercial culture, and specific issues of application such as health claims in advertising, marketing to children, tobacco and alcohol advertising, and the role of sexual imagery in modern marketing.

This took time. I would like to thank my board of directors and colleagues at the John Locke Foundation, a public policy think tank in Raleigh, North Carolina, for allowing me the opportunity to pursue this research and offering many useful observations and suggestions. Conversations with longtime friends such as Virginia Postrel, Jeff Taylor, Roy Cordato, Karen Palasek, and Steve Margolis helped to clarify some key points and sent me off in directions I would not otherwise have contemplated, directions that turned out to be critical in defining and advancing my thesis.

My deepest gratitude extends to the John Templeton Foundation for its instrumental role in providing financial assistance for the project, and to Jim Dunton and Nick Philipson at Praeger Publishers for their interest in the final product. Most importantly, thanks to my family for putting up with my lengthy weekend absences from home. Getting them to go along with that was certainly the most successful sales job of my life.

# Introduction

In the 1990 Paramount film *Crazy People*, Dudley Moore and Paul Reiser play two advertising executives. Moore's character is disenchanted and stressed out about his role in the business. He comes up with a new campaign for their Volvo account using this slogan: "Buy Volvos. They're boxy, but they're good." Reiser's thoroughly cynical character responds with profane disbelief, which prompts Moore to explain himself:

> **Moore:** Hey, I thought this would appeal to a no-nonsense type consumer.
>
> **Reiser:** Who the hell ever heard of advertising that a car is boxy?
>
> **Moore:** But they *are* boxy. An intelligent buyer knows that. Hey, let's not fool the public anymore. Let's not lie. Let's level with America!
>
> **Reiser:** We can't level, you crazy bastard. We're in advertising!

Thinking Moore to be literally out of his mind, Reiser has him committed to a mental institution. But then the campaign becomes wildly popular, so Moore is asked back—only he refuses to leave the institution. He then gets help from his mentally ill friends to come

up with other blunt slogans, only some barely suitable for family audiences:

> "United, most of our passengers get there alive."
> "Come to New York, it's not as dirty as you think."
> "You may think phone service stinks since deregulation, but don't
> mess with us, because we're all you've got. In fact, if we fold, you'll
> have no damn phones. AT&T—we're tired of taking your crap!"
> "Metamucil. It helps you go to the toilet. If you don't use it, you
> get cancer and die."[1]

It might seem as though the blatant message of the movie (which
degenerates into a star-crossed love story about halfway through) is
that you would have to be crazy to be an honest practitioner of advertising. But that is not the only way to read it. Since the bluntly
worded advertisements are actually *successful*—they appeal to jaded
consumers and result in more sales—a different conclusion might be
that you would have to be crazy *not* to use stark honesty in advertising. Indeed, some of the fake slogans in *Crazy People* became real advertising to the extent that the funnier ones got attached to their
real-world brands and have continued to be repeated and cited by
movie fans, consumers, and even textbooks and advertising professionals as examples of clever marketing practices.[2] Vincent Canby, reviewing the film unfavorably in the *New York Times*, caught on to the
underlying trick but did not like it very much. He called the movie "a
feature-film equivalent to those commercials that pretend to be sending themselves up" and observed that the make-believe slogans
"knowingly celebrate the system they are supposed to be satirizing."[3]
Indeed, the director of the film, Tony Bill, was himself a director of
television commercials and called advertising "a much easier, better
and more human way of making money" than his original career as a
Hollywood actor.[4] So portraying *Crazy People* as a full-throated screed
against advertising, as many contemporaneous observers and review-
ers did, was mistaken and simplistic—two adjectives that apply with
great frequency to discussions of advertising and its economic, social,
and ethical dimensions.

# THE MULTIFACETED IMAGE OF ADVERTISING

Americans have always been opinionated about advertising. That stands to reason, as Americans have had a long and intimate relationship with the practice and cannot fail to have drawn some pointed conclusions about it. It is not overreaching to call America the birthplace of much of what we think of as modern advertising, marketing, and commercial culture, including such basic innovations as the advertising agency, the advertiser-sustained news media, the catalog, the chain store, advertorials, commercial broadcasting, multilevel marketing, public relations, and product placement. On the other hand, many of these practices have analogues or antecedents in the distant past. Commerce comes naturally to human beings, as does salesmanship.

While American opinions about advertising have often been strong, they have also been mixed. You can find some of the most florid, over-the-top condemnation *and* praise of advertising from American writers, scholars, political activists, theologians, and advertising professionals.[5] Sinclair Lewis, whose novel *Babbitt* served as a sort of summary and rallying point for the anticommercialism invective of the 1920s, wrote that "advertising is a valuable factor because it is the cheapest way of selling goods, particularly if the goods are worthless." Another novelist of the day, F. Scott Fitzgerald, called advertising "a racket" and contended that one "cannot be honest without admitting that its constructive contribution to humanity is exactly minus zero." Voicing a common view of advertising as wasteful, the humorist Will Rogers snorted that if advertisers spent "the same amount of money improving their product that they do on advertising," then "they wouldn't have to advertise it." In public life, former Secretary of State Dean Acheson once complained that "time spent in the advertising business seems to create a permanent deformity, like the Chinese habit of foot-binding." And modern-day media critic Marshall McLuhan contended that "advertising is an environmental striptease for a world of abundance."

On the other hand, the adman and evangelical Bruce Barton wrote *The Man Nobody Knows* in 1925 to offer explicit comparisons between business marketing and the life of Jesus Christ, who was "a great advertiser in his own day," according to Barton. "As a profession advertising is young; as a force it is as old as the world," he wrote. "The first four words ever uttered, 'Let there be light,' constitute its charter. All nature is vibrant with its impulse." Barton, who was later elected to the U.S. Congress, also offered this celebratory insight: "Advertising is of the very essence of democracy. An election goes on every minute of the business day across the counters of hundreds of thousands of stores and shops where the customers state their preferences and determine which manufacturer and which product shall be the leader today, and which shall lead tomorrow."[6]

One of the most successful practitioners of the political form of American democracy, President Franklin D. Roosevelt, was ebullient in his high regard for advertising. "If I were starting life over again, I am inclined to think that I would go into the advertising business in preference to almost any other," Roosevelt said, adding that the "general raising of the standards of modern civilization among all groups of people during the past half century would have been impossible without the spreading of the knowledge of higher standards by means of advertising." One of Roosevelt's Republican predecessors, Calvin Coolidge, was no less effusive in his praise. "Advertising ministers to the spiritual side of trade," he told a gathering of executives. "It is great power that has been entrusted to your keeping which charges you with the high responsibility of inspiring and ennobling the commercial world. It is all part of the greater work of the regeneration and redemption of mankind."[7]

Popular depictions of advertising, public relations, and related professions in stories, books, movies, and elsewhere also reveal tensions and conflicts. For example, some movies about the industry have indeed contained bitter attacks, such as *The Hucksters* (1947), *The Man in the Gray Flannel Suit* (1956), and the British film *How to Get Ahead in Advertising* (1989). But others, such as *Will Success Spoil Rock Hunter?* (1957) and *The Out-of-Towners* (the 1970 original starred Jack Lemmon, and the 1999 remake Steve Martin), have taken a more lighthearted, comical approach to the subject and portrayed ad professionals as more naïve rather than villainous, as manipulated instead of manipulator. In fact, while advertising came in for some clever satire in *Will Success Spoil Rock Hunter?* with the protagonist (Rockwell

Hunter, played by Tony Randall) deciding by the end to leave the profession in favor of rural chicken farming, 20th Century Fox chose to imbed advertising for other Fox films within the movie. Again, as was with case with *Crazy People*, boiling down the film's theme to a straightforward attack on the advertising industry proves surprisingly difficult.[8]

One way to illustrate the varying popular takes on the industry is to compare the Cary Grant–Myrna Loy film *Mr. Blandings Builds His Dream House* (1948) to the characters and events portrayed by novelist Eric Hodgins in *Mr. Blandings Builds His Dream House* (1946) and *Blandings' Way* (1950). In the film, Cary Grant plays Mr. Blandings as a New Yorker lost in the country, as an advertising pro who turns out to be an easy mark for a series of rural operators as he builds a home in Connecticut. The main plot point associated with advertising is Blandings's inability to come up with a good, catchy slogan for Wham hams, an inability resolved happily by the end of the film. But in the books, Blandings undergoes much more of a personal crisis of confidence in his chosen profession, leaving it for a time and later returning to it—and to life in New York City—with misgivings.

While portrayals of advertising in modern American fiction have differed in many particulars, their characterization of advertising professionals has often been strikingly similar. One analysis of mid-twentieth-century novels described the typical character of the adman as "false in tone, tense in pace, vacant and self-hating, overheated and oversexed."[9] You can see versions of this character in film as well, such as in the 2000 movie *What Women Want*, in which advertising executive Mel Gibson gains the power to read women's minds and eventually comes to realize the error of his previously chauvinistic and unscrupulous ways. Sometimes, by the end of the story, the adman character (it is almost always a male) changes his behavior, as Gibson does, or his profession, as Randall does. Sometimes he does not. But he nearly always comes to the point of admitting the essential vacuity and amorality of the enterprise, as the main character Victor Norman does in *The Hucksters*: "We're all a bunch of hustlers and connivers in this business. . . . We don't steal, probably because it's bad for business, but we sure as hell do everything else for clients."[10]

# WHY ANSWER THE ADVERTISING QUESTION?

If the question were why advertising so often gets satirized or skewed in popular works of fiction—though often, as I have argued, with nuance and context—then devoting an entire book to answering it would be overkill. But the question, or really set of questions, that I address in this volume will prove to be far broader and more important than that. The image of advertising we see in modern fiction is but a reflection of a much more extensive critique, to be found over hundreds of years within the pages of both fiction and nonfiction books, in the law codes of governments ancient and modern, underneath much of the history of business and economic development, and among advocates and critics of capitalism itself. Debates about the economics, aesthetics, and ethics of advertising and other forms of commercial culture matter because they involve fundamental social issues. Do people buy more than they need, or what is truly good for them? What is the difference between good salesmanship and fraud? Do many corporations become large and profitable through unfair and monopolistic trade practices? Are Americans dangerously materialistic and narcissistic? Do they really exercise freedom of choice, or are they being manipulated? Are traditional moral values of chastity, sobriety, and humility inevitably at odds with modernity? Do the products we buy cost too much because of wasteful expenses unrelated to their manufacture? Do children grow up too fast, and get bombarded with messages and pressures they cannot withstand or even understand?

More basically, is our modern, advertising-laden culture a superficial and ultimately pointless one? Behind many critical examinations of advertising as a profession, industry, or social tool is the suspicion, sometimes explicit and sometimes implied, that it is all in the end little more than fluff. It matters little whether the goods being advertised are viewed as trifles or worse, such as when George Orwell called advertising "the rattling of a stick inside a swill bucket."[11] The point is that the advertising disguises what lies underneath, that it enables people to deceive themselves into believing they can be made healthier or happier by buying things.

A major theme of this book is that advertising is, indeed, far more than just a rote recitation of what is available, where it is available, and how much it costs. The title was inspired by a passage from a 1967 book by Ralph Glasser entitled *The New High Priesthood: The Social, Ethical, and Political Implications of a Marketing-Orientated Society*. In the book, Glasser argued that agenda setters and symbol manipulators—not just in commerce and media but also across many sectors, including government and religion—had "usurped the role of leadership in society" from traditional political or religious elites. In a previous work, Glasser had offered a definition of marketing that had become widely accepted: "Marketing, in a free economy, is the skill of selecting and fulfilling consumer desires so as to maximize the profitability per unit of capital invested in the enterprise." In *The New High Priesthood*, he sought to explain why he chose the word *desires* instead of the more familiar economic term *demand*:

> Demand is not a settled economic fact of life, like a river, but is the resultant of latent desires, dreams, and aspirations that may be fostered or not. Marketing does not sell a product—it sells a dream; a dream of beauty, of health, of success, of power.

A lipstick, Glasser explained, is not marketed "as a concoction of grease and coloring matter." It is offered as a way to obtain beauty, find romance, or gain confidence. Similarly, a beer ad is not really selling a drink. It is selling satisfaction, comradeship, or fun. "Long-term marketing success," he concluded, "depends on identifying latent desires and matching products to them," not simply coming up with evocative words, striking images, or catchy slogans.[12]

That advertising consists of selling not just things but also dreams is a concept that some see as inherently damning. I do not. Human beings are emotional and aesthetic creatures who have always invested the things they make, acquire, or use with meaning beyond the merely utilitarian. In the quirky and underappreciated 1957 musical *Silk Stockings*, a remake of an earlier film and play entitled *Ninochtka*, a

Soviet agent played by Cyd Charisse is sent to Paris to bring back a famous Russian writer who has defected. The defector's Western employer, a musical producer played by Fred Astaire, tries to deflect Charisse's mission, and soften her hard edges, by showing her the bright lights and luxuries of Paris. At first she resists, with humorous results, but eventually she receives a gift of silk stockings and retreats to the privacy of her hotel room. Away from seeing eyes, Charisse performs a lovely ballet in which donning the stockings begins her transformation from a cold, calculating servant of collectivism to a warm, passionate individual yearning for liberty. While this story is fiction, there are many real-world examples of émigrés, escaping from oppressive societies, citing a well-fitted suit, a well-made and sporty car, a small home of their own, and sometimes something as seemingly banal as lipstick as signifying their newfound freedom. They do, indeed, see these objects as deeply meaningful, with the meaning derived from an interaction between their concrete personal experience and the abstract imagery they have seen, heard, or read. Perhaps the stakes are lower and the dreams less lofty, but in our own lives we go through a similar process of investing meaning in our commercial transactions. Advertising is one of the tools we use—and, yes, sometimes misuse—to do it.

This book consists of a close examination of the history of advertising and other forms of marketing, their role in the broader development of market economies, and the sources and specifics of scholarly, literary, religious, and political criticism of these practices. There are also chapters devoted to what might be called the "hard cases" of advertising: health claims and the problem of fraud, the question of marketing to children, and the use of advertising to promote products or behaviors that many view as self-destructive, sinful, or harmful to others. The book is not offered as a comprehensive set of answers to the many intriguing and challenging questions posed about our modern commercial culture. But it is intended to identify and explore such questions, and in some cases as a reformulation of them.

# CHAPTER 1

# The Birth of Advertising and Commercial Culture

A summertime stroll down the street in a certain seaside resort on the Mediterranean was an excursion into unfettered commerce. Fresh produce, fine textiles and clothing, and manufactured goods from far and near were laid out to catch the eye of passersby, often with wares or signs hanging above a shopkeeper's stall to attract the most attention. Shoppers got an eyeful of the latest brand names and slogans. "One hundred percent pure," promised the maker of one fish sauce, a specialty of the region. "Quality strained sauce" was the answer from another brand. Off the street, signs for establishments such as restaurants and sports arenas used striking images and famous personalities to draw in foot traffic. One spa boasted that it was "good enough for Venus," while a tavern reminded sports fans that it was conveniently located on the way back from the stadium.

As the vacationer or local stroller continued down the street, sales pitches would reach the ear as well as the eye. The schedule for the day's races, the luxuriousness of the fabrics available at the corner stall, the number of comfortable beds at the local hotel—all were announced by hired orators, poets, and musicians. As it was nearly time for local elections in the city, political messages would have mingled with the commercial ones. "All the [city's] fruit sellers . . . urge you to elect" a prominent citizen as a local judge, read one painted sign. Nearby, a message for a rival judicial candidate stated that he was "a good man" and a worthy choice.

This being a resort town catering to many sailors, merchants, and travelers from far-off places, the goods and services being advertised were not limited to family fare. Images of beautiful women and athletic men, bountiful wine and beer, and other adult amusements were also easy to spot. A pair of dice and phallic symbols adorned a sign pointing the way toward a gambling house and brothel. For a good time, you should buy "frenzy wine," said another placard.

It is likely that while spending an afternoon walking along this street, you would be exposed to dozens of advertising and marketing pitches, at least. You might also have ended up buying something. But on the particular summer day that all of these signs, ads, and slogans were to be seen and heard, your shopping trip would have been cut short—as would your life. On August 24, 79 A.D., Mount Vesuvius erupted and buried the city of Pompeii as well as nearby Herculaneum under volcanic ash and lava.

Much of everyday life in ancient Rome would look, sound, and especially smell odd to a modern-day time traveler. But a walk through the markets of a Roman city, at least one catering to a wealthy or middle-class clientele like Pompeii's, would seem far more familiar. For about as long as human beings have sought to sell each other goods and services, they have made use of pictures, brand names, guarantees, slogans, and other kinds of images far removed from a simple listing of the items being purchased and what items or money would be given in exchange. Archaeologists and historians trace the evolution of commercial communication to the earliest civilizations in Mesopotamia and Egypt. At least 5,000 years ago, cobblers in Babylonia would hang shoes above their shop doors to promote what they did and how they did it. In Egypt, the earliest known commercial advertising was the port crier, who was compensated by the owner of an arriving ship to wander the streets announcing, for example, "a fresh arrival of oriental rugs from our special representative in the East." Frank Presbey, a popular American historian of advertising in the early twentieth century, wrote that the crier would not just tell passersby what was available and at what price. He "sang his story and gave further interest to his announcements by describing in florid language the regions from which the articles came and the difficulties under which they were obtained," Presbey wrote, describing a rhetorical style in salesmanship that has persisted into the present day.[1]

On the walls of the tomb of Qenamen, a mayor of Thebes who lived during the reign of the Egyptian Pharaoh Amenhotep III (1402–1364 B.C.), there is depicted a scene of trading ships pulling up to the docks and unloading their cargo. Among the characters in the scene are Egyptian merchants, men and women, sitting at their stalls near the waterfront to market their goods, apparently to foreign visitors as well as local buyers. Some of their goods, such as pieces of clothing and loaves of bread, are hanging above their stalls, probably as a handy way of catching the eye and announcing what was for sale.[2] These practices constituted the beginnings of the trade sign, that most basic form of visual advertising, which would later become ubiquitous in the cities of ancient Greece and Rome.[3]

For economic historians, Pompeii is a critical link to that past. The very nature of its disastrous end proved to be good fortune for future generations, as it served to preserve things that would otherwise have been lost to wind, water, and human hands over the millennia. Given that some artifacts of human cultures decompose more rapidly than others, one can get the impression that prehistoric man did little other than devise stone tools and hunt wild animals—unless he was fortunate enough to live near a cave and know how to mix colors. This would be misleading. Similarly, early human civilizations were not all about weapons, monuments, and pottery, though you can certainly get that impression by a casual examination of the way historians categorize them. By using the available written and pictorial evidence, ingenuity, and extrapolation, modern scholars have begun to weave together various strands of economics, culture, and social relations to give us a richer and more balanced sense of what life was like in an ancient city. These developments have been particularly welcome with regard to the commercial life of these early cities, in which one can find the beginnings of virtually all the business forms and practices we know in the modern world, including partnerships and corporations, multinational businesses, stocks and bonds, banks, insurance, and paper currency.

The history of advertising and commercial speech has been problematic here because of the fact that it was carried out to a large degree by the spoken word, on perishable writing surfaces, and on hand-painted signs that not only faded over the centuries but also were painted over with great regularity by store owners and their agents. In Pompeii, however, we find the archaeological equivalent of a snapshot, a moment of ancient commercial life frozen in time. The results are instructive. Present in the hustle and bustle of market life in this Roman vacationland are many early versions of advertising practices that some wrongly assume to be of more recent vintage.

**Product Branding** The aforementioned Roman fish sauce, called garum, was made out of the meat and entrails of sardines, mackerel, and other kinds of fish caught in the Mediterranean. It was pounded into a pulp and left in the heat to ferment over several weeks, after which the paste would be filtered and the drained sauce served in a variety of ways. Roman merchants offered for sale a variety of garum "brands" that referred to the ingredients, the processing, or the name of the manufacturer. A certain merchant named Scaurus seems to have become a sort of Procter & Gamble of the garum trade, maximizing his market share by offering many different brands. One was "Scaurus' tunny jelly, blossom brand, put up by Eutyches, slave of Scaurus." Sure, this brand name does not exactly trip off the tongue, but it is translated from Latin and separated from its target audience by centuries. Other brands of garum included phrases such as "best available" and "essence of the best mackerel."[4]

**Product Positioning** The wine market was also differentiated. In Pompeii, one researcher identified 200 different kinds of wines, most bearing a brand name that reflected a place of origin, intended use, or famous winemaker.[5] In an early case of product positioning, a tavern promoted its wines as intended for truly discerning customers who appreciated the best: "If you will give the sum of two donkeys, you will drink better wines; if you will pay four, you will drink Falernian wines."[6] Rome was most often considered the Polaris of product quality. A provincial bathhouse was represented as patterned after its Roman counterpart, while a showman would boast of attractions "fresh from Rome."[7]

**Product Placement** Modern-day writers and artists are often accused of being "sellouts" when they include the names of consumer products in their books, artwork, or television scripts for a fee. If so, they are in good company. Ancient Roman poets such as Martial and Virgil appear to have done the same thing, especially with fine wines. The poet Horace once wrote, "What would I rather do on the festival of Neptune? Come on, Lydia, hurry and bring forth the stored Caecubian [wine]." Another line from Horace sorrowfully concludes that neither "purple brighter than the stars nor Falernian [wine] soothes a grieving man," a sort of backhanded pitch for the latter but perhaps still an effective one.[8]

**Product Promotion** Although no mass media yet existed through which to promote goods and services, merchants in the Roman Empire and other ancient and medieval cultures made full use of the audio and visual techniques available to them. For example, the "sandwich board" form of advertising was said to originate in the city of Carthage, Rome's old enemy, where galley captains would send sailors or slaves into the city wearing garments bearing the names and images of their cargo. The aforementioned orators of the ancient world, compensated by shopkeepers and politicians to work the streets on their behalf, became the town criers of the medieval world with similar skills and customers. Indeed, in the thirteenth century the king of France required tavern keepers in Paris to hire licensed criers to advertise their wine prices even if the tavern keepers preferred to use other means of promoting their establishments, suggesting not only that this auditory form of advertising was ubiquitous but also that its practitioners had developed valuable political connections.[9]

**Product Endorsements** Archaeologists have found toy chariots with the names of famous charioteers, pocketknife handles with the head and name of a famous racehorse and his jockey, and lamps and bowls with images of famous gladiators on them.[10] Some of the many political ads found on the Pompeii site—the volcanic eruption appears to have occurred just before a scheduled election—may have been not just attempts to win votes on the part of politicians but also an attempt to associate a product or industry with a popular political leader in the city.[11] Centuries earlier, some Greek merchants had attached advertisements on statues of gods and goddesses to make sure people saw them—and to invoke divine favor on their wares.[12]

Of course, it is important not to exaggerate the parallels between ancient and modern commercial communication. In the ancient and medieval world, the majority of the population engaged in subsistence or manorial farming and spent little time in cities buying goods and services in the marketplace. Coins being scarce, they still often resorted to bartering with neighbors for the necessities of life, while being able to afford few of the luxuries that were imported at great expense from the spice and silk markets of the Far East, the amber and fur markets of Northern Europe, or the ivory, salt, and slave markets of sub-Saharan Africa. To the extent that peasants and villagers purchased trade goods at all, they were probably not acquired in market cities such as Pompeii but from traveling salesmen. Among the evidence for this fact are the derivations of many of the colorful words we still use today to refer to the selling and marketing professions. Both the terms *hawker* and *huckster* derived from an old Germanic word meaning "to crouch or bend, as if carrying a burden." The term *peddler* comes from an old English word for a basket.

*Advertise*, on the other hand, reflects a combination of two Latin roots: *ad*, for the preposition *to*, and *vertere*, a verb meaning *to turn*. Literally, an advertisement is something that induces you to turn your attention away from where it was directed, and toward whatever is being advertised. In other words, the very concept of advertising assumes the presence of competition, of competing demands on your time and effort. Advertising is not worth much if its intended audience has no capacity to make choices and to act on them. Moreover, as demonstrated by the literal meaning of the word, advertising has always been about getting someone's attention, not just about providing raw facts about something to be bought or sold.

As such, large-scale commercial advertising—as distinguished from the marketing of political regimes or religions through such devices as coinage, public art, and town criers—was not either necessary or feasible until large numbers of potential customers were in a position to see or hear it, and then to act on it by deciding what to buy and where and how to live. Thus, it would have to wait until the development of major cities, major avenues for long-range transportation, and the printing press.

## PRINTING AND ADVERTISING

Ancient Rome, once again, was the setting for what most historians believe was the first "newspaper." Indeed, the creation of *Acta Diurna*—or "Daily Events"—is traditionally attributed to none other than Julius Caesar in 59 B.C. Handwritten and distributed to readers primarily by being posted in prominent areas through Rome, *Acta Diurna* provided a steady stream of official edicts and announcements, news from the military front, schedules of sporting events, court proceedings, religious writings, omens and astrological signs, and election results. Although limited in its readership to certain classes in Rome and supported neither by subscriptions nor advertising, *Acta Diurna* contained most of the elements that make up modern print or broadcast news.[13] A key element for allowing a broader distribution was manufactured paper, not yet available in Europe. In China, where paper was invented, the earliest newspaper that has survived was apparently circulated in Beijing in the year 748. Only three years later, the Arab Empire would defeat Chinese forces at the battle of Talas, in central Asia, and carry the secret of paper back with them to the Mediterranean world. In the Middle East and in Moslem-ruled Spain, Arab mills produced paper that was apparently sold in Europe as early as the twelfth century. By the end of the thirteenth century, Italian and other Europeans were making their own paper.[14]

In Europe, the tradition of the *Acta Diurna* continued into the Middle Ages with the occasional release of handwritten notices, from either rulers or church leaders, that would be read by criers in a town square or passed around in handwritten form among the (literally) cloistered, educated elite. These notices became known as "newssheets" by the sixteenth century, during which some became actual sources of revenue for their official publishers. In Venice, for example, the republican government issued newssheets on the latest news from the front during wars with the Ottoman Turks, and then charged citizens an admission fee to attend public readings of each edition. The original fee was a small Venetian coin called a *gazeta*. Eventually, *gazette* became one of the most popular names for a newspaper.[15]

A more commercial kind of newsletter circulated among members of prominent European trading families during the late Middle Ages and early Renaissance, such as the de Medicis in Italy and the Fuggers in Germany. It contained not just price and product information for the various markets in which the families traded but also updates on the political and military conflicts of the day, which obviously would be of great interest to merchants. These trader newsletters were sometimes passed along to businessmen and other wealthy citizens, thus becoming an early news medium for the commercial classes.

Johann Gutenberg's invention of the printing press allowed for both kinds of printed materials—notices released by secular or clerical leaders and newsletters produced by tradesmen—to begin their evolution into true popular newspapers. It also facilitated the introduction of printed advertisements, though the two trends took centuries to converge. Shortly after the press debuted in the mid-fifteenth century, shopkeepers began to have handbills printed and posted across a city to advertise goods for sale. The first known English-language circular appeared in 1480. It was the handiwork of William Caxton, who had introduced printing itself to the British Isles. But printers needed more than periodical advertising handbills to stay in business. During the sixteenth century, the primary source of printed news they came up with was the pamphlet, or "newsbook," which usually focused on a particular event such as a battle, plague, scandal, or reported miracle. These were important sources of information and entertainment, but they were not regularly published. As printers proliferated late in the century and began looking for ways to keep their expensive new machines busy, they began to issue periodical summaries of items they picked up from newsbooks, trading reports, official pronouncements, and other sources. The first real newspapers began circulating just after 1600 in Holland, Germany, and Switzerland. Printers in Austria and England joined in by the 1620s; France, Denmark, and Italy in the 1630s; and Scandinavia and Eastern Europe by midcentury.[16]

Some of these newspapers were independently owned. Others were little more than extensions of governments or clerical offices, such as a Paris newspaper backed by the infamous Cardinal Richelieu. But even the independent printers were usually involved to a large degree with their home governments and state churches, for which they often performed lucrative printing work. Comparatively, revenue from the sale of their early newspapers was limited and unreliable. Then, as now, it proved difficult to ensure that copies, once sold, would not be recirculated widely throughout a town, village, ship's crew, congregation, or social circle. Thus, printers were often reliant on their other work to pay the bills, and much of this regular work was for the state or the church. Neither relationship was particularly conducive to editorial independence. During much of the 1600s, a combination of censorship and incessant military conflicts—such as the Thirty Years' War on the Continent and the English Civil War—kept these early newspapers from establishing a firm and independent identity, as paper and other raw materials were either hard to find or highly taxed.

In the late 1600s, a fundamental change in the printing business ushered in the beginnings of an independent press. Newspapers developed stable sources of revenue outside the control of political or religious authorities by marrying news with commerce. In England, Edward Lloyd owned a coffeehouse near the docks where merchants and sailors often congregated. He founded *Lloyd's News*, and later *Lloyd's List and Shipping Gazette*, to provide regular shipping news as well as coverage of general news events. By serving a target audience with a strong and constant need for its news, *Lloyd's List and Shipping Gazette* sustained itself nicely by direct sales.[17] Also near the end of the seventeenth century, newspapers began to run formal, paid newspaper ads on a regular basis. By then, printed handbills and advertising pamphlets had existed for nearly two centuries, used to promote such widely divergent products as bibles, circuses, and berths on ships carrying colonists to the New World. Indeed, some historians consider the efforts of trading companies and land speculators to encourage mass emigration to the Americas to be the world's first large-scale advertising campaign.[18] And the idea of paid advertising in newspapers had actually cropped up as early as 1525, when a German newspaper advertised a drug for sale (beginning a relationship between advertising and medicine that has continued to stir controversy until the present day, as Chapter 6 describes). But the practice was not widely adopted for more than a century.

In 1672, the earliest surviving newspaper ad in the English language offered a cash reward for the return of twelve stolen horses.[19] By the turn of the century, advertising began to generate a significant stream of revenue for some European printers. In America, where newspapers were already starting to proliferate, the first known ad— a real estate notice for a Long Island estate—ran in 1704 in the *Boston News Letter*, itself the first regularly published newspaper in the English colonies. Its publisher was Boston Postmaster John Campbell, who saw a business opportunity in the regular news summaries he prepared for the Massachusetts General Court. Unfortunately, the authorities' condition for allowing Campbell to found the *Boston News Letter* was that they would retain control over what he printed, so advertising did not yet facilitate editorial independence.[20] That would come over the next two decades, in both Europe and America, as entrepreneurial printers began to attract a diverse and interesting array of advertisements that frequently proved to be more compelling to readers than the often-dated news items and official proclamations filling the rest of the papers. Indeed, President Thomas Jefferson would later assert that "advertisements contain the only truth to be relied on in a newspaper."

An early pioneer in commercial advertising, as in so many other fields, was the brilliant printer Benjamin Franklin. Shortly after settling in Philadelphia in 1723, Franklin became the editor of the *Pennsylvania Gazette*. By providing clearly written, often funny articles on a wide variety of topics, Franklin made the *Gazette* the most widely read newspaper in the American colonies. He also made it the most successful at attracting commercial advertising, by changing the way it was presented to the reader. Before Franklin came along, newspaper ads closely resembled the rest of the publication. They contained only text—rows and rows of it. Franklin added pictures to illustrate what was being marketed, and was apparently the first printer to use "white space" to distinguish one block of advertising from another. Later, Franklin founded *The General Magazine* in 1741 and printed the first-known American magazine ad. His advertising was more attractive, more distinctive, and thus more easily sold to skeptical merchants.

Franklin was not just innovative with regard to presenting ads. He also influenced their content. Rather than simply listing the available product, perhaps with a helpful illustration, along with its price and availability, Franklin's ads emphasized how the good or service would make a consumer's life happier and better—and how competing products might not be able to offer the same benefits. For example, in advertising his own invention of the Franklin stove, he stressed the health, safety, social, and efficiency aspects of the product:

> Your whole room is equally warmed, so that people don't need to crowd so close around your fire, but may sit near the window and have the benefit of the light for reading, writing, needlework, etc. . . . You have not that cold draft of uncomfortable air nipping at your back and heels . . . by which you may catch colds, coughs, toothaches, fever, pleurisies, and many other diseases. . . . As very little heat is lost when this fireplace is used, much less wood will serve you, which is a considerable advantage were wood is dear. . . . And lastly, the fire is secured at night, that not one spark can fly out of the room to do damage.

What other reason could there be for choosing the Franklin stove over its rivals? Well, the clever marketer sought to tap into the basic human discomfort with the aging process. Other stoves, Franklin warned, "would damage the eyes . . . and shrivel the skin, bringing on the early appearance of old age."[21]

As advertising historian Christina Mierau tells the story, by the mid-eighteenth century Benjamin Franklin was living in not only the second-largest city in the British Empire and America's commercial center—Philadelphia—but also the center of a proliferating commercial culture. While shopkeepers from Boston to the Carolinas made use of centuries-old devices such as trade signs and handbills, Philadelphia merchants took them to a new level of marketing acumen. Artist Matthew Pratt made a living in the city by painting many of the trade signs. One depicted a gathering of political delegates in front of a tavern at the corner of Fourth and Chestnut Streets. Folks walking by began playing a sort of parlor game to see how many of the actual political figures in the picture they could name. Many would then enter the tavern to continue the game and get a drink. "As he refilled his customers' drinks," writes Mierau, "the tavern owner realized a simple truth—it paid to advertise."[22] This kind of gimmick is still around; where I live in Raleigh, the state capital of North Carolina, a local seafood restaurant and popular political hangout still has a large mural on the wall depicting several of the state's most prominent politicians, who also happened to be patrons of the restaurant.

The mid-eighteenth century saw innovations in printing and journalism that spread across the American colonies and Europe. The first daily paper had already appeared in London earlier in the century, but in the 1750s the dailies began to adopt a four-column style that allowed for greater flexibility in laying out both news and advertising. The first French daily of a similar style appeared in 1777, and the first colonial one, the *Pennsylvania Packet*, in 1784. What made the American press stand out was not the frequency or quality of publication but its commercial content. Catering to an expanding, literate, and mercantile population, American newspapers were more innovative with advertising and more willing to display it prominently. These trends would culminate in the nineteenth century in the rise of mass marketing and, later, the rise of truly mass media.

## MASS MARKETING AND THE NINETEENTH CENTURY

Early America's commercial culture already stood out to a large extent from the European cultures from which it sprung. But developments throughout the nineteenth century would accentuate the differences. As Americans moved westward to found new settlements, towns, and cities, the trading impulse moved along with them. So-called Yankee peddlers—though their places of birth were varied, including overseas—began to travel the country's paths and early roadways to sell manufactured goods, jewelry, alcohol, medicine, and other high-value items that could be moved economically by foot or wagon. At the same time, salesmen headed in the opposite direction, back east, to sell land and promote commercial opportunities to potential settlers. Both peddlers and "boosters," as the latter came to be called, made use of the spoken and written word to market their offerings. And as the new settlements began to expand, one sign that they were becoming real towns was the arrival of a printer and the founding of a newspaper. Real estate and government advertising were often the mainstays of these early publishing enterprises.

American newspapers were numerous by the 1830s but their circulation remained relatively small, in part because most of the population still lived on the farm or in small towns and in part because of pricing. Printers were still trying to recoup a significant share of the cost of each issue by newsstand sales or subscriptions. In response, copies were shared among friends or read in common areas. Benjamin Day, a publisher in New York, realized that the strategy of charging a lot for each issue was penny-wise and pound-foolish. It made more sense to maximize a newspaper's circulation, though this might require a lower price, if the resulting audience could be offered to advertisers as a valuable potential market. In 1833, he slashed the price of his *New York Sun* to a penny (the typical newspaper's price in the city was 6 cents) and was selling about 2,000 copies a day within two months. By 1835, the *Sun* was selling more than 20,000 copies a day, making it the largest-circulation newspaper in the world. And it was obvious why Day's business bet had paid off: two-thirds of each day's pages contained advertising, a rate far higher than that of his competition.

The strategy would ultimately reverse the incentive structure for newspapering and make it far more efficient and profitable. Previously, publishers worried about what we now call the "pass-along rate," the extent to which a single copy of their newspaper was circulated among friends and family. Every instance represented a lost sale. But by slashing the price to a penny and paying the bills through advertising, Day had turned a worry into a goal. The more copies were passed along to other readers, the more advertising messages were conveyed—and thus, assuming credible estimates of the practice, the more advertisers could be charged without adding the cost of printing and distributing more copies. By adopting an advertising model, Day had fundamentally changed the business of journalism and offered journalists a feasible way to establish editorial independence from political patrons, parties, and government contracts.

The *Sun* did not have the new "penny press" market to itself for long. In 1835, James Gordon Bennett began publication of the *New York Herald*. By offering more sensational news coverage and more innovative advertising, Bennett soon pushed the *Herald's* circulation above that of the *Sun*. A key selling point of the *Herald* was the daily publication of rows of so-called noncommercial advertising from private individuals looking to buy or sell a vast array of goods and services—what we now called the classifieds. Later, advertisers bought blocks of the small-type classified space and configured the text into attractive shapes or even large numbers and letters in an attempt to grab the attention of classified readers looking for clothes, jobs, household help, or romance.

The penny-press concept soon spread beyond New York City. Across the country, newspapers large and small began to experiment with lower subscription prices and more advertising pages. Readership surged. Indeed, only in recent years has an accurate picture of nineteenth-century newspaper circulation come into view. Traditionally, it had been counted on a per-person basis. But because families were far larger than they are now, the more appropriate measure is newspapers per dwelling (or household), and on that measure there were 2.6 copies per urban dwelling in 1900—the highest diffusion of newspapers in America before or since.[23]

Still, many local businesses were reluctant at first to invest in newspaper marketing. During much of the nineteenth century, banks would lower the credit rating of firms that were known to use advertising, as it was considered a sign of financial weakness.[24] Also, many publishers were still leery of some eager would-be advertisers such as brand-new businesses without a track record of paying their bills. So, a demand arose for placing ads from established businesses in out-of-town newspapers. Seeing an opportunity, Philadelphia salesman Volney Palmer opened a brokerage in 1843 to link potential advertisers with local newspapers across the country. By 1850, this early version of an advertising agency had been replicated in New York and other East Coast cities. In 1867, the New York agency Carlton & Smith began placing national advertising in religious magazines, and the practice soon spread to secular ones. A year later, another Philadelphia marketing whiz, Francis Wayland Ayer, opened up the nation's first commission-based ad agency, N.W. Ayer & Son (named after his father).[25]

A year after that, in 1869, a former teacher and newspaper employee from New England named George Rowell sought to distinguish his new agency from rivals by offering a more research-oriented and outcome-based approach. Rather than simply attempt to talk manufacturing and retailing firms into buying any and all kinds of ads on one side of the transaction, and then trying to convince newspapers to take the risk of not being paid on the other, Rowell commissioned the first-known circulation counts and readership surveys of newspapers across the country to determine what kinds of products would likely sell best in particular localities. He published some of his results in 1869 as the *George P. Lowell Newspaper Directory*, which included dozens of small papers across the country that few East Coast ad buyers knew much about. He also purchased advertising space directly from the newspapers, getting a discount because he paid cash up-front, and then resold the space to his advertising clients. During his first year in business in New York, Rowell bought $600 in ad space and sold it for $2,000. Naturally, his profitable ideas caught on in the industry. In 1873, New York hosted the first convention of American advertising agents. In 1877, New York–based James Walter Thompson bought the magazine-advertising business of Carlton & Smith and became a key figure in the early development of the industry, inventing the position of account executive. The industry spread west with the creation of the pioneering firm Lord and Thomas in Chicago in 1881. By 1888, Rowell was ready to start publishing *Printer's Ink*, the first trade magazine for the advertising industry.[26]

While commercial advertising in the mass media was certainly on the upswing, it is important not to equate it with marketing and commercial communication. There were many other ways for nineteenth-century industries to market their wares to consumers, and these ways were often considered more important. Among these were newly redesigned storefronts and word-of-mouth promotions as well as new tools of the sales trade such as prepackaged samples and direct-to-consumer advertising.

A fascinating example of the latter trend was the trade card. As advertising scholar James Twitchell told the story, the trade card was the natural outgrowth of the personal calling card that began life in the early days of the printing industry and survives today as the business card. During the eighteenth century, printers produced cards on behalf of individuals and businesses that included increasingly attractive and sophisticated engravings. "In the 1790s a Bavarian inventor learned that he could vastly expand the artistic possibilities [of engraved cards] by using specially prepared blocks of limestone, a greased crayon, and water," Twitchell wrote. "The engraver could draw rather than carve the images." By the 1820s, printers switched from engraving to lithography. Later, the introduction of color made these cards far more visually compelling than the images readers could typically find in newspapers. With the introduction of steam power and other technologies, card printing ramped up by several orders of magnitude. By the 1880s, hundreds of thousands of trade cards were being printed on behalf of a host of companies selling seed, thread, soap, cereal, pencils, farm machinery, and especially patent medicines, which by themselves accounted for more than half of all the cards in circulation.[27]

How did they get into circulation? Manufacturers bundled cards with products leaving their factories. They armed their sales representatives with stacks of cards to hand out to customers, potential customers, retailers, and local community leaders such as elected officials, educators, and publishers. Trade cards soon became trading cards, as friends and family members collected and swapped their favorites in a practice that later became familiar with cards promoting sports teams and motion pictures.[28] Some chose to make a gift of their favorite trade cards, a trend that coincided with the parallel introduction of holiday-themed cards by many printing companies. Valentine's Day was the most popular occasion for such exchanges, beginning with short commercially printed verses in the 1840s and then full-fledged color lithographs in the 1850s and 1860s.[29] Eventually, the card companies began to cater more to household than business customers as other forms of national advertising overtook the trade card by the early twentieth century. Thus, today's baseball cards, *Yu-Gi-Oh!* and *Star Wars* game cards, greeting cards, and business cards all share an intriguing history with that of commercial advertising.

# THE REVOLUTION IN RETAIL

If trade cards allowed American businesses to put their messages and images in the hands of consumers across the far-flung country, the growing urbanization of the late nineteenth century presented increasing opportunities for retailers to engage in direct marketing in front of and inside their burgeoning stores. At the country's founding in the late eighteenth century, some 90 percent of Americans lived on the farm. As the new nation grew and developed, the rural share began to shrink as settlers built small towns and as some displaced farmers began moving to the cities on the coast and on rivers. After the Civil War, this trend intensified, so that the 1880 census was the first to record fewer than half of Americans living on the farm. Both farms and small towns would yield to cities over the ensuing four decades, with the share of Americans residing in urban areas doubling by 1920 from one-quarter to one-half.[30] Home ownership rates show a similar trend, actually declining for most of the second half of the nineteenth century and the first half of the twentieth as those who previously owned and worked rural homesteads moved to cities and become urban renters.[31]

The scale of retail grew in tandem. In New York, for example, the 1820s saw the opening of small stores on Broadway by Alexander T. Stewart (1823) and Samuel Lord and George Washington Taylor (1826). By the 1840s, Stewart had opened his Marble Palace in Manhattan, which attracted 1,000 visitors an hour and displayed $600,000 worth of merchandise. It grew rapidly over the next fifteen years, by 1870 employing 2,000 people, offering $42 million in goods in several specialty departments, and extending credit to consumers for large purchases. In the still-bustling commercial hub of Philadelphia, John Wanamaker had cofounded a store selling men's and boy's clothes in 1861, and then expanded it during the Civil War in part by aggressive price cutting. Seeing opportunity in Stewart's growth rate in New York, Wanamaker opened his first store there in 1869.[32]

Meanwhile in Europe, the mid-nineteenth century had ushered in some new concepts and designs for retailing, too. Whereas most fashionable stores in cities such as London and Paris had paired up customers with sales representatives who brought out wares by request, the 1840s and 1850s saw the development of larger stores with goods pre-positioned to show off their styles and colors. In emulation of Middle Eastern bazaars, European shopping districts began to be covered with ceilings and later with glass skylights. These "arcades" were a sort of proto–shopping mall, with customers able to wander through a variety of small boutiques and specialty stores. With the advent in the 1850s of Grand Expositions in London, Paris, and other cities, shoppers and tourists became more comfortable with larger, sprawling retail centers where products were displayed in massive quantities rather than doled out by shopkeepers. Retailers learned that visual presentation was at least as important as vocal salesmanship. They duplicated the concept of the traveling exposition in the form of permanent emporiums. In Paris, owners of a drapery shop in the 1860s began to rebuild it as such a structure, what would become the famous Bon Marche that opened in 1872.[33]

Wanamaker traveled to Europe in 1871 looking for clothes to import, and came away inspired by what he saw. He acquired the abandoned freight depot of the Pennsylvania Railroad and began to renovate the huge structure into America's first true department store, which opened in 1876 as the Grand Depot. The result was less a store than a huge tourist attraction and publicity machine. It was lit during the day by stained glass skylights and at night by elaborate chandeliers. And it was so huge—at 129 counters over 3 acres served by 2,000 clerks—that Wanamaker's store offered guidebooks, which soon became illustrated "souvenir" booklets printed at the store and including its history and philosophy.[34] The Bon Marche, the Grand Depot, and the other department stores that quickly followed suit made use of massive signage, complex and intricate design, artwork and fountains, and presentations intended to invoke the mystery and glamour of faraway lands as well as the comforts of hearth and home. By piling up merchandise nearly to the (high) ceilings, they implied to consumers that virtually anything they wanted might be found within. By putting products in their context—plates and saucepans in a mock kitchen, clothes and jewelry on mannequins—the department stores allowed shoppers to visualize themselves using the merchandise rather than just examine the merchandise itself. The Bon Marche generated excitement with periodic "white sales," still familiar today, during which the sprawling store would be decorated entirely in white.[35]

The debut of the department store had important implications for advertising and its related field, public relations. Stewart, Wanamaker (who acquired Stewart's company after his death in 1876), and other innovative retailers made use of in-house periodicals, newspaper and magazine advertising, circulars, signs, and word of mouth to promote their attractions. Wanamaker hired John Powers, a former *Nation* editor and skillful copywriter later considered "the father of modern advertising," to serve as the firm's advertising counsel.[36] Wanamaker also founded the *Farm Journal* periodical in 1877 and published it for some years. From its inaugural issue, *Farm Journal* contained full-page advertisements for his Philadelphia store. His *Ladies' Journal* emphasized the women's department. Most retailers made assiduous use of press releases, interviews, and publicity agents to encourage newspapers to write up the latest store renovations, the newest line of clothing, and the upcoming personal appearance at their store by major figures from the worlds of politics, entertainment, or sports. Newspapers responded. These businesses were a seemingly inexhaustible source of news and feature articles, in areas as diverse as art (the Marshall Field store boasted "the largest single piece of glass mosaic in the world"), music (Wanamaker's Grand Depot had a musical court featuring the largest organ in the world), family life (Macy's Christmas displays became a staple of holiday feature writing in the 1870s), and business (these massive establishments employed thousands and affected even more with decisions about location, access, lighting, street improvements, and water and electric service).[37]

The department stores did not just advertise particular products or amenities. They sought to communicate an overall philosophy. Wanamaker did so directly, with what we would now call "advertorials." His newspaper ads included personal statements on business and public affairs, philosophy, travel, even nature. An 1889 ad placed by Macy's explained the "Seven Lamps of Architecture of Our Business," such as standardized pricing and liberal return policies. Both advertising and in-house publications emphasized the personal philanthropy and generosity of store owners, such as Lyman Bloomingdale's gifts to the Metropolitan Museum of Art. That company's *Blooming-dale's Diary* also celebrated its treatment of its employees to a "large, light, airy, sanitary lunch room" and to "medical attendance . . . furnished to those who may be unfortunate enough to be confined to their houses by illness."[38]

# REACHING OUT ACROSS THE COUNTRY

The early success of America's early department stores mostly benefitted from the minority of the population who lived in big cities, though of course this proportion was growing during the later half of the nineteenth century. Country folk or tourists might schedule a special trip to Philadelphia, New York, or Chicago to shop, but such practices precluded the repeat sales that many retailers craved. Fortunately, markets abhor a vacuum. Retailers opened mail-order departments so that customers could reorder the products they had purchased during their store visits. But some entrepreneurs saw the marketing opportunity to be far greater than that. In 1872, a salesman named Aaron Montgomery Ward founded in Chicago the nation's first business devoted solely to marketing goods directly to consumers by means of a printed catalog. The first Montgomery Ward catalog listed 163 items on a single sheet of paper. By 1883, the catalog had grown to 240 pages listing 10,000 different items, and had coined the phrase "Satisfaction Guaranteed or Your Money Back." Millions of dollars in Montgomery Ward merchandise was being shipped along the nation's railroad lines and then distributed by mail to customers in cities and towns not yet boasting their own department stores.[39]

A railroad agent in Minnesota took note of the Montgomery Ward phenomenon but noticed that it still had not truly brought the cornucopia of American capitalism to rural areas. Then fate turned the agent, Richard W. Sears, into a salesman. At his railroad depot in Redwood Falls, Minnesota, Sears accepted delivery of a carton of gold watches on behalf of a local jeweler, who protested that he had not ordered them and would not pay for them. Stuck with the inventory, Sears went out and quickly sold the watches for a handsome profit.

Intrigued by the experience—and by the possibilities of the mail-order business—he moved to Chicago in 1887 and took on a partner, a watchmaker named Alvah C. Roebuck. Their Sears and Roebuck watch company soon branched out into other goods and introduced a catalog of its own in 1891.[40]

By 1895, the catalog exceeded 500 pages and had grown far beyond its watch and jewelry offerings to include silverware, bicycles, sporting goods, firearms, furniture, books, clothes, eyeglasses, and many other goods. Part of the appeal of Sears, Roebuck and Co. (the name stuck even though Roebuck had soon retired due to illness) stemmed from pricing policies: bulk buying drove the company's prices far below its competitors', and in the 1895 catalog it introduced no-money-down purchases, discounts for cash purchases, and various guarantees. But the catalog, named *The Book of Bargains: A Money Saver for Everyone*, was not just a list of products and prices. It told a story. The catalog, nearly entirely the product of Sears' own mind and hand, used compelling pictures and words—about 100 words, on average, per product—to allow rural customers to imagine what it would be like to own a new fishing pole, a bigger stove, or a new set of chairs. Another way to help readers picture themselves as satisfied Sears customers was to, well, print letters from satisfied customers, bearing titles such as the sunny "Proud of the Buggy," the bubbly "Everyone Says the Watch Is a Dandy," and the somewhat disquieting "Perfectly Satisfied with the Revolver." Sears wrote in a simple and familiar style, and soon the company became known as "the farmer's friend." In 1896, Sears began a spring and fall catalog to replace the previous annual edition. Color came in 1897. The catalogs were popular enough for Sears to begin charging customers for them. In 1900, Sears surpassed Montgomery Ward for the first time to become the largest mail-order retailer in the United States.[41]

While rural folks read and ordered from their Sears catalogs, their urban peers were the driving force behind another important development in advertising and marketing during the latter decades of the nineteenth century: the debut of the truly national general-interest magazine. Book publishers had already created nationally circulated magazines such as *Harper's* (formed in 1850 by Harper & Brothers publishing company) and the *Atlantic Monthly* (created in 1857). At first these magazines republished European authors and original American fiction, but soon they added other material and, importantly, illustrations to attract a sizable circulation base. *Harper's Weekly* had a circulation in 1860 of 200,000, and soon its famous in-house illustrator, Thomas Nast, was reinventing the political cartoon. But these magazines often considered advertising to be unsuitable for their readers, and even when accepting it tended to consign their ads to the "back of the book" so as not to offend readers or interrupt the flow of articles. The publisher of *Harper's* once spurned Boston ad agent George Rowell's offer of $18,000 for a single sewing machine ad and on another occasion refused to disclose the magazine's circulation to him.[42]

The 1880s brought change. In 1883, Cyrus and Louisa Curtis converted their previous *Tribune and Farmer* magazine into one aimed directly at female readers. Renaming it *Ladies' Home Journal*, they sliced the yearly subscription price to 25 cents (compared with $3 to $4 for *Harper's* and other national magazines) and sought to make their money by aggressive advertising, much like the earlier penny press had revolutionized the economics of city newspapers. It worked. *Ladies' Home Journal* was aimed at a broad audience and soon had more than half a million readers. Famously, Curtis explained his concept to a convention of national advertisers:

> Do you know why we publish the *Ladies' Home Journal*? The editor thinks it is for the benefit of American women. This is an illusion, but a very proper one for him to have. But I will tell you the real reason, the publisher's reason, is to give you people who manufacture things that American women want and buy a chance to tell them about your product.[43]

Another Curtis success story was the *Saturday Evening Post*. In 1897, Curtis bought the languishing *Post* for $1,000. It had only 2,300 weekly readers. Within a couple of years, the *Saturday Evening Post* was one of the biggest-selling magazines in the country. By 1909, its circulation was over 1 million a week, which doubled to 2 million in 1913. Again, the secrets of success were a lower price, content made accessible to the common reader (including copious illustrations), and a methodical search for advertisers interested in the markets Curtis could offer them.[44] Effective use of illustrations was also significant in the success of *Scribner's* magazine, introduced by the publisher Charles Scribner's Sons in 1887 to compete with *Harper's* and the *Atlantic Monthly*. With the first-known publication of a full-color illustration, in 1900, *Scribner's* soon had more than 200,000 subscribers.[45]

The trade-card phenomenon had already demonstrated the appeal of attractive color prints, so other magazines scrambled to make use of color illustrations while at the same time dropping their prices— innovations in the production of paper in the 1880s and 1890s helped by reducing production costs—and accepting more advertising along the lines pioneered by *Ladies' Home Journal*.[46] Maine publisher Frank Munsey was one of the first to "give in" to the advertising-based model Curtis had championed. *Munsey's Magazine* was nearly defunct in 1893 when he slashed his price to 10 cents, jacked up his print run to 200,000, and guaranteed his readership to national advertisers, who responded eagerly. By 1900, even *Harper's* began to accept large amounts of advertising. Half of its pages were ads in 1908.[47]

It would be a mistake to think of the magazine surge of the late nineteenth century as occurring solely in the form of national, general-interest periodicals. The printing and advertising innovations of the day "produced an unprecedented proliferation of newspapers and journals," wrote cultural historian William Gabler. "Every major industry, occupation, way of life, and special interest had its own il-lustrated weekly or monthly containing advertisements offering the latest products and equipment."[48] These included farm periodicals, magazines and newspapers circulating among trade associations, nu-merous small-circulation political and literary journals, and publica-tions produced by major department stores, railroad firms, banks, and other national corporations. By the turn of the century, magazines and other periodicals had an estimated total weekly circulation of nearly 17.5 million in the United States, representing almost as many Americans as those who read a daily newspaper (19.6 million).[49]

# MARKETING AND COMMERCE IN THE EARLY TWENTIETH CENTURY

The first three decades of the twentieth century saw earlier developments in print advertising, marketing strategy, salesmanship, and public relations transformed into coherent systems backed up by market research, standardization, college-based education and training, and technology. For example, around 1900 the first college courses in selling and marketing appeared in Germany and the United States. Both educational institutions and companies began to develop encapsulated presentations and guidebooks for positioning products and explaining their features to retailers or consumers.[50] In part, this was a response to competition. During the latter years of the nineteenth century, salesmen found that their roles as purveyors of information and setters of fashions and trends were being supplanted by the emerging, nationwide mass media. Their status was declining, as were the travel and expense budgets of their employers now making greater use of paid advertising. So the direct-sales business had to change.[51]

One of the leaders of this movement in America was John H. Patterson, who had founded the National Cash Register Company (NCR) in 1884 and proceeded to develop one of the most sophisticated systems for training and deploying a sales force in the business world. He wrote out scripts for sales representatives to commit to memory and held conventions to excite his employees and attract new ones—perhaps serving as a precursor to the emotional events and promotional literature popular today among those in sales and multilevel marketing. Patterson also made effective use of publicity by inviting the public and the media into his Dayton, Ohio, factory, which included a cafeteria, hospital, library, and recreational facility. NCR sported an elaborate lawn and garden, and showed motion pictures and hosted lectures during the employees' lunch hour. By the early twentieth century, Patterson's model at NCR had become much emulated by the likes of Eastman Kodak and General Motors, and its core elements survived later at International Business Machines (IBM), which was led by a former NCR executive, Thomas J. Watson.[52]

More generally, the process of bringing goods to market underwent dramatic change in the early twentieth century. Changes in postal practices in the 1870s had already led, as we have seen, to the development of a burgeoning mail-order business. In the 1890s, refrigerated rail cars became more than just occasional luxuries and led to a much wider array of produce in grocery stores. After 1900, trucks began to traverse the growing road systems of America and other countries, thus freeing up delivery routes and bringing goods more quickly into smaller communities. By 1918, U.S. companies alone were manufacturing 230,000 trucks a year. Highway spending skyrocketed accordingly, from $4 million in 1902 to $514 million in 1927. Just from 1921 to 1929, paved road mileage in the country nearly doubled.[53] These trends, in turn, allowed for the development of chain-owned retail and department stores, which made extensive use of both the in-store marketing techniques developed by Wanamaker and his contemporaries as well as the mass media of newspapers and magazines. Mail-order houses already knew how to do both, and began to open their own storefront chains. Montgomery Ward opened its first store in 1926 and had 531 operating by 1929. Sears opened its first store in 1925 and had 319 by 1929. Montgomery Ward declined Sears' merger offer in 1930.[54] The following year, Sears sold more merchandise from storefronts than from its venerable catalogs. Another important development was the introduction of coin-operated vending machines (starting in the 1890s) and self-service counters and stores (1910s and 1920s), again showing how audio and visual promotions and advertising were replacing the spoken word of sales attendants.[55]

The advertising business went through a similar period of systemization and maturation. Advertising agencies conducted more extensive market research, as did media companies themselves. Curtis Publishing set up a commercial research division in 1910 to investigate consumers' buying habits in areas of interest to its magazine readers. The *Chicago Tribune* conducted its first door-to-door survey in 1913. In 1916, Hollywood got into the act when Paramount decided to promote its trademark and films directly to consumers. Through market research, the studio determined that women were most likely to determine a family's viewing habits and focused its movie advertising on outlets such as *Ladies' Home Journal*.[56] These efforts matured during the 1920s into more wide-ranging research that include practical applications, such as testing advertising copy on sample customers. At Procter & Gamble, a young economist named Paul Smelser joined the research department in 1923. While colleagues examined the nation's commodity markets, Smelser was far more interested in the behavior of consumers. He would ask questions such as "What percentage of Ivory soap is used for face and hands and what percentage for dishwashing?" P&G executives found that they had no idea. They tapped Smelser to create a market research department in 1925. He soon employed dozens of "investigators," often young female college graduates, who would conduct door-to-door interviews in cities across the country. The interview scripts were standardized and memorized. Even the answers were to be remembered, not written down, so that consumers would not be made ill at ease by clipboards and paperwork.[57]

Perhaps the most compelling example of how the period's advertising industry functioned can be found in the new automobile industry, which by 1915 was the single-largest spender of ad dollars in America. While the United States was not the birthplace of the automobile, it was the birthplace of large-scale automobile advertising. After inventing the country's first gasoline-powered motor vehicle in the early 1890s, Charles and Frank Duryea of Springfield, Massachusetts, ran the first illustrated ad for a car, their Duryea Motor Wagon, in 1896. Interestingly, the ad showed a woman driving a female companion. Other ads in newspapers and national magazines followed. By 1906, fifty-seven American car companies were spending hundreds of thousands of dollars in national magazines such as the *Saturday Evening Post* and *Collier's*. Over the next several years, newspapers became still more of a promotional vehicle for the industry, not only through paid ads but also via news coverage and publicity. Car manufacturers hired agencies and pitchmen to rebut the message advanced by many highbrow magazines and commentators that automobiles were only an expensive luxury for the wealthy. For example, Henry Ford hired a former press agent for a circus, LeRoy Pelletier, to head up his publicity department. One 1915 campaign dreamed up by Pelletier had the Ford Motor Company place ads in 143 newspapers nationwide promising that if the company sold 300,000 cars that year, each buyer would receive a cash rebate. Sales surged.[58]

Some of the most creative writers, artists, and strategists gravitated to the automobile industry during this period. The ads made use of powerful imagery, some evoking rural or Western themes of freedom and abandon while others emphasized convenience and luxury in a more stylish urban setting. A 1905 ad for Ford's Model F stressed its "high-climbing power" and low price. Enjoy "a summer day and a Cadillac," urged a 1904 newspaper offering. Peerless Touring Cars— the self-described "embodiment of grace and elegance"—reinforced the message with an enticing image of a "Peerless Girl." Readers could order their own pictures (of the girl, that is) by sending in 10 cents.[59]

During the 1920s, automobile advertising was more sophisticated, much more copious, and often in color. Alfred Sloan, who took the helm at General Motors in 1923, acted as the pacesetter for the industry by using advertising and publicity to differentiate his growing diversity of offerings, offering "a car for every purse and purpose." An innovative manager, Sloan broke down GM into semiautonomous divisions to foster competition and creativity. The company was a pioneer in market research and public relations, seeking to substitute hard data for guesswork and to align prominent brand names such as Cadillac and Chevrolet to the varying preferences of millions of current or potential consumers. Henry Ford, by contrast, had used advertising primarily to communicate how much his product cost, how reliable it was, and where it could be purchased. He thought it was a waste of money to use ads to elicit emotions, to help consumers visualize themselves at the wheel, or to associate a car with treasured memories of the past or hopeful aspirations about the future. When Sloan took over GM, it had only one-fifth of the American automobile market. Ford had more than half. But Sloan's managerial and marketing innovations began to reverse the trends. By 1927, Ford felt compelled to introduce a new design, the Model A, and to run colorful newspaper ads across the country touting its "choice of four colors" and "beautiful new low body lines." Still, the following year GM surpassed Ford for the first time in auto production and sales.[60]

Companies such as Procter & Gamble and General Motors were helping to form the commercial culture of America. The significance of the trend can hardly be overstated: after doubling from 1880 to 1900, inflation-adjusted, per capita spending on advertising in the

United States doubled again from 1900 to 1929. Indeed, as a share of gross domestic product (3.3 percent) and personal income (4 percent), advertising expenditures had in 1929 reached its highest point in American history before or since. By that pivotal year, in other words, the basic ideas, strategies, and economic position of modern advertising had been established. But also established by then was an important and influential counterculture of criticism and antipathy toward this commercial culture, as evidenced by the work of University of Chicago scholar Thorstein Veblen (who died in 1929) and other economists, philosophers, and social critics who saw most advertising practices as anticompetitive, manipulative, and even obscene. And also in the 1928–1929 period, the basics of advertising would be put to use by another auto company, Dodge, in one of the first effective nationwide campaigns employing a new medium that would become compelling force in advertising and commercial communication: broadcasting.

# CHAPTER 2

# A Carnival of Conspicuous Consumption

To paint a picture of the history of advertising and other forms of marketing, you must start with a timeline, a succession of dates and innovations. But this constitutes just the first few brush strokes, mostly in a single direction. Forms of mass communication proliferate. Businesses find an ever-increasing number of tools available to package and sell their wares. Consumers find themselves increasingly courted, even fawned over. One innovation breeds another. It is a broad outline that only begins to resemble its subject as other strokes, other colors and shapes, are added. For example, far from being perceived as an irresistible force of (economic) nature, advertising has often provoked annoyance, disgust, fear, loathing, and despair. It has been condemned as sinful, challenged as wasteful, shunned as disgraceful, and suppressed as harmful.

The selling impulse has been both ubiquitous and controversial in most cultures and civilizations. While it has drawn many vociferous critics from the ranks of clerics, bureaucrats, academics, and intellectuals, some of the most lugubrious rhetoric has come from a surprising source. Advertising, wrote one author in 1894, is misspent energy "which results from competition, and which does no good except to increase the cost of goods to purchasers." At least half of all advertising is nothing but sheer waste, said another commentator at about the same time. By 1910, one analyst stated that the "consumer nearly always purchases in unconscious obedience to what he or she believes to be the dictates of an authority which is anxiously consulted and respected," suggesting that advertising was capable of implanting an impulse to buy so deeply that consumers need never realize how easily they were being manipulated.

All of these statements came from advertisers or their agents. In reverse order, the "unconscious obedience" assertion came from the pen of one Lee Mahin, the head of an advertising agency in Chicago.[1] The previously mentioned department store magnate John Wanamaker famously is said to have made the statement that "half of my advertising is wasted; I just don't know which half." And the notion that advertising accomplishes little except raising the price of goods to consumers comes from a book, *The Human Drift*, published in 1894 by a man who would shortly thereafter become one of the most successful entrepreneurs and advertisers of the era, King C. Gillette.[2] His story is a fascinating one, and typifies the apparent contradictions and ironies that surround the rise of mass-market advertising and media.

By 1895, the 40-year-old Gillette had gained little public notice either as an author or as an inventor, having already secured several patents for devices with no apparent market. He made his living as a traveling salesman. His most successful client was William Painter, who had invented and marketed the cork-lined bottle cap. In 1895, Painter advised Gillette, who seemed to be undergoing something of a midlife crisis, to try to think of a product like the bottle cap that, once discarded, would have to be purchased again and again by consumers. Gillette had his "eureka" moment while shaving one morning with an impossibly dull blade. He reflected on the fact that, considering the need to sharpen the edge and treat nicks and scrapes, shaving with a traditional straight razor could take half an hour or longer. What if men need no longer be bothered with the time and trouble? Wouldn't they pay for the privilege? The result was Gillette's safety razor. After bringing on a more talented inventor, the pointedly named William Nickerson, as well as some majority stockholders, Gillette's company brought out his new safety razor in 1903.[3]

The product did not sell itself. The Gillette Safety Razor Company proceeded to make masterful use of the techniques of packaging, advertising, and publicity that had arisen in the latter decades of the nineteenth century. Its first magazine ad read simply, "We offer a new razor." Subsequent pitches promised "no stropping, no honing"—emphasizing the potential time savings—and an end to the "barbershop habit," emphasizing the potential money savings. In an early version of the now-familiar "Put your money where your mouth is" line, Gillette had his own face plastered on ads and razor-blade packages, stating, "If my Razor wasn't good enough for me to use, I wouldn't ask you to try it." Gillette recognized that he was not getting men simply to buy a new razor (and, more importantly to the company, a continuous supply of razor blades). He was asking them to adopt a new shaving *system*. Gillette encouraged newspapers and magazines to run articles describing how to use the new razors, and wrote his own piece describing how best to dispose of used blades safely. To rebut suggestions that shaving with a safety razor was somehow effeminate, he hired Honus Wagner, a Hall of Fame shortstop from major league baseball, as a spokesman.[4] To exude even more manliness, he used images that compared shaving to forest clearing and other means of lording over nature. To get a laugh, Gillette put a baby in a 1905 color ad with a face covered in shaving cream and the slogan "Begin early, Shave yourself."[5]

A key theme of Gillette's early ad campaigns was freedom. "The Gillette Company declared that a man's personal freedom was compromised by the need to pay another man to shave him," wrote Gib Prettyman, a scholar who has researched Gillette's career. "At the same time, shaving could become a more telling expression of personal values if a man was potentially responsible for shaving himself."[6] So, was Gillette implying that to purchase his safety razor was to issue a sort of Declaration of (Shaving) Independence? No. This was not an implication. A 1906 ad in the *Saturday Evening Post* made the point explicitly, with a picture of George Washington holding a traditional straight razor in one hand and a Gillette razor in the other. "George Washington Gave an Era of Liberty to the Colonies," the ad stated, and "the Gillette Gives an Era of Personal Liberty to All Men." Farther down, it argues that the new safety razor "gives men freedom

from the slavish habit of being shaved by another." And just to up-
date the message for the modern reader—the ad bore prominently
both the dates "1776" and "1906"—it tied the freedom theme into a
current issue about American expansion and freedom of navigation:
"If the time, money, energy, and brainpower which are wasted in the
barber shops of America were applied in direct effort, the Panama
canal could be dug in four hours."[7]

Gillette went from selling 51 razors and 168 blades in 1903 to an
astounding 90,000 razors and 12 million blades in 1904. The next
year, he doubled the amount spent on advertising per razor, and sales
soared again. "The whole success of this business depends on advertising," he later reminded his board. "We must be the aggressor—we
must be continually advancing and drive [competitors] back at the
point of the bayonet, and our ammunition must be money for advertising," which was like a "Gatling gun" to "drive them from the field."[8]

So what are we to make of the fact that this seemingly militaristic
commander of a modern marketing army was at the same time writing about advertising as if he were the commercial equivalent of a
pacifist? Very much reflecting the intellectual trends of his day, and
probably bearing the direct influence of socialist Edward Bellamy's famous 1888 novel *Looking Backward*, Gillette was by the 1890s a full-
throated advocate of central planning, socialist economics, and social
engineering on a massive scale. His aforementioned 1894 tome, *The
Human Drift*, probably requires extensive reading to be fully appreciated as a methodical and horrifying blueprint for the eradication of
difference, the repudiation of commerce, and the redefinition of "freedom." Proposing to build a utopian "Metropolis"—he was probably
the first to use the term as a proper noun—that would straddle the
boundary between New York State and Canada, Gillette went as far
as to offer engineering specs, building materials, and the optimum mix
of industries for his concept of densely packed skyscrapers housing
the entire population of America in a strip 120 miles long and 30 miles
wide. He stated repeatedly that "no system can ever be a perfect system, and free from incentive for crime, until money and all representative value of material is swept from the face of the earth."[9]

Gillette's condemnations of advertising and commerce were inspired by his own career as a salesman—"one of that nomadic frater-

nity" who were as important to modern capitalism as the entrepreneur, banker, or merchant, he wrote. From Gillette's experience, he drew the conclusion that competitive business was wasteful and blocked the application of reason and purposeful planning to economic and social problems. He said that the entire business sector could—and should—merge into a single, all-encompassing holding company. By eliminating the distractions of competitive enterprise, this entity would finally be powerful and forceful enough to take on the engineering challenge of the age: "The world is a diamond in the rough, and intellect, the only progressive entity, must cut the facets to discover its beauty and power." While there would be no room for advertising, public relations, salesmanship, and other marketing practices within his United Company, they would be useful tools during the transition, Gillette argued. "Promoters are the true socialists of this generation, and in a practical business way reaching results which socialists have vainly tried to attain through legislation and agitation for centuries," he wrote.[10]

Gillette's views on advertising and commerce are not as difficult to reconcile as they might first appear. Indeed, they represent one of several familiar—and often mutually inconsistent—objections that can be traced far back into history. Some critics thought advertising was an ineffective tool that served primarily to squander scarce resources. Others believed it was all too effective in manipulating consumers and making them buy products they did not need and could not really afford. Some scholars and merchants argued that aggressive advertising tended to help companies win monopolies in their respective industries, though they disagreed on whether this was a good thing (Gillette thought it was) or so deleterious as to justify government intervention. On the other hand, other scholars and business leaders believed that advertising subverted monopolies by allowing upstart competitors to challenge dominant industries, though again there was disagreement as to whether this was a benign outcome (some market leaders sought to restrict or abolish advertising to protect themselves from competition).

I find it useful to group these various challenges to advertising and other forms of commercial communication into four general categories: the argument from religion, the argument from culture, the argument from neoclassical economics, and the argument from institutional economics. Naturally, prominent critics of advertising often mixed several of these arguments together in their writings, speeches, or proposals. Nevertheless, I think that they are sufficiently distinct to merit separate treatment.

# ADVERTISING, RELIGION, AND MORALITY

For many condemnations of advertising, the spiritual and philosophical roots run deep. That is not to say that advertising per se was a subject of significant discussion in the world's major religious texts or in the writings of the great philosophers. Rather, the concepts that would inform later assaults on advertising and other marketing practices—concepts such as the sin of envy and the just price—were taken directly from religious teaching and the secular works of philosophy that both influenced and reflected such teaching.

For example, an important theme that runs throughout many critiques of advertising is that it wrongfully exploits human temptations, that it creates a desire for material goods that otherwise would not exist. Deleterious consequences are said to flow from this desire, including depression, envy, thievery, and violence. People are led astray to spend their money on luxuries rather than on the necessities of life. Parents ignore the needs of their children. The poor starve while the rich dine. God's creation is despoiled to provide extravagant clothes and gargantuan homes. And so on.

While few religious scholars and moral philosophers would question the morality of distributing basic information about how much a product costs and where it can be purchased, they have often frowned on "excessive" salesmanship that seems to emphasize images over facts. A recent statement by the Vatican's Pontifical Council on Social Communications expressed a centuries-old skepticism among many Christian theologians about "[a]dvertising that not only informs but also seeks to persuade and motivate—to convince people to act in certain ways, buy certain products or services, patronize certain institutions, and the like. This is where particular abuses can occur."[11] Although drawing inspiration from a number of scriptural references and teachings, critics from the religious traditions of Judaism and Christianity often consider the Old Testament's ninth and tenth commandments to be of particular relevance to the issue. One common translation of the two in the Book of Exodus reads as follows:

20:16 You shall not bear false witness against your neighbor.
20:17 You shall not covet your neighbor's house, you shall not covet your neighbor's wife, or his manservant, or his maidservant, or his ox, or his ass, or anything that is your neighbor's.

The importance of the ninth commandment to discussions of trade practices and business ethics would seem to be clear, though in the original Hebrew the rule against lying appears to apply only to legal disputes and governmental proceedings and thus had to be interpreted more broadly later to encompass a prohibition against falsity in business dealings. Still, understood in the context of other religious teachings, a rule against merchants trying to defraud their suppliers and customers would seem to be straightforward—and indeed has had great relevance to discussions and criticisms of advertising and salesmanship. The issue resisted simplification, however. While some theologians and ethicists thought of commercial fraud in literal terms—a salesman using unambiguously false claims to make a good seem more attractive or to obscure its real cost—others took the concept to mean more generally that it was wrong to emphasize any selling points about a good other than basics such as price. For example, some Jewish scholars interpreted the commandment to create a severe limitation on commercial behavior. "A storekeeper can't even polish his apples to make them more attractive than his competitors' fruit if there is no different in quality," according to one interpretation.[12] Obviously, if using audio or visual techniques to make a good more attractive to potential customers was wrongful, much of what constitutes advertising and marketing was morally suspect.

But why was the tenth commandment, warning against the sin of covetousness, considered relevant to the acts of commercial persuasion? Because, critics said, these acts really constituted attempts to make an audience want what others possessed. As early as the first century A.D., the Hellenic Jewish philosopher Philo argued that the tenth commandment was intended to warn against "desire" itself. He wrote that "desire is a thing fond of revolution and plotting against others; for all the passions of the soul are formidable, exciting and agitating it contrary to nature, and not permitting it to remain in a healthy state, but of all such passions the worst is desire. On which account each of the other passions, coming in from without and attacking the soul from external points, appears to be involuntary." For Philo, then, the desire to obtain something one did not already possess was the genesis of sin; indeed, sinful feelings and actions were "involuntary" outgrowths of covetous desire.[13] Many theologians who followed Philo also equated coveting with desiring, and saw the tenth commandment as a warning against materialism and commercialism. Many early Christians combined this thought with references throughout the New Testament to greed, idolatry, and the manifest wickedness of "the wealthy" to denigrate the pursuit and accumulation of worldly possessions.[14]

But on this matter, as on so many issues of scriptural interpretation and religious principle, there has always been disagreement. With regard to what "coveting" is, and how business practices might encourage or avoid it, the disagreement started with the translation of the Hebrew text. The word *hamad*, which was translated into Greek and later into other languages with words such as *covet* and *crave*, also originally bore the meaning of "to attempt to attach something to oneself illegally"—or, to put it another way, to attempt to steal or defraud another. It referred not just to feelings but also to actions. Scholars interpreting the tenth commandment in this literal way did not see it as redundant with the eighth, traditionally rendered as "you shall not steal," because in that case the original Hebrew word actually translated as "enslaving a neighbor's labor," essentially a form of kidnapping.[15] Christians who adhered to this interpretation of the commandment against coveting cited as evidence the words of Jesus in the Gospel of Mark, in which he restated several of the commandments and used the phrase "do not defraud" to convey the meaning of the tenth commandment.[16]

This quite different understanding of the commandment, and more generally of the Bible's teachings about acquisition and commerce, was understandably more popular among those believers who engaged in trade and were successful in their business. As far as trade practices were concerned, this understanding of the commandment could still lead to strong criticism, as Martin Luther was offering by the sixteenth century:

> Such is nature that we all begrudge another's having as much as we have. Everyone acquires all he can and lets others look out for themselves. Yet we all pretend to be upright. We know how to put up a fine front to conceal our rascality. We think up artful dodges and sly tricks (better and better ones are being devised daily) under the guide of justice. We brazenly dare to boast of it, and insist that it should be called not rascality but shrewdness and business acumen.[17]

Still, within this tradition what was condemned by scripture and teaching was not acquisitiveness or ambition, not a desire for a better life for oneself and one's family, but instead (1) illegal actions to obtain goods belonging to someone else, and (2) wishing that others did not have what they had, a kind of envy that these believers thought led to unjust acts and social disharmony. A Calvinist catechism in 1647 read that "the 10th Commandment require[d] full contentment with our own condition, with a right and charitable frame of spirit toward our neighbor, and all that is his. The 10th Commandment forbid[s] all discontentment with our own estate, envying or grieving at the good of our neighbor, and all inordinate motions and affections to anything that is his." More recently, the sociologist Max Weber observed the distinction that "greed for gain is not in the least identical with capitalism, and is still less its spirit." Condemnations of the wealthy and praise for the poor in the teachings of Jesus and the early apostles must, according to this view, be understood in the context of a Roman world in which it was exceedingly difficult to amass wealth outside of a web of government corruption, tax-farming contracts, exclusive monopolies, and outright (and officially sanctioned) thievery and fraud.[18]

Characteristically, the Catholic Church charted somewhat of a middle course between these two interpretations of the tenth commandment and, more generally, the Christian duty to reconcile religious principle with commerce and the worldly life. A believer was not enjoined from desiring material comforts altogether, or seeking to meet them through trade and commerce, but neither was the believer free to engage in any and every form of consensual commercial activity. According to the second edition of the *Catechism of the Catholic Church*, the commandment "forbids greed and the desire to amass earthly goods without limit." An earlier version warned that while it was not a sin to desire to obtain things belonging to someone else, as long as they were obtained by just means, the definition of *just means* extended beyond just the absence of force or fraud. At risk of violating the commandment were "merchants who desire scarcity and rising prices, who cannot bear not to be the only ones buying and selling so that they themselves can sell more dearly and buy more cheaply; those who hope that their peers will be impoverished, in order to realize a profit either by selling to them or buying from them . . . physicians who wish disease to spread; lawyers who are eager for many important cases and trials."[19]

Another strand of religious thought that influenced perceptions of advertising and marketing was the theory of the *just price*. If the goods and services we buy include promotional and advertising costs in their price, some critics said, then they impose an unjust burden on consumers because the price is higher than it needs to be. Discussions of economic value and price actually began in the West centuries before the birth of Christ in the early legal codes such as that of the Babylonian ruler Hammurabi—whose famous law code included regulations of wages and prices—as well as the writings of several important Greek philosophers. Plato, for example, exhibited deep hostility to money and trade, calling them "necessarily evils" and appearing to grope for some way for societies to order their economic affairs through central planning and enlightened regulation. Other Greek thinkers such as Xenophon and Protagoras seemed more favorably disposed to the idea that, for example, there was no way to determine objectively what a good "should" be worth. Plato's student Aristotle also grappled with issues of price and value, observing that "what is rare is a greater good than what is plentiful. Thus gold is a better thing than iron, though less useful; it is harder to get, and therefore better worth getting." But Aristotle did not succeed in explaining the interaction between value in scarcity and value in use, and could not solve the apparent paradox that water seemed to be much more valuable to human beings, but less valued by human beings, than diamonds were.[20]

As these ideas percolated through the later Roman world, and began both to influence and be influenced by early Christian teaching, a distinction became evident between price and value, the former referring to the amount of goods or currency typically asked in exchange for a given good in a given place and the latter referring to the satisfaction or enjoyment the purchaser found in the good. St. Augustine wrote in *The City of God* that "according to the utility each man finds in a thing, there are various standards of value," as one person might value a slave over a horse and another value the horse over the slave. Consensus on the issue was impossible because "every man has the power of forming his own mind as he wishes."[21] By the sixth century, the legal code promulgated by Emperor Justinian clearly distinguished market prices from the values that consumers might assign. "The prices of things function not according to the whim or utility of individuals, but according to the common estimate," the code stated. ". . . Time and place, however, bring about some variations in price. Oil will not be evaluated the same in Rome as in Spain."[22]

Later, after the fall of Rome and the onset of the medieval period in Europe, some religious scholars began to address price and value directly. In the thirteenth century, two Christian theologians—Albertus Magnus and his student Thomas Aquinas—framed the debate over the just price by focusing attention on the cost of producing a good. Following the lead of both Aristotle and St. Augustine, Magnus recognized a distinction between the natural order and the economic order in determining the value of something. In the latter case, he wrote, one could estimate the economic value of a good by determining the "labor and expenses" consumed in producing it. If the price offered in the marketplace was lower than this cost of production, then the good soon would not be produced for sale at all. Economic historians Robert Ekelund and Robert Hebert argue that Magnus had made "an important analytical leap" by describing what economists would later call the "equilibrium" between supply and demand, with cost then acting as a "regulator of value."[23] Aquinas then followed up Magnus's focus on cost as a determinant of economic value, or the value in exchange, by observing the role of human wants in determining a product's value in use. Later economists seized upon this distinction to develop a coherent theory of the market process, often expressed in graphs where supply curves (influenced by the cost of production) and demand curves (influenced by consumer preferences) met at an equilibrium point that represented the market price of a good at a particular point in time.

But the writings of Aquinas were not interpreted by theologians of his day or in the ensuing centuries as constituting a defense of markets in determining the price of goods. Instead, they pointed to his discussions of a just price that would guarantee fairness and an equality of all men before God. Aquinas applied the New Testament's Golden Rule—"Do unto others as you would have them do to you"— to economic exchange and concluded that each side should gain the same value from a trade. "No man should sell a thing to another man for more than its worth," Aquinas wrote in his *Summa Theologica*, meaning that the price offered to a consumer should be the same as the price that a vendor would feel justified in paying. The sage economic advice to "buy low and sell high" was, in other words, a form of injustice, as was charging interest on borrowed money, though Aquinas was willing to accept the reality of profit as long as it was tightly regulated and put to good use: "as when a man uses moderate gains acquired in trade for the support of his household, or even to help the needy."[24]

By no means was the Aquinas just price concept considered the last word in Christian thought about the issue. Other scholars refined the concept, expanding the original focus on individual needs to encompass a broader notion of aggregate and effective demand. In the sixteenth century, the so-called Salamanca school of theologians and philosophers in Spain took a skeptical look at the theory of the just price. "Those who measure the just price by the labor, costs, and risk incurred by the person who deals in the merchandise or produces it, or by the cost of transport or the expense of traveling . . . are greatly in error," wrote Luis Saravia de la Calle in a 1544 work. Thus, a producer could not work out a just price by simply tallying up his costs. A well-written book produced inexpensively by a printing press should not cost less than a poorly written book written out laboriously by hand, he explained. Instead, a just price had to come from a "common estimation," by the collective judgment of many producers and consumers.[25]

Still, the Aquinas doctrine was immensely influential, and remained so through the seventeenth, eighteenth, and nineteenth centuries when the mass media were born and ways of advertising products exploded. Members of the clergy, with their suspicions of striving and extravagance rooted in their reading of the Old Testament and their suspicions of consumer exploitation rooted in the New Testament, were key early critics of these trends. In 1829, the famous Congregationalist Reverend Lyman Beecher (father of the even more famous author of *Uncle Tom's Cabin*, Harriet Beecher Stowe), warned that "the power of voluntary self-denial is not equal to the temptation of an all-surrounding abundance." Writing in the first issue of the *Atlantic Monthly* in 1857, the journalist Parke Godwin wrote of "a whole commercial society suddenly wrecked" by excessive demand for "fine upholstery," "costly dinners," and other luxuries. "When the times comes—as come it will—for paying for all this glorious frippery, we collapse, we wither . . . we sink into the sand," he predicted.[26]

Susan J. Matt, a historian at Weber State University, has studied the American reaction to the rise of the mass consumer market. "In the late nineteenth and early twentieth centuries, many Americans worried about the influence of the expanding consumer economy on morality and behavior," she wrote, adding that churchmen and other moralists attacked the role of in-store, newspaper, magazine, and catalog advertising in provoking dangerous feelings of envy and disenchantment and in raising the price of goods to consumers.[27] She cited the example of Edward Bok, editor of *Ladies' Home Journal*, who worried that if, because of mass advertising of fine clothes and other luxuries, "a woman succumbed to her envy, she would soon engage in other types of immoral behavior that might threaten family peace and welfare and endanger female purity."[28] Even commentators more favorable to capitalism in general, such as Baptist minister and Brown University President Francis Wayland (who wrote one of the most popular economics textbooks of the nineteenth century), warned against excessive consumption and extravagance.[29]

# CRITIQUES OF THE CARNIVAL CULTURE

As the nineteenth century progressed, a movement toward secularism, in some cases shading into agnosticism or atheism, yielded a new generation of social critics. They often espoused views about capitalism and the emerging consumer culture similar to those of their religious counterparts but relied on different kinds of evidence and argumentation. The poet Arthur Hugh Clough, for example, was born in 1819 in Wales but also spent some of his childhood in Charleston, South Carolina, and was reared and educated within the bounds of traditional religion. During his university days at Oxford, Clough began to move away from orthodox religion, even giving up his college fellowship in order to escape ordination in the Church of England. After time spent on the Continent in the revolutionary movements of France and Italy, Clough became an educator, social reformer, and poet. Commenting on what he saw as the hypocrisy of English society, the gap between biblical teachings and actual human behavior, he wrote a famous verse that included these lines:

> Thou shalt not steal; an empty feat,
> When 'tis so lucrative to cheat:
> Bear not false witness; let the lie
> Have time on its own wings to fly:
> Thou shalt not covet, but tradition
> Approves all forms of competition[30]

In America, Ralph Waldo Emerson challenged the artificiality of much of commercial culture, attracting many followers and admirers (including Clough) to his views about authenticity and the imperative of transcending fashion. Later American writers and commentators picked up this strand of thought to denigrate advertising as frivolous (Mark Twain wrote that "many a small thing has been made large by the right kind of advertising"), manipulative ("Advertising," said Will Rogers, "is the art of convincing people to spend money they don't have for something they don't need"), and wasteful (as previously noted, Sinclair Lewis contended that advertising was "the cheapest way of selling goods, particularly if the goods are worthless").[31] Sherwood Anderson, who spent twenty years as an ad agency copywriter, said that he had been "soiling his tools" as a writer in the business and that advertising was a "universal whoredom."[32]

In his intermittently engaging and exasperating *Fables of Abundance: A Cultural History of Advertising in America*, Jackson Lears portrays this criticism as in part a reaction to the carnival and medicine-show culture of mid- to late nineteenth-century America. The rise of mass media advertising during the period did bear the unmistakable imprint of such traveling showmen. Slogans and imagery in print advertising were often reminiscent of the barker and the circus sign. As for the sale of medicines of questionable composition and effectiveness, there was no doubting the ease with which it made the leap from the back of a traveling salesman's wagon to the back page of national magazines (as discussed in greater detail in Chapter 6). There is also no doubt those engaged in the advertising business recognized this early relationship between the carnival and the commercial and its potential for embarrassment and invalidation. As early as 1850, newspaper publisher Horace Greeley was seeking to distinguish legitimate advertising from what he considered the bawdy intrusions of carnival culture:

> There is a large class who delight to shine in newspapers as wits and poets, and announce their wares in second-hand jokes, or in doggerel fit to set the teeth of a dull saw on edge. If their object is notoriety or a laugh, this is the way to attain it; but if it be business, it would seem better to use the language of business. Leave clowns' jests to the circus, and let sober men speak as they act, with directness and decision.[33]

Greeley might well have had a particular person in mind when he wrote that passage: Phineas T. Barnum, often credited with originating the concept of an organized advertising campaign. "I knew that every dollar sown in advertising would return to me in tens, and perhaps hundreds, in a future harvest," the famous circus owner and promoter wrote in the same year (1850) as Greeley's jeremiad. Born in 1810, Barnum actually pioneered a range of techniques in commercial persuasion, including not just formal print advertising but also public relations, press releases, publicity stunts, outdoor advertising, and word of mouth. After learning the selling trade as a bartender, publisher, and ticket vendor, Barnum came to New York in 1834 and began work as a promoter. The next year he managed a famous attraction at the American Museum featuring a purportedly 161-year-old woman who was the former slave and nanny of George Washington. After interest in the improbable show dwindled, Barnum wrote letters to New York newspapers under assumed names alleging that Barnum was defrauding the public. The ensuing controversy boosted attendance again.[34]

Later, Barnum took a troupe of performers on the road for seven years, then returned to the American Museum as owner and proprietor. It boasted such famous fakes as the "Wooly Horse" and the "Feejee Mermaid" (in reality a monkey's upper body sewn to a fish's tail). He made lots of money. He later lost lots of money in bad investments, going bankrupt and finding the need to reinvent himself in the 1860s. He began to work more live animals into his museum attractions, and then took advantage of the new national railroad lines to "take his show on the road," quite literally, and eventually to boast "the Greatest Show on Earth."

Was Greeley right to consider Barnum and other manifestations of the carnival culture as reflecting poorly on the legitimate advertising business? And further, were critics of advertising right to dismiss even the concept of a distinction between the two, to view advertising and other kinds of commercial persuasion as little more than a giant three-ring circus? It depends on the extent to which Barnum, particularly in the ventures of his mature years, truly sought to trick and swindle or to amaze and entertain. "The public appears disposed to be amused, even when they are conscious of being deceived," he wrote in his own defense.[35] While false claims about patent medicines might defraud or endanger the lives of customers, false claims about a woman's age or a strange animal's parentage were "all part of the show," Barnum seemed to be suggesting, and added to the humor and self-parody that he was offering to audiences. Clearly, it is one thing to make children's eyes light up with ridiculous tales and visual sleights of hand. It is quite another to promise a sewing machine that will not break down, only it does; or vegetable seeds that turn out to be mostly grass seeds; or a "traditional Indian medicine" for serious ailments that turns out to consist in large measure of an undisclosed shot of grain alcohol.

For many of advertising's critics in the late nineteenth and early twentieth centuries, however, its roots in the periphery of popular culture were damning. After all, as Lears and others have noted, the cultural "establishment" has often associated the traveling salesmen, the fast-talking carnival barker, and the medicine-show practitioner of dubious medical pedigree with untrustworthy outsiders. Many felt both a visceral revulsion toward such characters—toward Yankee traders in the American South and West and toward Jewish or Asian peddlers across the country—as well as a sort of perverse, "forbidden fruit" attraction to the same. Moralists might express displeasure with commercial culture as violating biblical commandments or purveying dangerous temptations, but these cultural critics tended to view advertising as sordid, as beneath their dignity, as behavior that did not measure up to their expectations of how people should spend their time and money and what they should think about. As economist Israel Kirzner once put it, this argument reflects a "deep-seated contempt for the low tastes of the masses," but it is "all the easier to blame the vulgarity of mass tastes upon the businessmen who minister to them."[36] A related theme of this critique was the association of the new consumer culture with urbanity, with a lifestyle less authentic and meaningful than the traditional realm of the family farm. President Theodore Roosevelt complained in 1908 that "there is too much belief among all our people that the prizes of life lie away from the farm," a belief than he and others blamed in part on the new mass media and their advertising messages.[37]

While religious and secular attacks on advertising are distinguishable, they are not entirely separate. Sociologist Michael Schudson divides cultural attacks on advertising and the consumer society into four categories. One is the Aristocratic critique, which I just described. Two others, the Quaker critique and the Puritan critique, obviously have their roots in religious tradition but their expression has little to do with theology. The Quaker critique sees the use of persuasion as one of a set of commercial practices that generate wastefulness and extravagance. It sees materialism as the problem and simplicity, perhaps even austerity, as the solution. The Puritan critique, on the other hand, can be interpreted as suggesting that the *wrong kind* of materialism is the problem. Consumers *should* invest their own meaning in goods, based on their utility and personal experience, instead of allowing advertising to invest "surplus meaning" to them. "If we were sensibly materialist, in that part of our living in which we use things, we should find most advertising to be of an insane irrelevance," one critic of this camp wrote. "Beer would be enough for us, without the additional promise that in drinking it we show ourselves to be manly, young in heart, or neighborly." Schudson's final category, the Republican critique, argues that advertising and consumer culture lead individuals to become too passive, too indulgent, and too "privatized." This idea—which, like the others, has a profoundly backward-looking, conservative ring to it despite its provenance among the secular left— is that modern commerce cheapens and displaces public life.[38]

## THE MIXED MESSAGE IN NEOCLASSICAL ECONOMICS

As previously noted, one of the great unsolved mysteries in the proto-economic writings of ancient and medieval thinkers was the question of price and value. In the eighteenth century, Adam Smith had grappled with some of the same issues in his classic *Wealth of Nations*, restating the old paradox that a diamond has a high value in exchange but little in use, while "nothing is more useful than water" but "scarce anything can be had in exchange for it."[39] Smith could not resolve the paradox either, and focused his attention on changes over time in the exchange value, in the price of one good relative to another. His efforts in this regard, and across a host of important economic topics, may not have all been entirely as original as commonly believed, but there is no question that Smith was effective at integrating ideas. He was a system builder. And his system, expanded over the decades of the late eighteenth and nineteenth centuries by other thinkers such as David Ricardo and John Stuart Mill, became known as classical economics. Even Karl Marx, while helping to lead a radical revolt against classical economics in the mid-nineteenth century, accepted many of its basic tenets and definitions. His labor theory of value, for example, was a version—albeit a narrow and deeply flawed one—of the old classical concept that the value of a good was determined from the cost of producing it.[40]

During the 1870s, at least three separate schools of economic thought developed and promulgated the solution to the problem of value. This solution was called marginal utility, or marginalism. While differing in particulars, theories of marginal utility contained the fundamental insight that consumers place their own value on goods and services quite apart from how much it costs to produce them; that these value preferences can differ dramatically based on time, place, and personal preferences; and, most importantly, that they happen "on the margin." That is, consumers place a value on a prospective purchase based on how much of that good they already use or possess. This is how marginalists resolved the water-diamond paradox: obviously water in general is more valuable to human life than are diamonds in general, but the real question is how much the next amount of water is valued over the next amount of diamonds. If I own a well and rarely feel thirsty, your offer of a gallon of water will not interest me much. But if I live in a desert and have limited stores of water, your offer might be worth a great deal. (Still, to the well owner, the total benefit that he derives from all the water he uses is large, even if the marginal value—the value of one more gallon—is small.)

Two of the three schools espousing the marginalist revolution in economic thought were based on the European continent: the Austrians, centered on Vienna and including Carl Menger, Eugene von Bohm-Bawerk, and Friedrich von Wieser; and the Swiss, Italian, and French followers of Leon Walras at the University of Lucerne. The third school was founded in Britain, where William Stanley Jevons published his seminal work, *Theory of Political Economy*, in 1871. Marginalism and other ideas became embodied in a neoclassical school of economics that came to be associated with a prolific author and teacher at Cambridge University, Alfred Marshall. One of his important contributions was a careful and systematic approach to building models for how an economy functions across markets and time. Another was his sound knowledge of mathematics and its application to economic analysis. Unfortunately, despite Marshall's own attempts to warn against excessive theorizing and mathematical formulations, his work helped to form a mindset among later generations of economists that downplayed the role of advertising and other forms of salesmanship in communicating critical information between and among buyers and sellers. As economists Robert B. Ekelund, Jr., and David S. Saurman put it in their pathbreaking 1988 work, *Advertising and the Market Process*, economists in the Marshallian tradition "have traditionally been in the vanguard of those stressing advertising as wasteful activity" because of their "long honeymoon with the conclusion of a perfectly competitive model in which advertising is regarded as superfluous."[41]

Anyone who has taken a basic college course in economics can, upon reflection, see the effect to which Ekelund and Saurman were referring. The familiar graphs of curving lines, used to demonstrate how market equilibrium is found and why prices change in relationship to changes in supply and demand, are based on so-called perfect information. It is assumed that if the quantity of goods changes, consumers as a group find out about this and respond. It is also assumed that if consumer preferences change, producers as a group find out about that and respond. The problem is that in a real world of complexity, diversity, disorder, and competing claims on attention and resources, there is nothing automatic about the exchange of economic information. It is costly to collect and to distribute. If producers want consumers to know that they can now manufacture a good more quickly or at a lower cost, thus allowing them to make more such goods for sale, they have to make an effort to do so. Similarly, if consumers find that they have too much of one thing or too little of another, they need some effective means by which to make their changing preferences known to potential suppliers.

Marshall had thought enough about how the economy worked in practice, not just in theory, to recognize that businesses often found it wise to advertise. Surprisingly, he was one of the first major economists known to have even discussed the subject, in this case in his 1919 book, *Industry and Trade*. He wrote that some producers needed to spend significant sums communicating to potential consumers about goods that the latter might never have thought about buying before. Marshall cited the example of the typewriter. "When the idea of a typewriter was first conceived, very few people were inclined to take seriously the suggestion that it could rival the pen in efficiency," he wrote. Thus, typewriter manufacturers needed to advertise to convince consumers that the product would satisfy a need of theirs.[42] More generally, Marshall observed that advertising served to communicate where goods and services could be purchased, and at what price. These messages helped consumers to "satisfy their wants without inordinate fatigue or loss of time," he wrote, thus potentially reducing the real cost of goods and services to these consumers.[43]

But Marshall failed to develop these insights further. Moreover, his work also contained significant challenges to advertising in theory and practice. While advertising might be useful in clueing consumers in on the existence of a new product, Marshall argued that its use in more mature markets with familiar goods and established producers was likely to be wasteful. After all, if competing firms used repetitive commercial messages to boost their brand names without communicating any additional information, how could consumers be benefiting from it? The advertising campaigns merely added to the cost of bringing the goods to market, a cost frequently passed on to buyers in the form of higher prices. Some of his students went further in the denunciation of advertising. One of the most famous, Arthur C. Pigou, listed advertising as one of the tactics companies could use to establish and protect a dominance in a particular industry. He wrote that in this case, "extensive advertising or a distinctive trade mark may have established a sort of monopoly of reputation, which it would require heavy advertising expenditure on the part of any would-be rival to break down."[44] Thus, while Pigou opened the door to advertising as a potential threat to monopoly, he saw most would-be competitors as being unable to afford enough of it to break through the power of brand names and consumer habits established by the advertising of monopolies or cartels. So on balance, he suggested, advertising was often injurious to consumers and the public interest.

It is not surprising that Pigou and other economists and social scientists advanced this criticism during the 1920s. The content of advertising was then changing from 1800s-era blocks of dense text and near-anatomical photographs of products to a modern, looser style that placed products in a cultural context. Depending on the target audience, the layout might depict urban sophisticates, housewives, businessmen, teenagers, or children using and enjoying what was being advertised.[45] Many other economists and thinkers influenced by the neoclassical tradition of Jevons and Marshall would make more pointed criticisms of the business of advertising in the coming decades. Their concern was typically greater to the extent that advertisements went beyond simple declarations of a product's price, characteristics, and availability to employ powerful images, to introduce fads and fashion, and to differentiate and perpetuate brands. What, these scholars asked, did any of this have to do with communicating basic information to consumers?

## THE INSTITUTIONALIST CHALLENGE TO ADS AND ACQUISITION

If the neoclassical economists of the late nineteenth and early twentieth centuries were of two minds about the benefits of advertising in the emerging modern economy, adherents to a rival school of thought, the institutionalists, were of one mind: advertising harmed the public welfare. This distinctly American tradition in economics was founded by Thorstein Veblen, a Midwesterner of Norwegian ancestry who was trained at Yale University as a philosopher and later taught political economy at the University of Chicago, Stanford University, the University of Missouri, and the New School for Social Research. Veblen's most famous work was the 1899 book *Theory of the Leisure Class*, which savaged the basic assumptions and common applications of classical and neoclassical economics and popularized the concept of *conspicuous consumption*, which was to play a key role in debates over advertising and consumer culture.

While Veblen was a unique thinker in many respects, his approach to economic issues was not without antecedents. Beginning in the decades prior to the marginalist revolution of the 1870s, scholars in both Great Britain and the Continent had challenged the theoretical basis of the classical economics of Adam Smith, David Ricardo, and John Stuart Mill. These critics argued for inquiry more closely tied to case studies and a methodology that eschewed grand systems and sweeping insights in favor of analysis that takes into account the particular cultures, customs, and social norms of individual nations or regions. The German historical school, for example, questioned the universality of liberal, free market ideas as well as those of Marxism. Its adherents sought a "middle way," a culturally appropriate socialism that did not require or anticipate revolution. Among English-speaking scholars in Britain and the United States, a similar vein of thought emphasized historical study and pragmatism over the formation of generally applicable laws of economic behavior (Veblen himself studied at Johns Hopkins University under Charles Sanders Peirce, the founder of the American pragmatist school of philosophy).[46]

But Veblen's skepticism about classical economics was far deeper. He questioned its fundamental presuppositions about utility, about why people desire goods and how they go about trying to acquire them. In typically rich language, he wrote that the classical writers had employed a "conception of man" as "a lightening calculator of pleasures and pains, who oscillates like a homogeneous globule of desire of happiness under the impulse of stimuli that shift him about the area, but leave him intact."[47] In reality, Veblen wrote, human beings are creatures of habit as well as whim, of status as well as comfort, and of emotion as well as reason. In describing how humanity came to desire and produce things, Veblen's theory reflected a fascination with the new Darwinian science of evolution. Peering back into the prehistory of primitive man, he argued that people did not seek to acquire goods only to satisfy their innate desires or ameliorate their pains. He suggested the concept of *pecuniary emulation*, the idea that people often acquired goods either to improve their status within their peer group or at least to fit into a peer group enjoying a certain degree of comfort or luxury. Initially, Veblen thought, human societies offered honor and respect to those who accumulated great wealth through physical prowess—through war, violence, and plunder. Over time, even as such behavior grew to be less commonly accepted as normal and acceptable, the pursuit of wealth through other means still served as a means of demonstrating one's honor and might. Indeed, one might earn social respect not only by acquiring lots of things but also, and perhaps just as importantly, by no longer exhibiting the need to work hard. Leisure would itself become something that would be conspicuously consumed, just as spacious homes, sumptuous clothes, or scrumptious meals would be.

In other words, Veblen's take on the market process was not limited to the argument that, left to its own devices, it might not consistently deliver the goods and services consumers might want at prices driven down by competition among providers. Economists within the neoclassical, Marshallian tradition sometimes came to that conclusion because they still operated within the classical framework of maximizing utility, and as we have seen, Marshallians such as Pigou drew such a conclusion about much of the advertising industry. Veblen's point was more subversive. It was really questioning whether consumers' perceptions of utility were useful in the first place. If they wanted to buy a new and larger house not to enjoy its spaciousness or to accommodate the needs of their changing families, but primarily because other people they knew owned larger houses, then no real social utility was being accomplished, Veblen asserted. There is a contrasting ethic within human societies, an ethic that he called "workmanship" and praised as the better standard for determining whether something is truly valuable. But pride of workmanship was frequently pushed aside by the dynamic of pecuniary emulation, with the result being a waste of society's resources:

> The test to which all expenditure must be brought in an attempt to decide [its wastefulness] is whether it serves directly to enhance human life on the whole—whether it furthers the life process taken impersonally. For this is the basis of award of the instinct of workmanship, and that instinct is the court of final appeal in any question of economic truth or adequacy. It is a question as to the award rendered by a dispassionate common sense. The question is, therefore, not whether, under the existing circumstances of individual habit and social custom, a given expenditure conduces to the particular consumer's gratification or peace of mind; but whether, aside from acquired tastes and from the canons of usage and conventional decency, its result is a net gain in comfort or in the fullness of life. Customary expenditure must be classed under the head of waste in so far as the custom on which it rests is traceable to the habit of making an invidious pecuniary comparison—in so far as it is conceived that it could not have become customary and prescriptive without the backing of this principle of pecuniary reputability or relative economic success.[48]

While the institutionalist school founded by Veblen contained broad implications for economic theory and practice, for our purposes his critique of the tools of commercial persuasion is most directly relevant. Obviously, if consumer desires are not assumed to be mostly, or perhaps even significantly, illustrative of true consumer needs, then the entire modern apparatus of production and marketing could potentially be seen as wrongheaded. If consumption is just conspicuous, not satiating, then advertising and marketing are part of a vicious circle; the more images there are of new and enticing goods and services to purchase, the more consumers will purchase them in order to "keep up with the Joneses," but then those seeking greater social status will need still more luxuries to be produced and advertised, and so on.

Veblen's system brought together many of the differing strands of anti-advertising sentiment together, in that he sought to offer scholarly support for such propositions as (1) advertising leads people to buy things they do not really need, (2) advertising is a wasteful process that pushes up prices, and (3) advertising and other kinds of marketing are distractions from the real problems that businesses and policy makers must address within a modern production economy, problems that are essentially technical in nature and thus require the talents of engineers, or "technocrats," to address rather than those of entrepreneurs, salesmen, and publicists.

When employed purely as a staid means of communicating the price and availability of goods, Veblen wrote in his 1905 book, *The Theory of Business Enterprise*, "advertising is a service to the community." But the "greater part" of advertising is "competitive" (a term he did not use as praise) and thus wastefully seeks to persuade consumers to switch from one brand to another, or to purchase one good over another, similar good. This is "of slight if any immediate service to the community," he continued, but businesses left to their own devices have little choice but to squander their resources:

Such advertising . . . is indispensable to most branches of modern industry; but the necessity of most of the advertising is not due to its serving the needs of the community nor to any aggregate advantage accruing to the concerts which advertise, but to the fact that a business concern which falls short in advertising fails to get its share of trade. Each concert must advertise, chiefly because the others do. The aggregate expenditure that could advantageously be put into advertising in the absence of competition would undoubtedly be but an inconsiderable fraction of what is actually incurred, and necessarily incurred under existing circumstances.[49]

Suggesting that as much as 90 percent of the cost of a product can be generated by the cost of marketing and distributing it, Veblen railed against the magnitude of the waste associated with modern business practices: "It is evident that the gains which accrue from this business of competitive selling and buying bear no determinable relation to the services which the work in question may render the community."[50]

The institutionalism of Thorstein Veblen was a direct assault on the mass advertising and consumer culture of his day, the early twentieth century. His ideas did not remain cloistered in academia. In fact, Veblen was not himself a particularly good fit in the academic world. He lost at least two teaching posts, at Chicago and Stanford, because of his odd and unkempt manner, weak teaching skills, and flagrant sexual dalliances with female students. He gained notoriety as an editor of the *Journal of Political Economy*, and then after World War I as the editor of a radical political magazine in New York City, *The Dial*, and as an essayist for *The New Republic* and *The Nation*. His books actually became much more famous after his death in 1929, but political activists had already read and digested them during his lifetime. Two Veblen acolytes, Frederick Schlink and Stuart Chase, published a book in 1927 entitled *Your Money's Worth*, which questioned whether consumers were truly getting what they deserved from the heavily advertised and marketed products they were buying in record numbers during the so-called Roaring '20s. The book sold well and led to the creation of Consumers Union, the organization that published (and continues to publish) the magazine *Consumer Reports*—noted for its refusal to accept business advertising.[51] Another follower of Veblen, James Rorty, published *Our Master's Voice* in 1934. A former advertising copywriter himself, Rorty fulminated against the industry and its role in sustaining competitive capitalism.[52]

Schlink, Chase, and Rorty were early leaders of the consumerist movement, an offshoot of the Progressivism of the period that had enjoyed early success in the 1906 passage of the Pure Food and Drug Act. As discussed in subsequent chapters, the consumerist movement was to enjoy both advances and retreats in the coming decades, as were critics of advertising as a whole. While each of the main strains of skepticism about commercial persuasion—the religious, the cultural, the neoclassical, and the institutionalist—has persisted into the twenty-first century, powerful forces were about to be unleashed within the industry that proved difficult to contain. Chief among them was the birth of broadcasting and the increasing commercialization of everyday life.

# CHAPTER 3

# Broadcasting Revolution, Advertising Evolution

The nineteenth and early twentieth centuries saw the rise of true mass marketing in America and much of the developed world. The magnitude of the change can be partly measured by dollars: in 1929, total advertising expenditures in the United States were estimated at $3.4 billion, up from $200 million in 1880. Even after adjusting for inflation and population growth, it was a 300 percent increase, and advertising represented a significantly larger share of the national economy (3.3 percent) than in 1880 (1.8 percent).[1] However, these events did not constitute a sudden invasion of advertising and commercial persuasion into a previously pristine experience of daily life. As we have seen, marketing in various forms has been part of economic life since the dawn of history. More recently, the invention of the printing press and the birth of newspapers and journals were followed by hundreds of years of steady change and experimentation. Printers offered space for advertisers, but not much at first, and the messages began as plain and simple statements of prices and other basic information. The eighteenth century brought more creativity in ad sales and presentation, particularly in Britain and the United States. By the 1830s and 1840s, the economics of media and marketing reached an inflection point with the creation of the penny press and the opening of the first display-oriented retail stores and shopping districts. The ensuing decades brought ad agencies, trade cards, magazine ads, national campaigns, catalogs, and the origins of public relations and marketing research. They also brought resistance and controversy—as some publishers dragged their feet in opening up their periodicals to advertising, some small-town retailers fretted about the impact of department stores and mail order, while critics from the realms of religion, letters, and academia blasted the influence of materialism and consumer culture on traditional social and economic institutions.

It had taken centuries, in other words, for the tactile technologies of human communication—print, pictures, and display—to become inundated with commercial messages. It would only take a few years for broadcasting to, as some might put it, succumb to the advertising temptation. But while broadcasting may have constituted a revolution in how people in America and around the developed world got their news, information, and entertainment—the share of U.S. households with radio sets rose from 11 percent in 1927 to nearly half in 1930 and 82 percent by 1940—the word *evolution* better describes broadcasting's growth within the advertising market. It took a comparatively long time for radio and, later, television to muscle aside print periodicals as the largest purveyor of advertising messages. Believe it or not, measured in ad expenditures, this did not happen until 1980.[2] Still, a focus on expenditures understates the significance of broadcasting in transforming the consumer culture, since one of its functions proved to be to reduce the cost of transmitting commercial information.

## THE PIONEERS OF BROADCAST ADVERTISING

The retailer Sears had begun life as a watch company, and jewelry and clockmakers were among the mainstays of the turn-of-the-century advertising market. So perhaps it is not surprising to learn that a single watch company, Bulova, played a formative role in both radio and television advertising. Joseph Bulova, an immigrant from the Czech lands of the Austro-Hungarian Empire, opened his first clockmaking shop in New York City in 1875. By the early twentieth century, Bulova was on contract to multiple retailers across the country to manufacture timepieces designed for nightstands, pockets, and wrists. World War I was a transformational event for the watch industry, as soldiers raved about the value of reliable wristwatches and after the war formed a new national and international market for men's watches.

Meanwhile, World War I had served to transform another preexisting technology: radio. Guglielmo Marconi and Nikola Tesla had experimented with wireless transmission in the 1890s. After proving itself in maritime and other limited uses before World War I, wireless became an indispensable tool in the war effort, on land and especially at sea. On contract with the armed forces, the American firm Westinghouse manufactured large quantities of radio parts: tubes, crystal receivers, transmitters, and amplifiers. After the armistice was signed in 1918, the company found itself with a large surplus of inventory it could no longer sell to the government. Its solution was to cultivate a consumer market for radio sets. In 1920, Westinghouse founded the first radio station, KDKA in Pittsburgh. A few more stations began broadcasting around the country in 1921, but the real critical mass appeared in 1922 as hundreds of stations suddenly sprung up across the country, most of them owned and operated by educational institutions.

During these early years, many national leaders were expressly opposed to the introduction of commerce to the new medium. Then–Commerce Secretary Herbert Hoover spoke for many when he said that it was "inconceivable that we should allow so great a possibility for service . . . to be drowned in advertising chatter." He distinguished between print ads, which a reader could just skip over, and radio ads, which would be harder to avoid. Hoover warned that if the serious content of the early radio stations—such as classical music and news—"became the meat in a sandwich of two patent-medicine advertisements," that would be "the quickest way to kill broadcasting." Early federal regulations prohibited the use of the "public airwaves" for profit, and the ubiquity of university broadcasters seemed to auger well for maintaining radio's pristine and noncommercial quality.[3]

It was not to be. It was never really even a possibility. As early as 1921, the telephone monopoly AT&T was making plans for a network of thirty-eight company-owned stations across the country that would broadcast programming with commercial sponsorship. It expected to dominate the market because of its patented control over telephone transmission, which would be used to link the network together. AT&T established the nation's first commercial broadcasting stations in 1922, beginning with WEAF in New York City. Its earliest commercial message advertised, ever so delicately, some new apartments in Queens. They were all sold within a week.[4] Other advertisers purchased time, too, though these were not really "commercials" in the modern sense. They did not mention prices, selling points, or retail offerings. Often, companies tried to build brand familiarity by attaching their names to musical performers, such as the A&P Gypsies and the Kodak Chorus.

Before AT&T could implement its idea of an ad-based radio network, other companies sought to get there first. Westinghouse and General Electric, working through their jointly owned subsidiary the Radio Corporation of America (RCA), founded WJZ in New York City and sought to evade AT&T's telephone-line bottleneck by using telegraph lines, shortwave, and high-powered transmitters to form a network. Sensing that it would not be able to capitalize on its telephone monopoly, AT&T decided to exit the business in 1926 and sold out to RCA, which then formed the National Broadcasting Company (NBC). The WEAF-based group of stations became known as the NBC-Red Network and the WJZ-based group became known as the NBC-Blue Network.[5]

Here is where Bulova reenters the picture. True advertising-based radio networks would need to offer advertisers far more than a sponsorship mention or a bland, spoken-word announcement. Just as nationwide print advertising had become a sophisticated business that mixed slogans, artwork, endorsements, and other design elements, radio would need to produce and air a prepackaged inventory of commercials that could be used repeatedly and tied in with a company's overall marketing strategy. As a watch company, Bulova's product was the perfect subject for the nation's first radio-network commercial spot. Its jingle went like this: "At the tone, it's 8:00 P.M., B-U-L-O-V-A Bulova watch time." To finish the marketing circle, in 1928 Bulova introduced the world's first clock radio.[6]

Bulova was not finished with advertising firsts. As radio quickly became a dominant force in the popular culture, tinkers and entrepreneurs began working on another promising medium of communication: television. While demonstrations and even some limited regular broadcasts occurred during the late 1920s and early to mid-1930s, television began to come into its own in the late 1930s with packages of news and entertainment programming. Sports broadcasting began in 1939. Two years later, on July 1, 1941, NBC began its broadcast of a baseball game between the Brooklyn Dodgers and Philadelphia Phillies with a 10-second advertisement. It consisted of a picture of the United States with a watch superimposed. In both bold lettering and a voice-over, the commercial stated, "America runs on Bulova Time."[7]

# EARLY BROADCASTING STRATEGIES FROM ADVERTISERS

The automobile industry, already the single-largest source of advertising dollars for the print media by the early 1920s, did not take much urging to pursue the new marketing possibilities afforded by broadcasting. Just one year after the debut of network ads, the radio industry had sufficiently straightened out its technical and organizational problems to establish the national network as a viable competitor for advertising dollars. That year, 1928, Horace and John Dodge were the first automakers to use it. In a national advertising launch for the new Dodge model, they spent about $715,000 (in 2004 dollars) to sponsor an hour-long broadcast, of which only about four minutes were devoted to direct commercial spots.[8] Dodge's strong results showed how the new national medium could be used to differentiate products and create consumer excitement. Other manufacturers pursued means of building up their brand name over time, such as Chrysler's 1928 sponsorship of a national radio broadcast of Amelia Earhart discussing her trans-Atlantic flight, General Motors' subsequent decision to sponsor Sunday night concerts from New York's Carnegie Hall, and Studebaker's creation of a radio show and orchestra bearing the name of its line of cars, the Studebaker Champions.[9]

Of course, automakers faced a obvious challenge in using radio. Their print advertising made extensive use of pictures, both of cars themselves and of more abstract or conceptual images. How could the spoken word be used to supplement or amplify the visual images? Associating brand names with shows and orchestras was one solution, while another was to coin slogans that would stick in consumers' minds. One of the most famous catchphrases of the period, introduced in ads for Duesenberg automobiles, was "It's a Duesey." In the spots, characters used the phrase to compare other beautiful objects to the graceful lines of a luxurious Duesenberg roadster. While the homophonic term *Dusey* was already in limited use as a synonym for *unique* or *outstanding*—apparently deriving from an older use of *daisy* and the name of a famous Italian actress, Eleanora Duse—many etymologists believe that it only became commonly used slang (and got transliterated into *doozy*) after the advent of Duesenberg's advertising campaign, demonstrating the influence of radio in building a truly national commercial and popular culture during the 1930s and 1940s.[10]

The year 1928 was pivotal in another way: the industry contracted with the Massachusetts Institute of Technology to produce the first market research on radio. It found that the prime listening time across the country was 8:00 P.M. to 10:00 P.M., but that differing regions, ages, and sexes had different scheduling and content preferences. Rural listeners liked religious programs and crop reports, while urban listeners preferred classical and orchestral music. Families with children liked stories and popular music (though demands by composers to be paid licensing fees for playing their songs severely limited the latter programming). Unlike the case of newspapers, which circulated for hundreds of years before advertising became their chief source of revenue—and allowed them to become independent of political and religious authorities—potential sponsors were involved with the creation of radio networks virtually from the beginning. As one advertising executive put it in 1930, "The public wants entertainment. The advertiser wants the public's attention and is willing to pay for it. Therefore, let the advertiser provide the entertainment."[11]

Instead of NBC, it was to be a new network, CBS, that worked closely with advertisers to pioneer the programming that would later become standard fare. After the 1929 stock market crash, a New

Yorker with family roots in the tobacco business, William Paley, bought a financially strapped group of stations and created CBS. Unlike NBC, which saw itself as a supplier of programming to local stations and charged them accordingly, Paley chose to purchase as many stations as he could directly. For the independently owned affiliates that remained, he began a policy of offering programs free of charge to be broadcast in prime time in return for running the network's national advertising. By 1930, Paley's new network was actually larger (with seventy-nine stations) than NBC (which had sixty-one) and structured quite differently. From the start, Paley consulted with leading figures on Madison Avenue, including John Orr Young and Raymond Rubicam, and with key clients such as George Washington Hill, whose North Carolina–based American Tobacco Company dominated an industry Paley already knew well. The result was a close integration of product and program, such as *The Cremo Military Band Program* (Cremo was a cigar brand), the *General Motors Family Party*, and the *Palmolive Hour* (starring "Paul Oliver" and "Olive Palmer").[12]

Local innovators went further than just associating brand names with the names of programs or hosts. A major center of activity was Chicago, where the hugely successful (and eventually controversial) program *Amos 'n' Andy* debuted on WMAQ in 1928 and later went national on NBC. The managers of WMAQ and its rival, WGN, had solid revenues during the evening hours but little during the day. Assimilating the findings of early marketing research, they realized that daytime audiences were overwhelmingly female and that women made 80–90 percent of the buying decisions in American households. As an advertising journal then put it, "The proper study of mankind is man . . . but the proper study of markets is woman."[13] So WGN hired a former ad agency representative to develop sponsored programming for daytime. He came up with the idea of a continuing serial, like *Amos 'n' Andy*, but in which characters would bear the name of a product. To the Super-Suds Company, he pitched a drama about an Irish American family called *The Sudds*. The answer was no. He changed the name to *Good Luck Marie* and offered it to a margarine maker. Another no. The station then hired a former schoolteacher, Irna Phillips, who brought the show to the air in late 1930 as *Painted*

*Dreams* and eventually secured sponsorship from a Chicago meat-packing company. This was the first "soap opera," though the phrase had obviously not yet been coined.[14]

Two years later, Phillips left to create a carbon-copy program on WMAQ entitled *Today's Children*, soon sponsored by two General Mills laundry products: La France Bluing Flakes and Satina starch. The link to soap was finally established. Later, Pillsbury picked up the program and was its sponsor throughout the decade. Phillips worked Pillsbury flours and other baking products directly into the script. The central character, Mother Moran, spent much of her time in her kitchen. Cake baking was a frequent plot device, as were kitchen-table conversations about the latest innovations from Pillsbury. In one story, Moran wrote to a "Mrs. Pillsbury" for help with kitchen aids and was later treated to a tour of Pillsbury's Minneapolis facilities.

Listeners reportedly saw explicit placement of companies and products into their radio shows as anything but an intrusion. According to surveys, they *preferred* product placement to clearly distinguished advertising spots because the latter took "time away from the story." Product placements also were seen as a way to make programs more accessible to ordinary people by bridging the gap between reality and fantasy. By 1933, both CBS and NBC were broadcasting these kinds of daytime programs nationwide. CBS picked up *Today's Children*, while NBC picked up two other Chicago-originated shows, *Betty and Bob* (again sponsored by General Mills' soap products) and *Ma Perkins* (sponsored by Procter & Gamble's detergents). Product placements were commonplace. General Mills' trademarked character Betty Crocker made guest appearances to promote bread making. On *Today's Children*, Mother Moran's granddaughter Lucy entered Pillsbury contests and once had to write a paper for school entitled "The Story of Bread."[15]

The close coordination of programming and advertising, both daytime and evening, was no accident. Advertising agencies, not radio networks, created and produced shows for broadcast. This business model persisted for both radio and, later, television for more than two decades. The *Happiness Boys* program had the title characters singing popular tunes as well as interspersed commercials. General Foods' Jell-O picked up Jack Benny's comedy show in 1932 and benefited from an intriguing marketing gimmick. The program began and ended with a straightforward promotional message for Jell-O by the announcer, Don Wilson. But the middle "commercial" consisted of Wilson working his way into whatever comedy routine was underway and, not very gracefully, slipping in a mention of Jell-O. Benny and the other cast members would then typically offer up some good-natured jokes at Jell-O's expense before continuing the show.[16] General Mills' breakfast cereal Wheaties offered *Jack Armstrong, the All-American Boy* in 1933, beginning a lengthy relationship between cereal companies and youth-oriented action and adventure shows that included *The Adventures of Superman* from Kellogg's Pep and several programs sponsored by Quaker Oats' puffed cereals—the only cereals, young listeners were told, that were "shot from guns." The popular comedy *Fibber, McGee and Molly* featured a disproportionately large number of scripts involving floor wax, particularly the brand manufactured by its sponsor, S. E. Johnson.

## CHALLENGE, RESPONSE, AND PUBLIC RELATIONS

While radio transformed American culture, it did not immediately transform American advertising. It attracted about 7 percent of total advertising dollars and then rose to a peak of 15 percent in 1945 before dropping to below 6 percent during the onset of television in the 1950s (it has since risen to about 8 percent of advertising expenditures, thanks to increased automobile commuting). Radio did become the medium of choice for packaged-goods advertisers and similar industries, but for many others it was not really a natural fit. Print media—newspapers, magazines, catalogs, yellow pages, and direct mail—lost some business but continued to dominate the marketing mix for many decades. (Indeed, the combined print category retained slightly over 50 percent of the advertising market as late as 2002.) The real challenge faced by the advertising industry in the 1930s and 1940s was not the need to adapt to new technology but rather the business slump created by the Great Depression, the New Deal, and World War II. Adjusted for population and inflation, advertising spending sank like a stone after 1929, dropping 41 percent to its low point in

1935 and then recovering to its pre-Depression height only by the early 1950s. After its 1950s growth spurt, advertising underwent relatively modest growth in the 1960s and 1970s, and actually decreased as a share of gross domestic product until 1980.[17]

The factors such as contracting money supply, rising unemployment, and heightened consumer parsimony affecting advertising agencies and clients in the 1930s were soon joined by another one: the rise of the consumerist movement and other activist, academic, and ideological challenges to commercialism. As previously mentioned, in the late 1920s Stuart Chase began a series of books and articles—including *The Economy of Abundance* (1934); *Rich Land, Poor Land* (1936); and *Idle Money, Idle Men* (1940)—criticizing media, advertising, and corporate America in general. "Advertising creates no new dollars," Chase wrote early in his career. "In fact, by removing workers from productive employment, it tends to depress output, and thus lessen the number of real dollars."[18] An early collaborator of Chase's, F. J. Schlink, wrote *1,000,000 Guinea Pigs* in 1933 to excoriate the drug and cosmetic industries for their advertising practices. Chase and Schlink, devotees of Thorstein Veblen, helped to spearhead a movement during the 1930s that published other books alleging fraud and waste in advertising, founded interest groups and consumer organizations (including Consumers Union in 1936), published periodicals (including *Consumer Reports*, various left-wing political journals, and *Ballyhoo*, which satirized advertisements themselves), and pushed for legislation in Congress.

A previous organization, the National Consumers' League, had been established in 1899. Reacting to the journalistic work of the "muckrakers" of the period, the League pushed for government regulations to ensure the safety of food and medicine, efforts that helped to enact the Pure Food and Drug Act in 1906 to combat fraud and require accurate labeling. In 1912, Congress amended the measure so as to more clearly ban false curative claims on drug labels. Two years later, it created the Federal Trade Commission (FTC), which would eventually give competitors a legal recourse if they alleged damage from false or misleading advertising. More important was the adoption of state statutes banning dishonest advertising, because most of them—unlike the federal law—did not require that plaintiffs prove advertisers intended to do harm, or had done harm, with false claims. Ohio was the first to enact such a statute, in 1913, and by 1921 twenty-three states had done so.[19]

But by the early 1930s, many activists were not satisfied with trying to rebut or rein in false advertising claims. Their legislative goal, according to one sympathetic historian, was "to outlaw advertisements that were ambiguous or made inferences."[20] Essentially, they did not believe that advertising should do anything other than provide basic facts about the ingredients, function, price, and availability of products. No more imagery, no more jingles, no more differentiating products or building brands. In 1933, as part of the early New Deal, sympathetic congressmen introduced the Tugwell Act, named after President Franklin Roosevelt's assistant agriculture secretary and "brain trust" confidante Rexford Tugwell. It would have revised the previous Food and Drug Act to hold companies responsible for an ad "creating a false and misleading impression"—and thus would have in a single stroke vastly expanded the federal government's power, shifted the burden of proof to advertisers in defending their claims, and fundamentally reshaped the advertising industry.[21] It was a very loud, very scary wake-up call. The industry, agents and advertisers, responded by making extensive use of the rapidly maturing field of public relations.

## A BACKTRACK AND A DETOUR

Corporate America's early bids for publicity and use of what would later be called public relations techniques were discussed briefly in a previous chapter. A closer look at the history of this key element of the marketing mix is necessary at this point, however, because of the ways in which public relations soon diverged from advertising, both in ends and means. Of course, the ultimate end of any business strategy is, or should be, to maximize long-term profitability, to deliver as much value as possible to the owners or shareholders of the firm. But firms in highly competitive industries such as food and medicine, consumer products, automaking, and retail were at the forefront of the innovations in mass market advertising. They were spending dollars to attract consumers. In contrast, the firms that pioneered the use of public relations to advance their bottom lines were in subsidized or regulated industries such as railroads, telephony, and electric power. They were spending dollars increasingly to attract political favors.

Writing as a professor of journalism at the University of Texas at Austin, the journalist Marvin Olasky chronicled the history of corporate public relations in the late nineteenth and early twentieth centuries. During the antebellum period, when competing private firms began to lay down track in the Northeast, South, and Midwest, the federal government played little role in the business, and even most state governments (after being burned by failed investments in canal companies decades before) spent little or no effort subsidizing the industry or regulating its affairs. That changed during the 1850s. Officials of the Illinois Central line decided to lobby Congress for federal funds to build a new road. They were among the first companies to employ a large team of lobbyists in Washington. Around the country, their agents encouraged newspapers to run articles calling for a new North-South railroad to bind the country together and avert civil war. The hardest sell for railroad companies was among Southern Democratic lawmakers, so the outbreak of war in 1861 opened the way for more federal largesse, much of it secured by aggressive lobbying and favorable publicity. The culmination of the railroads' efforts was a decision by Congress to offer massive land grants to most (but not all) of the companies building transcontinental railroads.

American railroad executives became increasingly oriented away from robust competition on price and service and toward pooling—or the coordination of previously separate enterprises—and public relations. They engaged in practices such as "puffery," or out-and-out bribery of newspapers to print railroad publicity as news stories, and "deadheading," or the offer of free tickets to politicians and journalists in hopes of generating "good will" and favorable publicity. The railroad companies also gave sizable sums to endow university chairs, fund college scholarships, and build hospitals and asylums. By the 1880s and 1890s, a new generation of railroad executives sought to downplay the role of free enterprise and profit in the transportation industry, seeking instead the status of a "public trust" that worked hand and glove with governmental authorities. Chicago railroad president Robert Harris suggested that "reason," not market competition, should set rates and policies for railroads. Competition may advance "private interests," he suggested in 1885, but public service required "that the wealth and happiness of the whole should be increased—hence I conclude that the policy of the state should be rather to prevent competition than to encourage it."[22]

At the turn of the century, it was the turn of the electric and telephone companies to seek the status of a "public trust" rather than a competitive business, this time in the formal sense of a franchised monopoly. Early leaders of the electric industry, such as Samuel Insull of Chicago Edison, crafted a conscious strategy of convincing federal, state, and local officials to end the vibrant early competition in wiring cities for electric power. They employed teams of spokesmen and press agents to make speeches, plant newspaper stories, and work the halls of legislatures and Congress. Part of their message was that if "rationality" was not brought to the electric power industry, savage competition among private companies would inevitably lead to collapse, a takeover, and direct government provision of electric service. Similarly, Theodore Vail of American Bell sought first to establish the company's nationwide grip on telephone service by arguing that only a monopoly firm could guarantee that telephone users would be able to talk to each other across town or across the country. When that argument failed to persuade government officials to ban American Bell's competitors—the notion of a "natural monopoly" in telecommunications clashed with the reality of dozens of competing firms often holding their own against Bell—Vail decided on a different course. In 1915, he changed the company's public relations strategy to demonize competition itself as "vicious" behavior that inhibited gains in economic efficiency (remember the similar viewpoint expressed by King Gillette and a number of leading economists at about the same time) and harmed the reputation of the business community. "Relations between the public and the corporations have not fully adjusted themselves to that nicety of balance which is possible, and which will give each of them all that either is entitled to, or could get," Vail wrote in the *Atlantic Monthly*.[23]

While businesses seeking government favors sought to blur the lines between private enterprise and public franchise, most of corporate America saw publicity as an adjunct to other advertising and marketing practices. Their press offices sought to attract attention to new stores or new product lines. They urged newspapers to write about satisfied customers or the latest technological marvels. To the extent that such publicity efforts later became redefined as "public relations," as communication designed to strengthen a company's reputation and defend it from critical inquiry or punitive regulations, most corporations put relatively little effort into them. After all, most perceived little need to do so. During the 1920s, business was growing by leaps and bounds. There seemed to be no reason to worry a great deal about a political backlash or a general deterioration of the public's perception of business. The emerging public relations field was dominated by Ivy Lee, who disliked capitalism and was attracted to some of the aspects of totalitarian governments being established in Russia and later in Germany. Lee encouraged all kinds of companies, not just the railroads and utilities, to downplay talk of competition—even suggesting that it reflected an un-Christian failure to love one's neighbor.[24] By following his advice, the American businesses that were devoting sustained attention to public relations were doing little to explain and defend the principles of a free market economy. They sought to answer the criticisms of the Progressives during the early twentieth century not by rebutting their factual charges or questionable economic assumptions, but by partial compliance with their regulatory demands and by promises not to indulge in the "vicious" competition of the nineteenth century. For this error, they were to pay a price—and to embark on an only partially successful attempt to make up for it in the years following the onset of the Great Depression.

## THE INDUSTRY COUNTEROFFENSIVE

By the 1930s, many business leaders found that they could not rely on platitudes about "serving the public trust" or "working hand and glove with government" to protect their freedom to conduct their business, including the freedom to advertise their wares. In reaction to the social, ideological, and political forces targeting advertising and corporate America itself, individual businesses as well as trade associations and other groups began to make use of a variety of persuasive and lobbying techniques. Newspaper and magazine ads, op-eds, letters and circulars, and other print media were among them. J. Walter Thompson, one of the biggest names in the advertising business, published *A Primer of Capitalism* in 1937 (about the same time the J. Walter Thompson Company began publishing *People* magazine) and worked with many clients to include statements about free enterprise in their display advertising. Ad agency employees wrote articles for popular magazines extolling the virtues of advertising and fanned out across the country to make speeches and teach on college campuses. On the client side, General Motors began an extensive public relations effort in 1931 that relied on publicists, press releases, public events, and the creation of organizations such as the Automotive Safety Foundation to reassure the public and head off proposals for heavier government regulation.[25]

But for many businesses, it was radio that took center stage. Early survey research had demonstrated that Americans actually trusted radio news and commentary more than they did print, perhaps because it seemed like a more personal and intimate means of communication (a phenomenon that, some might argue, was demonstrated once again with the rising political and social importance of commercial and public news/talk radio in the 1990s). So in addition to advertising products on the radio, American corporations advertised themselves—and free enterprise. Sometimes, the messages were explicit. In 1934, CBS begin airing the *Ford Sunday Evening Hour*. The program consisted of classical music interspersed with "intermission" talks by William J. Cameron, director of public relations for Ford Motor Company. Cameron's addresses defended the free market, extolled Ford's workplace practices and retirement policies, and questioned the "alluring schemes" of labor unionists and left-wing activists for "sharing the wealth" through government intervention. While not strident in tone, Cameron's speeches were intensely skeptical of Roosevelt's New Deal policies and legislative attacks on corporations. Millions of listeners responded to Ford's offer to send them copies of the speeches.[26]

Other efforts to combat the radicalism of the 1930s were subtler. The DuPont family, sensitive to allegations of war profiteering during World War I and at least as outraged about the leftist turn in Washington as Henry Ford was, created a history program on CBS in 1935 called *Cavalcade of America*, which was broadcast on NBC after 1940 and later as an ABC television series in the 1950s. DuPont's advertising agents were heavily involved in reviewing scripts for the show, which dramatized the lives of historical figures such as Thomas Jefferson, Daniel Boone, Thomas Paine, and Roger Williams. Later, particularly in its television form, *Cavalcade of America* included contemporary stories that showed average Americans overcoming adversity and showing courage. The stories were designed to reinforce traditional American ideals, including freedom and self-reliance. Implicitly, they served to question the public policies of Roosevelt and Truman, and what company leaders called "many strange and bewildering doctrines" perpetrated by political and social activists. To protect the program from allegations of bias and to facilitate an aggressive outreach effort to families, educators, and academia, DuPont contracted with famous Yale University historian Frank Monaghan to review scripts. The company sent out tens of thousands of promotional pamphlets to schools and hosted dinners for state education officials. These efforts were rewarded with dozens of broadcasting awards from industry and educational associations.[27]

Another technique was for companies to sponsor radio news commentators who espoused views supportive of free enterprise and inimical to labor unions and leftist political movements. Beginning in 1933 with newspaper columnist Boake Carter's daily commentaries on CBS, the practice grew to include George Sokolsky and Fulton Lewis (sponsored by the National Association of Manufacturers), Upton Close (Shaeffer Pen), H. V. Kaltenborn (Pure Oil), and Henry Taylor (General Motors). The National Association of Manufacturers (NAM) represents a particularly interesting case of industry seeking to make use of the mass media to combat its opponents. In addition to sponsoring commentaries, NAM also created its own dramatic series on the radio in 1934. *The American Family Robinson* portrayed a small-town family dealing with the economic effects of the Depression while resisting the siren songs of unionism and socialism. Here is how scholar Elizabeth Fones-Wolf summarized the early content of the show:

> In the first series of episodes, Luke Robinson, the "philosophical and kindly" editor of the *Centerville Herald*, defended his friend Dave

Markham, owner of the local furniture factory, which was on the verge of closing due to exaggerated charges of running an unsafe plant and exploiting his workers. . . . Robinson defended Markham by demonstrating that the plant had been running for three years at a loss and that conditions had deteriorated when a government agency, presumably the [National Recovery Administration], had forced him to increase pay and shorten hours.

The story concluded with the revelation that one of the organizers of the labor unrest was a fugitive from police custody and the townspeople's realization that "the welfare of the town—and the nation too—is tied up with the success of private enterprise."[28]

At this point, it might be asserted that corporate America's response to the challenges of the 1930s demonstrate precisely what its critics said they were afraid of: that corporations had too much power and were too willing and able to mislead the public through public relations propaganda to believe in the status quo and to resist change. But that would be a hasty conclusion, based on only part of the story. The reality was that by the 1930s, Americans were getting a steady stream of news, commentary, books, movies, magazine articles, and other material painting a relentlessly negative and even creepy picture of everyday economic and social life—while portraying Roosevelt and other self-styled "reformers" as heroic champions of the common man and the public interest. The president himself was "a master advertiser of government," as cultural historian Jackson Lears put it, "using Blue Eagles to symbolize the National Recovery Administration and Fireside Chats to win support for all his programs."[29] These efforts bore fruit. The public perception of business and many of its marketing practices became and remained stubbornly skeptical. "The positive attention that had been paid to business in the 1920s had turned to criticism and condemnation for bring[ing] on the catastrophic economic events of the period," according to a perceptive history of the American marketing profession. By the end of the 1930s, "serious questions existed about the ethics and efficiency of selling and distribution methods."[30]

Corporate public relations efforts were far from uniformly successful. The more politically charged and overwrought the messages they sought to convey through their print and broadcasting vehicles were, the more the messages were to provoke backlash and to sow dissension among the business community itself. For example, many of the political commentators sponsored by American corporations later found themselves dropped by their sponsors and networks on the basis of their excoriation of the Roosevelt administration. NAM's *American Family Robinson* was rejected by all three radio networks (including newcomer Mutual Broadcasting) for being, in NBC's words, "decided propaganda." It had to be syndicated directly to local affiliates, where it became a sensation with nearly 300 nonnetwork stations carrying the program by the late 1930s.[31]

More generally, corporations and the advertising industry only blunted the government's regulatory thrust rather than fully deflecting it. The 1933 Tugwell bill did not make it out of the relevant congressional committee, but subsequent legislation did give the Federal Trade Commission the power to issue "cease and desist" orders against specific ads. And once Roosevelt used his court-packing scheme after the 1936 election to cow the conservatives on the U.S. Supreme Court, the New Deal expansion of the federal government's power over the private economy was secured. The 1940s brought additional political pressure, such as then-Senator Harry Truman's investigation into the question of why advertising should continue to be viewed as a tax-deductible business expense.[32]

Within the advertising industry, many executives decided not to offer a full-fledged defense of commercial speech and free market competition but rather support for various self-regulation regimes and codes designed to head off more oppressive legislation.[33] Some of the efforts were merely extensions of Progressive-era institutions advocating "Truth in Advertising," and one might defend them as profit enhancing to the extent that they increased the credibility of advertising messages and thus the attractiveness of buying advertising.[34] However, the industry probably had its greatest success in reducing tensions with politicians and the public not by allaying their concerns about advertising and competition but by participating enthusiastically in the war effort during the 1940s. The creation of the wartime Advertising Council was, one left-wing writer has argued, "a major victory in the business counteroffensive against the New Deal."[35] That misunderstands the nature of the threat. Offering free ad space and expertise during wartime meant taking on a role akin to a public utility, not a competitive business that should be allowed to operate without interference. The image stuck in many minds.

## THE AUDIO BECOMES VISUAL

As the 1930s drew to a close, television began to change from an experimental toy to a true medium of mass communication. The programming that really took the ball and ran with it, so to speak, was sports. The stars of national radio shows were not about to go "slumming" on tv yet, but sports programming was obviously something that benefited greatly from the addition of pictures, even small and grainy ones. Early on, sports broadcasters saw the advertising potential of drawing a regular and loyal viewer base. While the Federal Communications Commission (FCC) had not yet allowed television officially to become commercialized, the visual nature of the medium allowed for some creative evasion. Two years before the first "legal" television ad for Bulova watches, the famous Brooklyn Dodgers announcer Red Barber managed to work a little product placement into the first nationwide broadcast of a major league baseball game. The radio coverage that day—July 1, 1939—had official commercial sponsors: General Mills, Procter & Gamble, and the company that became Mobil Oil. So Barber made a big show during the television broadcast of slicing bananas into a bowl of Wheaties, holding a bar of Ivory soap, and wearing a gas station attendant's cap. No words were spoken. But that was the point—both from a legal and a marketing standpoint. Soon tv ads demonstrated the powerful capability of marrying the immediacy and nationwide scope of broadcasting with print's traditional selling points of brand identification, design, and visual cues.[36]

The onset of World War II delayed the proliferation of commercial television. But after the Allied victory in 1945, the FCC lifted wartime restrictions on licensing tv stations and manufacturing tv sets, a consumer spending boom began, and technological innovations made broadcasts crisper and more attractive. The radio networks and their advertisers began to roll out television programs. At first, they were not exactly considered "top-flight" entertainment, and included professional wrestling, Vaudeville routines, B movies, and lots of amateur and professional sports. But viewership grew anyway, and the industry took notice. So did entertainers, who began to enter the medium following the 1948 debuts of Milton Berle's *Texaco Star Theater*, Ford Motor Company's *Ed Sullivan Show*, and George Burns and Gracie Allen's show, sponsored by B. F. Goodrich. In 1949, advertisers spent $58 million on tv—only about a tenth of the dollars that radio attracted that year. By 1954, ad expenditures on television ($804 million) shot past those on radio ($559 million), magazines ($668 million), and national newspapers ($635 million).

In just five years, the marketing landscape had changed significantly (though remember that local newspapers continued to be by far the largest advertising medium). To nationwide advertisers, the basic appeal of television was obvious: its ability to combine video with audio. You could not only talk about products but also demonstrate their use. The late adman Harry Matthei identified Sy Frolick, a young copywriter, as an early innovator of this practice in local television in New York City. Taking over the account of U.S. Rubber, the maker of Keds shoes, in 1946, Frolick took charge of a weekly science broadcast sponsored by the company. It asked Frolick to mention that Keds were washable. "Why don't we get a washing machine in here and show how clean the Keds come out?" Frolick replied. It worked so well that the company began sponsoring a Friday night show for teens, *Campus Hoopla*, where everyone wore Keds and an attractive gaggle of "Keds Cheerleaders" yelled out, "Keds are keen/Keds are neat/Keds are best for your family's feet."[37] Or consider the innovative advertising strategy of yet another watch company, U.S. Time. It began a campaign in 1948, first in print and soon afterwards on tv, that showed its new Timex watches subjected to all sorts of punishment—dropped from cliffs, tumbled over the Grand Coulee Dam, strapped to skis and boat propellers, shocked by electricity—and still continuing to function. A Timex "takes a licking and keeps on ticking," the famous slogan went. By the end of the 1950s, one of every three watches sold in the United States was a Timex.[38]

Once again, a telling sign that the new advertising medium, television, had finally arrived was the mid-1950s decision of America's automobile industry to fully embrace it. Actually, automakers and their ad agencies did not view tv with much relish at first. Accustomed to showing off their new models in print advertising that could accentuate the best angle and guarantee just the right color, executives worried that tv spots (then in black and white) would make their cars look bland. But the success of the Chevrolet-backed *Dinah Shore Show*—and its popular theme song "See the USA in Your Chevrolet"—shortly after its debut in 1951 began to change minds. Soon Ford was sponsoring, of course, the *Tennessee Ernie Ford Show*. Buick became Jackie Gleason's sponsor in 1956.[39] There was another twist that automakers had not foreseen: tv played a major role in broadening the market for trucks, which had previously been hard to advertise in print. "Pickups came bounding across the home screens, hurling from one arroyo to the next," wrote Victor Kenyon, a former senior vice president at J. Walter Thompson who managed Ford's advertising for decades. "TV encouraged all the truck images to get even tougher—downright snarly. People liked truck spots. They were all action, humor, and Western imagery."[40] Again, advertising was proving its ability to convey not just basic information—prices, availability, and specifications—but also the experience of owning and using the product. It was an appeal to the work ethic, to personal freedom, and to the frontier past.

The business model that worked for radio—having advertisers and their agencies create programs for the networks, rather than the other way around—at first proved equally successful with television. *Kraft Television Theater*, *Motorola Playhouse*, and the *U.S. Steel Hour* presented well-produced, often quite compelling dramas with such talented writers as Tennessee Williams and Rod Serling penning the scripts. But there were signs of tension in those early years as well. Some television producers chafed at the restrictions imposed by their advertisers, such as a rule for the detective show *Man against Crime*, sponsored by a tobacco company, that heroes but never villains could be showed smoking a cigarette.[41] On the business side of things, television advertising became such a lucrative enterprise by the mid-1950s that the broadcast networks began to think through the economics of essentially "renting" an hour or half hour to a single advertiser versus the alternative of breaking up the commercial time into individual spots and selling them piecemeal. Another group likely to gain from such a change would be a host of new advertisers, mostly smaller companies and those with fewer product lines, that could not afford to produce shows but could certainly buy flights of spots.

Networks and some farsighted advertising professionals salivated at the prospect of broadening their customer base. Still, initial efforts to renegotiate the terms of the television trade met with strong resistance from major advertisers and their agencies. In an early battle, NBC chose in 1950 to use its own talent to produce a daily television show based around the singer and radio personality Kate Smith. The network hoped to introduce a new concept of daytime television while capturing more revenue by selling 15-minute sponsorships within the *Kate Smith Hour* to four different advertisers each week rather than having just one producing sponsor. This "middle-ground" position between advertiser production and network production did not last. One sponsor demanded that the show be moved to a different time slot, which the network did over the strong protests of Smith and her production team—and to the detriment of the show's viewership. Other advertiser pressures led network executives to conclude that the *Kate Smith Hour* had shown the need for changing television's business model.[42] But only after the infamous quiz-shows scandals of the mid-1950s did the networks get their way, as it was the ad agencies that had rigged the questions and took much of the resulting public heat, though it is probably true that television production would have moved from advertisers to broadcasters (and contractors) in any event.

Television did not just change the business model for broadcasting. It also led to a fundamental restructuring of the print media, too. Print advertising had already become increasingly visual. One study of American magazines found that while about two-thirds of ad layouts in the decades before 1930 were devoted to words and specific information rather than visuals (photos, artwork, graphic design, etc.), the visuals become dominant shortly thereafter, averaging 58 percent of the layouts in the 1930s and 70 percent to 80 percent during the ensuing decades (though the proportion declined somewhat in the 1970s). While the arrival of television did not cause or even accentuate this trend, it did coincide with greater use of color and photography.[43] The more significant effects were found in the overall business model of the media. Suddenly, the general-interest magazines that had by midcentury become truly mass media with nationwide reach—including *Life, Look, Collier's,* and the *Saturday Evening Post*—could no longer compete on the basis of total audience. For years after tv reached its critical mass, magazines tried to keep up with cut-rate subscription drives. But the costs were prohibitive and national advertisers continued to chase after Nielsen ratings. So magazines and national newspapers responded by commissioning studies of their own. They pointed to the "pass-along rate," the number of readers per issue, and provided additional details to advertisers about the demographics of their readership base. To increase further the apparent efficiency of print-media buys, publications began to specialize, to target particular groups of readers attractive to certain companies or industries. Another mass circulation magazine, *Reader's Digest*, took still a different path. It pioneered a new measurement of readership—ad-page exposure, or the number of times a page is seen (particular useful for a publication opened multiple times by a single reader over the course of a month)—and relied on the direct marketing of branded goods and services to subscribers.[44] Eventually, many of the national magazines folded or transformed into specialty publications that previous generations would find unrecognizable (the original *Saturday Evening Post* finally disappeared in 1969 only to be reborn later with a health and nutrition theme, for example). Today, there are more national magazines and other print titles being published than ever before, but most of them are niche publications aiming for a relatively narrow slice of the marketing pie. This mind-boggling array of reading choices for consumers is itself a creation of the television age.

## HIDDEN PERSUADERS AND OPEN REVOLT

The triumph of television in America's consumer culture in the 1950s coincided with another wave of revisionism and invective aimed at advertising, public relations, and other means, according to which the "soulless corporation" allegedly used its power to manipulate the public. It seems certain that the two phenomena, commercial television and the new anticommercialism, were closely linked. The assault was broad-based. Popular Hollywood films such as *Will Success Spoil Rock Hunter?* and *The Hucksters* ridiculed the advertising profession or, alternatively, portrayed it as a menacing force. In the bookstores, novels and nonfiction alike offered millions of readers what was depicted as an "insider look" at how Madison Avenue really worked—its superficiality, its glitz and glamour, and its moral compromises. As discussed in greater detail in the next chapter, there was another revival of Veblen's institutional economics that represented the deeply skeptical view widely held in academia about advertising, corporate power, and the mass consumption culture. Back again was the notion that advertising was wasteful, that it induced consumers to spend beyond their means and for products they did not really need, that it propped up corporate monopolies, and that it substituted the questionable values of showmen and bamboozlers for the engineering ethic that modern industry truly needed to perform its proper social and economic roles. In politics and the media, the use of television and advertising techniques in election campaigns—begun in earnest with presidential candidate Dwight D. Eisenhower's creative use of the medium in 1952—led to a round of fretful hand-wringing about the debasement of the political process. In reality, the industry had never fully recovered from the pounding it took during the Depression years. The public had retained simmering suspicions of Madison Avenue that did not need much fanning to burst into flame.

Two events helped to spark the return of the anti-advertising critique. In 1957, a former market researcher named James Vicary began sending letters and making calls around the major advertising agencies in New York City to let them in on his amazing discoveries—and, of course, to offer his services for a hefty fee. Vicary explained that thanks to experiments with new camera technologies, he had developed a proven technique to impress compelling messages on the minds of viewers without them even realizing it. Specifically, he claimed that he had embedded frames in a motion picture that said "Eat popcorn" and "Drink Coke" and then shown the film, *Picnic*, to test subjects at a movie theater in Fort Lee, New Jersey. He further claimed that sales of popcorn had subsequently increased by an average of 57.5 percent and Coca-Cola sales by 18.1 percent. Declining to offer additional details, as this would compromise his pending patent application, Vicary offered to advise agencies and their advertisers on how to use the new techniques of *subliminal advertising*, a term he appears to have coined.[45]

In that same year, a journalist and author named Vance Packard scored a literary breakout with his bestseller *The Hidden Persuaders*.

Purporting to prove not just the isolated use of subliminal ads but also a more far-reaching manipulation of the American public through advertising, publicity, and propaganda, Packard used the term *brainwash* to describe the effects of mass marketing on consumers. He cited the advertising industry's sponsorship of motivational research and claimed that it had successfully probed the human psyche. "Large-scale efforts are being made, often with impressive success, to channel our unthinking habits, our purchasing decisions, and our thought processes," he wrote. "Typically these efforts take place beneath our level of awareness; so that the appeals which move us are often, in a sense, hidden."[46] The success of *The Hidden Persuaders* led to follow-up books from Packard. *The Status Seekers* (1959) featured a Veblen-like critique of social mores. *The Waste Makers* (1960) advanced the thesis that many corporations used "planned obsolescence" to guarantee an ongoing market for their consumer products. *The Pyramid Climbers* (1962) savaged the managerial culture of corporations, and *The Naked Society* (1964) warned of consumer culture's threat to privacy.

The news media seemed fascinated with the claims of Vicary and Packard, and spread them throughout the country in a matter of months. By May 1958, about 42 percent of Americans said in a poll that they had heard of subliminal advertising. Some broadcasting companies actually began to discuss the possibility of additional research into the technique, with at least one California television station announcing—and then retracting—plans to air subliminal ads. Reacting to the furor, the National Association of Radio and Television Broadcasters issued a statement urging stations not to use subliminal advertising pending a "review and consideration" by the association. Plenty of Madison Avenue firms returned Vicary's calls.[47]

But it was essentially a big hoax. Concerned policy makers in Washington, at Congress and the FCC, asked that Vicary replicate his experiment for their benefit. He came to the capital in January 1958 and offered a public demonstration. The technique did not appear to change viewer demands or behavior. Over the coming months, he began to back away from his more outlandish claims. Eventually, having pocketed millions in consulting fees, Vicary disappeared from public view for years, popping up in the early 1960s to admit that he had falsified the data from his initial experiment (and some analysts doubt that the Fort Lee test was ever conducted in the first place).[48] As for Packard, he helped to publicize Vicary and other frauds—such as "Dr." Ernest Dichter, who purported to be an expert on motivational research—while offering little real evidence for his paranoid theories of a massive conspiracy to brainwash and manipulate the public. As James Twitchell put it, the notion that advertisers would insert subliminal messages such as "Eat popcorn" into entertainment never made any sense as a widespread advertising strategy, even if it had not been based on preposterous scientific claims. "Ad execs don't want you to buy crackers or beer or cars," he pointed out. "They want you to buy Ritz, Schlitz, and Studebakers. What they sell is brands, not products."[49]

As is the case with many urban legends, however, the debunkers came later, and got less attention, than the initial and explosive claims. Far into the 1970s and 1980s, enough people still believed in the reality of subliminal advertising and hidden persuaders to allow Wilson Bryan Key, a Canadian sociologist, to find success with a series of books identifying "sublims" in a host of advertising images, most famously in ice cubes. It is likely that these flights of fancy stayed aloft because of a congenial climate. In the late 1950s, television was just beginning to be appreciated as a mass communication medium and a cultural force. Its power and reach were deeply disconcerting to many. Furthermore, it was not only frauds and publicity hounds who were claiming that modern marketing techniques induced consumers to spend what they did not have and to buy what they did not need. Scholars such as Dwight McDonald, David Riesman, Irving Howe, and John Kenneth Galbraith offered a similar critique. Often writing from reputable academic departments, these authors and essayists attracted a following among the highbrow opinion leaders who read political journals as well as the middlebrow readers of mass circulation magazine and books. They began to get the word out within an increasingly radical political movement that would spawn the counterculture of the 1960s. It is to the debate over the economics of advertising and marketing instigated in large part by Galbraith and his critics that our attention must now turn.

# CHAPTER 4

# The New Economics and Science of Advertising

"Learn About Admiral John Hood," the outside of the envelope stated enticingly. The letter came with a stack of other mail, much of it unsolicited, much of it discarded. But that personalized mailing label caught my eye. I did not remember that there *was* an Admiral John Hood. I looked at the return address: "Multieducator: The Multimedia History Company," it said. Beneath, in blue letters at a 45-degree angle, was another announcement: "It's New . . . www.his torycentral.com/ Check it out!" So, in the course of a few seconds, whoever had sent this marketing letter had piqued my interest in history and education, after first catching my eye with an intriguing namesake.

I opened the letter. Inside was a brief, polite letter informing me that I would find a short biography of Admiral John Hood, a history of the U.S. Navy destroyer named after him, and a catalog of the company's naval-related wares. "You can purchase products to proudly wear products with the name John Hood on it," the grammatically challenged missive stated. "What better time then [*sic*] when our troops are in harms [*sic*] way for you show [*sic*] your support then [*sic*] wearing a hat or jacket that proudly honors the ship named for you [*sic*] namesake."

While grimacing at the copywriter's apparent lack of third-grade writing skills, I was still interested enough to read on—after all, there was a war on at the time (in Iraq) and I *did* feel quite patriotic. It turns out that Admiral John Hood, an Alabama native, had served the country with distinction during the Spanish-American War and as a rear admiral during World War I. The destroyer bearing his name, the USS *John Hood*, was commissioned in 1944 and saw action against the Japanese in the North Pacific and then with the 7th Fleet off the coast of Korea in the early 1950s. Delighted by the discovery of information entirely unexpected and unknown to me, and right up my historical alley, I found that I simply could not pass up the opportunity to order some hats, shirts, and coffee mugs bearing the name and likeness of the ship. They would make perfect gifts for family and friends.

According to John Kenneth Galbraith, however, I had just been swindled. The famed professor, author, political commentator, and former ambassador to India brought the institutionalist economics of Thorstein Veblen to a popular audience in the late 1950s. His bestselling book *The Affluent Society*, published in 1958, portrayed the arrival of mass marketing and the consumer culture of capitalism it engendered as a grotesque waste of society's resources. Advertising, Galbraith wrote, was part of a process that manufactured human wants and then satisfied them at great cost. In good Veblenesque terms, he viewed the process as essentially pointless. "Among the many models of the good society no one has urged the squirrel wheel," he wrote.[1]

Galbraith used the term *the Dependence Effect* to describe this economic version of running in place. By definition, he said, truly important and urgent human needs will manifest themselves without the prompting of commercial messages. "Few people at the beginning of the nineteenth century needed an adman to tell them what they wanted," he scolded, and a man "who is hungry need never be told of his need for food." The group who really needed advertising was not consumers but producers, Galbraith continued, because the latter could not justify ever-increasing investment in productive capacity unless there was an adequate demand for the resulting output. The social value of satisfying such contrived demand could hardly be equated with the value of satisfying real consumer needs. "The . . . direct link between production and wants is provided by the institutions of modern advertising and salesmanship," he wrote. "These cannot be reconciled with the notion of independently determined desires, for their central function is to create desires—to bring into being wants that previously did not exist."[2]

Prior to receiving the direct mail piece, I obviously did not want T-shirts and coffee mugs with pictures of the USS *John Hood* on them because I did not even know the ship existed. The (apparently editorless) marketing firm in question had manufactured my demand for its products out of thin air, Galbraith and like-minded critics would say. The result has been a little more societal waste. The dollars I spent on the *John Hood* trinkets were diverted from some other, more important way to benefit me or my family. Meanwhile, the money invested in designing, manufacturing, and marketing all that useless junk could have been employed in a more redeeming enterprise, such as producing food or clothing for the poor.

## GALBRAITH AND HIS ANTECEDENTS

The publication of *The Affluent Society* in 1958 acted like a magnifying glass that focused a diffusion of ideas and criticism into a blaze of ideological and political activism. Plenty of prior thinkers and writers had made observations similar to Galbraith's, starting with his obvious intellectual progenitor, Veblen. What Galbraith brought to the effort was a brilliant mind, an ability to build conceptual systems, and a talent for communicating to audiences ranging from academic confabs to television viewers. His critique of advertising mixed various economic and cultural arguments, not just institutionalism, and in some cases harkened back to traditions of America's Puritan and Quaker past. Advertising contributed to the "unseemly economics of opulence" evident in the 1950s, Galbraith wrote, by stimulating demand for "tobacco, liquor, chocolates, automobiles, and soap in a land which is already suffering from nicotine poisoning and alcoholism, which is nutritionally gorged with sugar, which is filling its hospitals and cemeteries with those who have been maimed or murdered on highways, and which is dangerously neurotic about normal body odors."[3]

Galbraith's background had prepared him well for the role as one of the twentieth century's most famous economists. Receiving his

Ph.D. in agricultural economics from the University of California, Berkeley, after moving to the United States from his native Canada, Galbraith was briefly a professor at Harvard University before joining the wartime U.S. Office of Price Administration—an experience he appears to have relished, given his subsequent support for government price controls—and then in 1943 the editorial board of *Fortune* magazine. With experience in government and journalism, Galbraith returned to Harvard in 1949 to teach and write. His first book, *American Capitalism: The Concept of Countervailing Power* (1952), endeared him to the country's labor movement (unions were the "countervailing power" against corporations, the book suggested) and gained Galbraith some notoriety among intellectuals and politicians. The release of *The Affluent Society* six years later was the real breakout. Galbraith became to the 1950s what John Maynard Keynes had been to the 1930s and 1940s, though perhaps without the perceived scholarly heft. Professors and students on campuses across the country were discussing and building on his ideas. Galbraith was quoted regularly in the press and appeared frequently on television. Many officials of the subsequent Kennedy and Johnson administrations considered Galbraith their intellectual inspiration. They credited his ideas as paving the way for the Great Society and the War on Poverty.

Galbraith's anticommercialism had scholarly antecedents. In 1949, Harvard University Press had published James Duesenberry's *Income, Saving, and the Theory of Consumer Behavior*. Duesenberry questioned the neoclassical emphasis on marginal-utility theory and argued that consumer choices were not made from a fixed menu, like ordering dinner. Instead, consumers took notice of what others of their income level were buying, so that rising incomes exposed consumers to ever-rising amounts and qualities of goods. This Demonstration Effect, Duesenberry continued, actually harmed consumers by leading them to purchase goods they did not really need. "Our social goal of a high standard of living, then, converts the drive for self-esteem into a drive to get high-quality goods."[4] With regard to public policy, Duesenberry took his argument to its logical conclusion, suggesting that a steeply progressive income tax would produce an efficient allocation of resources by depressing the consumption of the wealthy and, in turn, reducing the Demonstration Effect on less affluent consumers.

Duesenberry's argument for tax-the-rich schemes was different from Keynes's earlier notion that high-income households saved too much and spent too little, thus reducing aggregate demand and necessitating the redistribution of income to poorer households to stimulate demand and prop up employment. Yet Duesenberry saw himself as expounding on the Keynesian model of consumer behavior. As a student in England, Keynes had studied with the philosopher G. E. Moore, a prominent critic of the theory of hedonic consumer behavior—of individuals pursuing pleasure and avoiding pain—that underlay classical economics. Keynes seems to have been influenced by Moore's rejection of the idea that individuals truly know what is good for them and can form personal preferences without recourse to the herd instinct. In his writings, Keynes talked about the "animal spirits" inherent in capitalism and described consumer behavior as consisting more of spontaneous urges than rational calculation.[5]

Two other scholars of the 1930s had been far more specific than Keynes in modeling and questioning the role that advertising and other kinds of marketing played in the economy. In 1933, Harvard economist Edward Chamberlin published *The Theory of Monopolistic Competition*. Resisting the older neoclassical practice of treating all goods within any competitive industry as identical, as perfect substitutes for each other, Chamberlin coined the now-familiar term *product differentiation* to describe the creation and maintenance of brand names. By employing advertising and promotion, Chamberlin suggested, companies could increase demand for their particular brand, expressed in the form of either attracting more customers or inducing existing customers to pay a higher price (or ignore the introduction of lower-priced goods from competitors, which is essentially the same thing).[6]

While Chamberlin thought that companies already dominant in their industry would be the most likely to be able to use advertising in this way to boost their profits, British economist Joan Robinson argued that the causality worked in the opposite direction. In her *Economics of Imperfect Competition*, which came out several months after Chamberlin's work, Robinson argued that companies used advertising to gain monopoly power in the first place and then to maintain it against future competitors. Whenever its dominance in an industry is threatened, she wrote, a company "can resort to advertisement and other devices which attach customers more firmly to itself."[7]

The link between advertising and market power, articulated by the likes of A. C. Pigou in the 1920s and Chamberlin and Robinson in the 1930s, influenced the work of still more economists in the 1940s and 1950s. The same year, 1949, that Duesenberry published his new theory of consumer behavior, a paper by Nicholas Kaldor distinguished between two uses of advertising: direct and indirect. The direct use was as a sort of companion good, sold below cost to customers by producers of the good being advertised. Kaldor viewed the bundling of these two goods as wasteful, because much of advertising's content had little to do with price or availability. But understood indirectly, Kaldor explained, advertising *might* contribute to social welfare to the extent that it increased the market share of a firm and thus allowed it to take advantage of economies of scale—the ability to spread fixed costs over a larger number of goods or services—with some of the resulting decline in production costs passed on to consumers in the form of lower prices. Kaldor considered this only as a possibility, and suggested that advertising's indirect effect of scale might also hurt consumers by muscling out competitors. On balance, he appeared to be skeptical that consumers were the net winner.[8]

A year after Duesenberry's and Kaldor's works were published, the economist Harvey Leibenstein wrote a key paper in the *Quarterly Journal of Economics* that brought together several different strands of thought about the mass consumption of consumers. There are three ways that the behavior of some consumers influences the preferences of others, Leibenstein wrote: (1) the "bandwagon effect," in which other people's purchasing of a good makes it more desirable; (2) the "snob effect," in which popular demand makes a product seem pedestrian, vulgar, and less desirable; and (3) the "Veblen effect," which asserts that a person will choose high-demand goods because they are more expensive, thus allowing him to show up his ability to afford them—to engage in "conspicuous consumption."[9]

Finally, in 1956 the economist Joe Bain—who would shortly afterward help to introduce the economic subdiscipline of industrial organization—attempted to layer some additional empirical support on top of the proposition that marketing practices harmed consumer welfare. Using interviews and survey responses, he examined barriers to entry in twenty manufacturing industries in the United States. Bain concluded that product differentiation was the most effective way that companies blocked competitors from entering the market, and thus could serve to create monopolies or oligopolies that raised consumer prices. While he did not conclude that advertising alone helped would-be monopolists differentiate their brands and thus impede consumers' willingness to consider better or low-priced alternatives, Bain argued that advertising was a key part of the process. In particular, he concluded, "The single most important basis of product differentiation in the consumer-good category is apparently advertising." More specifically, Bain pointed to the liquor-distilling industry as having used advertising and promotion so skillfully that significant competition from new firms was not "conceivable."[10]

Obviously, John Kenneth Galbraith did not invent a new reason to be suspicious of advertising and its role in consumption patterns and economic life. To him was left the task of organizing and popularizing prior criticisms, a task he performed with aplomb. For many, his vision of mass market capitalism and consumer culture as a spinning squirrel wheel, or perhaps a rat race, became the "conventional wisdom"—itself a term that Galbraith *does* appear to have invented.

## GALBRAITH AND HIS CRITICS

But Galbraith did not just draw a broad following among the intellectual and chattering classes. He also drew critics. Two famous ones in particular deserve some extended discussion at this point. Both were Nobel laureates in economics. Both published works in 1961, three years after the appearance of *The Affluent Society*, that served to undercut its central assumptions, although only one of these works was specifically designed to do so. And both were leaders of economic schools that were to generate alternative models for how advertising affected consumers, economic efficiency, and social well-being.

The first was George J. Stigler, a longtime professor at the University of Chicago and one of the founders of its "Chicago school" of free market analysis. A native of the Seattle area and graduate of the University of Washington, Stigler obtained an MBA at Northwestern

University and his economics Ph.D. from the University of Chicago, where he was influenced by the teachings of Frank Knight, Jacob Viner, and Henry Simons.

During the war, while Galbraith helped regulate the country's prices, Stigler began his own interest in prices while working at the National Bureau of Economic Research and later at Columbia University's Statistical Research Group. His subsequent work on the economics of advertising and consumer information was not directly inspired by the writings of Galbraith and other critics in the 1950s, as it partly predated them. But Stigler was certainly aware of Galbraith and had been highly skeptical of his previous book, *American Capitalism: The Concept of Countervailing Power*. Stigler demonstrated not only a keen intellect but also a good sense of humor in titling his review of Galbraith's volume "An Economist Plays with Blocs."[11] And certainly his explorations of the role that advertising and other forms of marketing played in the competitive process acted as a direct rebuttal to many of Galbraith's claims.

Stigler and like-minded scholars viewed prices not as simple tallies of the work effort bundled up in a product, or as a means of rationing scarce resources, but as bundles of information that were dispersed throughout the economy. They were not arbitrary or exploitative. They conveyed important information to producers and consumers about what was available, where it was available, how hard it would be to obtain, and whether there was enough demand for it to justify obtaining it.

For Stigler this concept of prices as information had many complex applications. For one thing, this information was itself an economic commodity. It had value but was also costly to produce. In his famous 1961 paper "The Economics of Information," Stigler articulated this seemingly simple point so effectively that many later observers—including Stigler himself—considered it to be his most important contribution to economics. "One should hardly have to tell academicians that information is a valuable resource: knowledge is power," the article began. "And yet it occupies a slum dwelling in the town of economics. Mostly it is ignored."[12] The real cost of a product is not the currency demanded for it but what the consumer gives up to acquire it. That is what economists called the opportunity cost, and it includes not only the things the consumer might have purchased instead but also the time and resources it takes for the consumer to find and acquire the product. The latter is known as the search cost, and it can tally up to a sizable sum. Previous economists arguing that advertising raised the cost of goods to consumers had looked only at dollar prices, and thus had missed an important way that advertising might *lower* consumer costs.

In the paper, Stigler pointed to search costs as an explanation for why prices for a particular good often differ even with a single community. Economists enamored with textbook models of competition—with its assumptions of perfect information on the part of producers and consumers—had long been troubled by price differentials, sometimes attributing them to monopoly power or "market failure." But Stigler explained that such price differentials reflect ignorance on the part of consumers. They do not know that a gallon of milk or loaf of bread might be cheaper at a grocery store a few blocks away than it is at the store where they usually shop. Acquiring that information by asking around, or driving from store to store, is costly.

But advertising can fill in the gap. It can let consumers know that lower-priced goods are available elsewhere. Armed with the information, consumers will then know where to shop to save money. Other grocery stores, in turn, will have to lower their prices and communicate that fact via advertising and promotion in order to compete. Thus advertising, Stigler argues, is an integral part of a market process that drives prices downward, not upward. The reason why this process is continuous—with retailers continuing to need to advertise—is that "knowledge becomes obsolete," he wrote. Factors affecting supply and demand change. New buyers and sellers enter the market. Thus, while "advertising is . . . an immensely powerful instrument for the elimination of ignorance," that elimination occurs at only a single point in time. Changing conditions bring it back, and so the process of reducing search costs continues.[13]

The implications of Stigler's point about search costs go beyond the issue of price competition, however. Advertising can benefit consumers even if it does not drive down the sticker price of goods. Consider an example. Suppose a consumer sought to buy a new refrigerator, and the brand she ended up purchasing cost her $1,000. Let us also say that out of that $1,000 in gross revenue, the manufacturer or retailer spent $40 on advertising and promotion (which appears to be roughly the industry-standard percentage).[14] If the consumer is thought of as paying that $40 as part of the purchase price, has the advertising caused her to spend 4 percent more than she would have without it? Not necessarily. What if, by running ads that emphasized the refrigerator's reliability and capacity, the manufacturer saved the consumer $60 in search costs? That might represent time spent researching the various brands, the purchase of guides or consumer magazines, and the time and fuel consumed in driving from store to store to discuss each refrigerator's characteristics with sales representatives. Under those conditions, advertising has served to *reduce* the full cost, the opportunity cost, of purchasing the refrigerator.

Of course, this represents only a first step in applying Stigler's point about advertising and information. My example assumes that the information the advertiser has communicated to the consumer will prove to be true and useful. If, in fact, the refrigerator is not reliable or does not hold as much food as promised, the consumer will not come out ahead. Whether advertising in a competitive market is likely to deliver true and useful information about price or quality, and thus to serve the interest of consumers in the long run, is a question discussed in detail later in this chapter.

The other critic of Galbraith with a relevant publication in 1961 was Friedrich A. Hayek, a prominent twentieth-century leader of the Austrian school of economics. Unlike Stigler's study of the economics of information, Hayek's April 1961 paper was directly aimed at Galbraith's *The Affluent Society*, as is evident in its title: "The *Non Sequitur* of the 'Dependence Effect.'" In it, Hayek granted the notion that consumer preferences were not formed in individual isolation, that advertising and marketing practices and the buying behavior of others influenced the choices of individual consumers. But he argued that the proposition did not prove what Galbraith thought it proved— or, perhaps more to the point, that it proved too much. It is not just consumer preferences for soap or automobiles that are formed in this way, Hayek wrote, but also preferences for fine art, music, painting, or literature. Once human beings are able to satisfy basic animal urges for food, clothing, shelter, and sex, it is difficult to imagine the specific desire for any other good without recourse to learning, persuasion, or some other kind of social cues. Did Galbraith really believe that all socially determined goals were inferior to the instinctual ones that humans shared with animals? "To say that a desire is not important because it is not innate is to say that the whole cultural achievement of man is not important," Hayek wrote.[15]

Indeed, the force of Hayek's argument can be felt without extending it beyond the scope of basic drives to acquire food, clothing, shelter, and sex. Practically speaking, these can be satisfied with gruel and broth, furs and rags, huts and tents, and furtive coupling in the dark. Is it really a "contrivance," to use Galbraith's word, for human beings to acquire a taste for well-prepared and varied meals, styled clothes, furnished homes, and the enhancement of beauty through cosmetics, lipsticks, and lingerie? It may not be surprising to find that some elements of the 1960s and 1970s counterculture found their inspiration in Galbraith, but his apparent aversion to culture, and attachment to the primitive, runs contrary to millennia of human experience—to behaviors and aspirations formed long before there were newspapers, magazines, radio, or television commercials.

## MODELS OF ADVERTISING AND MODERN EMPIRICAL FINDINGS

The ways that Hayek and Stigler responded to the critics of advertising are compatible but distinct. Perhaps a good way to see the distinction is to consider what modern-day economist Kyle Bagwell describes as the three major models for how advertising influences market outcomes.[16] In the past half century, an avalanche of studies and data has allowed economists to examine the rigor of these models and how they correspond to the realities of the modern economy.

The Persuasive View reflects the earlier, critical analysis of advertising presented by Pigou, Chamberlin, Robinson, Kaldor, Bain, and Galbraith. It argues that advertisers change consumer preferences in ways that serve the interest of advertisers, not consumers. The pre-advertising preference is considered the "true" one, so consumers are being induced to waste their money on things they would not freely choose to buy, just as I purchased the USS *John Hood* paraphernalia because of a direct mailing. Some years after Galbraith, Arnold Toynbee systematized the argument by positing the existence of three categories of economic demand: (1) needs (minimum material requirements of life, (2) "genuine" wants (which "we become aware of spontaneously," without "Madison Avenue"), and (3) "unwanted" demand (created by advertising).[17]

Hayek's function in the debate was to challenge not the existence of advertising's persuasive effect, but to question whether it truly harmed consumers as the early economists had alleged. The problem with their argument, as Hayek implied but did not state explicitly, was that it assumed consumers did not want their preferences to be changed! This rather bold assumption does not reflect human nature or personal experience very well. A world in which each individual knew with confidence exactly what he wanted, every day, at fixed times, and in fixed quantities, and merely sought to get these things as easily and cheaply as possible, would be a pretty dreary one. Fortunately, it is not the world we inhabit.

As Virginia Postrel explained in her critically acclaimed 2003 book, *The Substance of Style*, changing tastes in food, clothing, housing, cars, household products, and many other goods reflect in part the innate interest of most human beings in novelty, in being surprised. Offering further detail for Hayek's point about the arts, Postrel quotes a professor who has carefully studied the interaction between biology and art. Musical styles differ widely across cultures and generations, he said, but they all "depend on sounds, on pitch, on harmonies, on iterations—getting tired of something, being surprised. Novelty, surprise, echoing effects, repeating of themes, variations of themes—in all developed musics you find these things happening."[18] There certainly is a constant in consumer preferences: it is the constant desire for change, innovation, and adaptation. That this desire plays itself out as a persuasive process, one in which producers of a good seek to attract and retain consumer interest in their particular iteration, is not to suggest that consumers are necessarily being harmed or manipulated.

When those who espouse a negative version of the Persuasive View then turn to the broader economic consequences, they argue that advertising erects barriers to entering markets, shielding companies from competition and thus harming consumers with higher prices or degraded quality. Here they run headlong into an entirely different explanation of how and why advertising works: the Informational View, as articulated by Stigler and other Chicago school and free market economists. It does not model advertising as changing intrinsic consumer preferences. Rather, it examines how consumers already searching for goods and services can benefit from the information provided by the marketing efforts of producers and retailers, including but not limited to advertising. At its core, the Informational View serves as a powerful reminder that the old textbook version of competition is entirely an abstract with limited relevance to the real world. As one like-minded author put it in 1970, "The presence of advertising and other forms of differentiation is not responsible for the absence of perfect competition and the existence of an imperfect system; advertising came into existence *because* perfect competition does not exist."[19]

One could believe that both models accurately describe how advertising works some of the time. To determine whether it generally benefits consumers, then, one would need to try to gauge the frequency and magnitude of each effect and then compare them to see what the net effect of advertising is. A New York University professor, Jules Backman, presented one straightforward approach to analyzing the problem in 1968. Noting that classified and local newspaper advertising was overwhelmingly informational in content—providing prices, product descriptions, phone numbers, store hours and location, and so on—he simply totaled up the spending for each advertising category in an attempt to establish a ballpark estimate of how much advertising conveyed information. In 1966, classifieds and local newspapers ads (primarily retail) made up 29 percent of the total advertising expenditure of $13.3 billion. Even a lowball guess at the additional percentage of broadcasting spots, national print ads, and direct mail that conveyed information would raise the share above the 50 percent mark, Backman said. "These figures suggest that substantially less than half of total advertising is of the type [persuasive] that the critics are attacking as wasteful," he said, though "the exact amount cannot be pinpointed."[20] Updating Backman's approach, local newspaper ads and Yellow Pages listings (which also contain heavy amounts of pure information) together accounted for about 22 percent of the

$237 billion in advertising expenditures in 2002. If only half of the content of direct-mail pieces, billboards, and other nonbroadcast advertising was devoted to pure information—an assumption that seems reasonable given the kinds of products often marketing through these devices, such as credit cards, mortgages, hotel rooms, and gasoline—television and radio ads could be assumed to contain no information content at all and Backman's general conclusion would remain true.

Of course, it would be far more useful to assess the effects of advertising expenditures directly on measurable indicators of consumer welfare. Since the 1960s, there have been a large number of such studies, some specific to firms or sectors and some examining larger chunks of the economy. In general, the data appear to support the contention that advertising serves consumers more than it savages them. In their landmark work, *Advertising and the Market Process*, economists Robert B. Ekelund, Jr., and David S. Saurman summarized the findings of the major research in the area. In 1972, for example, a study looked at state regulations on the advertising of eyeglasses and eye examinations. Because of the variation of advertising regulations—some states completely banned the advertising of prices and some imposed no restriction—there was a sort of laboratory experiment going on. The findings were clear: eyeglasses cost 25 percent more in states with ad bans compared to those without them. Delving further into the data, the study compared the least restrictive states, Texas and the District of Columbia, with the most restrictive state, North Carolina. The latter's average eyeglass prices were more than double those in the former. In 1976, a different study found negative, albeit much smaller, consequences from state bans on prescription drug advertising. And in 1978, two scholars looked at billboard advertising of gasoline prices and found that, once again, when service stations were able to make more use of the practice, average gasoline prices were lower. "Though billboards are often singled out as eyesores by social critics, the information they contain yields net economic value to society," Ekelund and Saurman wrote in their summary. "Completely ignored is the additional time saved by consumers in price-searching activities that billboard price advertising makes possible."[21]

Other contributions to the advertising-and-price literature make use of game theory—modeling the behavior of producers and consumers within various scenarios and assumptions—and long-term studies of cost. In general, writes Bagwell, the research of the past couple of decades "offers support for the presumption that retail markets perform better when advertising is possible."[22]

## HOW ADVERTISING AFFECTS QUALITY AND COMPETITION

Again, it would be a mistake to think of consumer welfare entirely in terms of price. Advertising can help or harm consumers by influencing the quality of the goods and services they buy. In 1970, Phillip Nelson—now a professor emeritus of economics at SUNY–Binghamton and then a recent student of George Stigler's—introduced a useful distinction between "search goods" and "experience goods," suggesting that they lead to different uses of advertising. The characteristics of search goods are well-known to consumers from the get-go. You know what they do, how they work, and why you need them. What you may not know is where you can get them, and where you can find the best price. Experience goods, on the other hand, are harder for consumers to evaluate until after they are purchased and consumed. Later, two other economists—Michael Darby and Edi Karni—introduced a third category, so-called credence goods. These are goods for which it is difficult for consumers to judge their quality even after consuming them. Many professional services fall into this category. You might think your attorney, doctor, accountant, or auto mechanic is doing a good job serving you, but you may not be able to tell unless you lose a lawsuit, develop an illness, get audited, or throw a rod—and even then it might be difficult to attribute the adverse consequence to the quality of services previously received, since other factors can contribute to the calamity and no outcome can reasonably be guaranteed.

Advertisers make claims about the quality of all three categories of goods. Consumers find it relatively easy to evaluate claims about search goods. For example, typically one can leaf through a magazine before buying it, or determine whether a ream of copy paper is the right size and color. False advertising claims about search goods are unlikely to result in many purchases. For experience and credence goods, however, quality claims must be evaluated later. If a soft drink manufacturer claims that its new diet cola tastes the same as a regular cola, a drinker will not know until he tries it. But this fact does not mean that producers lack strong incentives to make defensible claims, as Nelson explained in an often-cited 1974 paper, "Advertising as Information."[23] For one thing, not many goods and services—particularly those advertised directly to consumers—can be profitable to produce over time if the producer can make one and only one sale per customer. *Repeat purchases* for experienced customers are critical for most businesses. If advertised claims of quality are followed by unsatisfactory experiences with products, repeat purchases obviously become less likely. Moreover, knowing that fact, even customers who have not yet experienced the good might well see advertising claims as useful *signals* of quality precisely because they are being advertised in the first place. Would a company consistently, at great expense, advertise a product as tasty if most consumers who buy it do not agree? If not impossible to conceive, the practice would at least be rare. A different version of the signaling argument came from economists Benjamin Klein and Keith Leffler in 1981. They argued that consumers see advertising as an indicator that a company is willing and able to maintain the quality of a good or service over time, of "the magnitude of the total brand-name capital investment." Such an effect explains why advertisers are willing to pay large sums to celebrity endorsers, Klein and Leffler say, and more specifically why they actually make public how large the sums are.[24]

Even for credence goods, the dynamics that Nelson described linking advertising and quality—the repeat-business effect and the signaling effect—will serve to link advertising claims at least with the perception of good-quality service. That such a perception might turn out, in the long run, to be false is no more a risk of trusting advertising claims about credence goods than it is of trusting other means of selecting a provider of such goods, such as word of mouth.

Once again, empirical studies in recent decades offer supporting evidence for the idea that advertising generally serves to identify, rather than obscure, true differences in product quality. A 1983 study for the Federal Trade Commission found that optometrists who advertised themselves on price and quality tended to do a better job of fitting contact lenses—measured objectively on the basis of prescription and injury to the cornea—than those who did not advertise. Earlier research had established that the more intensely a brand was advertised, the more likely it was to be rated highly in quality by *Consumer Reports* magazine.[25] More generally, a broad study of advertising expenditures in the United States from 1948 to 1995 found no evidence for what the authors called the "Galbraithian hypothesis"— that advertising served to stimulate overall consumer purchasing to justify ever-rising industrial production—and instead concluded that by signaling quality, ads help consumers "avoid regret from purchasing low-quality products."[26] Interestingly, work by Amna Kirmani and other marketing researchers in the 1980s appeared to show that above a certain point, advertising expenditures began to be perceived by consumers not as evidence of product quality but rather as evidence of defensiveness on the part of the producer. Kirmani's later research, using print ads of European consumer goods, suggested that consumers are particularly suspicious of constant repetition of quality claims, and of repeated use of bold colors and other attention-getting devices. Basically, they start to wonder if the company has something to hide.[27] As has already been demonstrated, a key element of the modern economic approach to advertising is the realization that consumers typically buy more than once, they learn through experience, and their preferences and responses to advertising are not as controllable by sellers as earlier generations of analysts seem to have assumed.

It would be reasonable to question whether such findings for particular products and services can be generalized to advertising as a whole. The problem for economists who suspect that advertising in general harms consumer welfare is that the mechanisms they assert for causing the harm—increasing industry concentration and monopoly power—also appear to be difficult to demonstrate in the real world. For example, a 1964 paper by Lester Telser tracked advertising expenditures and market shares from 1948 to 1955 for three industries: cosmetics, soap, and food. He found that while the market shares of the four leading brands declined in all three industries, the decline was greatest in precisely the industry, cosmetics, that featured the most intensive advertising. Studies of European markets for consumer goods in the 1970s found a similar result: the more intensive the advertising, the less stable were the market shares of the leading companies. Nor can large advertisers count on economies of scale to blow their smaller competitors out of the water, as it turns out. Research by Julian Simon and other economists in the late 1960s and 1970s found that there appeared to be no economy of scale in advertising for many common items. Simon found that for drugs, cigarettes, milk, and liquor, there were decreasing rates of return to advertising expenditures and repetition.[28]

And remember Joe Bain's prediction back in 1956 that advertising and promotion had erected insurmountable barriers to entering the distilled liquor business? In 1967, a different scholar took another look at the industry and found that one-third of the companies making whisky in 1965 did not exist before World War II, and that the four leading brands—despite spending increasing sums on advertising— saw their market share drop from 75 percent in 1947 to 54 percent in 1967. Bain's predictions did not turn out to be accurate.[29]

As Chicago school legal theorist Richard Posner observed, seeing product differentiation as a barrier to entry requires assumptions that, like the one about consumers desiring not to have their preferences changed, are upon reflection highly questionable. If consumers are capable of being persuaded via advertising to prefer Brand X to Brand Y, why are they not capable of being persuaded by subsequent advertising to prefer Brand Z? Marketing may represent a significant upfront cost for a new company entering a particular industry, but that property makes it no different from other up-front costs such as building a plant, buying equipment, or finding a skilled workforce. Advertising constitutes "brainwashing," Posner wrote, only if there are no competing claims from rivals or would-be rivals. "No proof has yet been offered that it is easier for the first advertiser to win a consumer's patronage than it is for the second advertiser to shift it to him." Indeed, there may be a sort of "free rider" problem in that the first advertiser may spark consumer interest in a new product that can later be marketed, at lower cost, by a competitor. And in a point that ties back to the notion of consumer preference for change, not stability, Posner observed that established manufacturers of goods such as soap are frequently introducing new brands or subbrands, despite the fact that they have already differentiated and established their old, reliable brands. This "suggests a taste for novelty on the part of the consumer that does not square with the theory of the first advertiser's advantage," he wrote.[30]

To return to the initial discussion, Stigler's presentation of an alternative Informational View to Galbraith's negative Persuasive View—and Hayek's denunciation of Galbraith's negativist assumptions about persuasion—served to erode the economic underpinnings of the anti-advertising movement. A useful distinction between the advertising pessimists and the optimists is that the former assume that consumers do not want or need advertising to accomplish their goals. The latter disagree. Stigler and his Chicago school contemporaries and descendants described a competitive process in which information is costly, so rational consumers will want and need advertising claims to help them reduce the cost of finding lower-priced and better-quality goods and services. According to this view, advertising is a tool for eliminating *rational ignorance*, or a lack of knowledge that is understandable and predictable because of the very real costs associated with acquiring it. Hayek and later analysts within the Austrian school, most notably Israel Kirzner, described a competitive process in which information is not only costly to acquire but also so dispersed and idiosyncratic that advertising becomes an indispensable tool of entrepreneurs seeking to attract consumer attention. The question for Austrians is not just what consumers do not yet know (and advertising can help them to find out), but also what consumers do not know that they do not know, a concept that Kirzner termed *utter ignorance*.

What some might call "persuasion" or perhaps something more sinister, Kirzner called "injecting a pleasant surprise into the world of the consumer." While Hayek's initial rejoinder to Galbraith strikes many as biting and devastating, the Austrian critique is actually a more cordial one to the old-school critics of advertising than the Chicago school's, which essentially argued that these critics had been asking entirely the wrong questions about advertising. No, Austrians say, the older economists were asking the right questions but had, perhaps understandably, drawn erroneous conclusions. It *looks* like persuasive advertising might allow the seller to get the better of the buyer, because specific consumer preferences are indeed being changed from what they would have been in the absence of advertising. But that is a superficial and unrealistic depiction of what is going on. "The advertiser, it should be emphasized, has not *responded* to preexisting consumer demand," Kirzner wrote, "but neither has he, necessarily, violated that preexisting pattern of demand by invasively altering it through psychological manipulation. He has merely opened the consumer's eyes to see what he had earlier failed to notice."[31] Another way to think about the Hayekian argument against Galbraith and his predecessors is that their method for answering questions about persuasion is not a neutral one. To say that consumers are harmed by advertising claims, you have to assert that what consumers would have purchased or done without them would have more effectively advanced their interest. But who is to say? Presented with new information and alternatives, consumers have in reality changed their minds. Galbraith was claiming the right to change it back. Why was his judgment superior?

For his part, Galbraith never really recognized how devastating the early criticisms of Stigler and Hayek had been to the institutionalist and Keynesian strains within his critique of advertising. Writing in 1988, Galbraith claimed that after the publication of *The Affluent Society*, free market economists had simply pretended not to notice his assault on the notion of consumer sovereignty—this is not a fair reading even of the Chicago school's exploration of advertising as information, much less of the Austrian response—and that these economists had done nothing to reconcile their theories with real-world experience. This tendency "to put the advertising industry outside the realm of respectable economic thought and discussion is inexcusable," he wrote, in part because it is "damaging to the industry itself, for it leaves it in a vaguely functionless limbo. I look back with a certain satisfaction on my efforts to correct this error but with somewhat less satisfaction on my record of success."[32]

I will say this at least for Galbraith's odd take on what was then a robust thirty-year debate: it certainly established beyond any potential refutation that information is not perfectly distributed and comprehended.

# THE NEW ECONOMICS AND REGULATORY CHANGES

For social scientists who worry that their work will never have an impact outside the cloisters of academia, the development of the new economics of advertising in the 1960s and 1970s constitutes a hopeful tale. It turns out that government policy makers were, indeed, paying attention to the ebbs and flows of debate about the role that advertising and commercial claims played in the market process.

The 1960s and early 1970s were a difficult time for the advertising industry and its traditional regulators. A new generation of activists and self-styled "consumer advocates"—many inspired by the likes of Veblen, Chase, Packard, and Galbraith—began to attack the federal government as a weak-kneed and ineffective guarantor of the public interest. At the very beginning of the decade, in 1960, there were more than 100 bills in Congress targeting various aspects of advertising and marketing practice. As the Kennedy administration prepared to take office in 1961, presidential confidante Arthur Schlesinger resurrected President Truman's old idea of ending the tax deduction for advertising.[33]

A few years later, Federal Communications Commission Chairman Newton Minnow famously proclaimed that television was "a vast wasteland." Ralph Nader began to sound the alarm, asserting that Johnson administration regulators were either in the pocket of big business or overly worried about the consequences of taking controversial stands. Newspapers and magazines ran numerous exposés of fraudulent and manipulative claims, and were joined by a new wave of "consumer reporters" working for local and national television news media. In 1969, newly elected President Richard Nixon asked the American Bar Association (ABA) to examine some of Nader's claims. The ABA report urged an overhaul of the Federal Trade Commission (FTC) to strengthen its enforcement powers and redirect its energies away from merely responding to charges of false advertising and toward the idea of requiring advertisers ahead of time to substantiate their claims.[34] In addition to general criticisms of advertising, activists and regulators during this period zeroed in on spe-

cific areas of concern such as advertising aimed at children (as discussed at length in Chapter 7).[35]

As a consequence of these and other challenges, Congress and the
Nixon administration basically reconstituted the FTC through legislation. Then in 1971, the FTC held a major series of hearings on
"modern advertising practices" that helped define a shift of strategy.
The preemptive doctrine of "advertising substantiation" became FTC
policy. As John Calfee, who formerly served in the FTC's Bureau of
Economics, later wrote, the burden of proof had shifted somewhat in
the direction that the activists of the 1930s had originally sought:
"Previously, the FTC had to demonstrate that claims were false; now
it could require firms to demonstrate that claims were true."[36] Soon
prospective advertisers were sending in piles of documents and files
for regulatory review and potential public scrutiny, and it looked like
a heavy dose of stultifying regulation was in the offing.

But it did not last. As Calfee explained, "It turned out that the FTC
and the U.S. courts were paying remarkably close attention to the new
economic thinking on advertising."[37] Particularly influential were
studies in the Stigler tradition that uncovered the critical role that advertising claims played in informing consumers and heightening competition on the basis of both price and quality. By the late 1970s, the
FTC had adopted an entirely different critique of what kinds of advertising claims were truly fraudulent, and thus potentially appropriate for regulators to police, while embracing a new role in demanding
an end to advertising restrictions and bans that in practice harmed the
welfare of consumers. For example, while the FTC no longer pursued
so-called fictitious prices cases—such as saying a product was on sale
at "50 percent off" some unstated list price—it actually pressed professions such as medical doctors and attorneys to loosen rules that,
supposedly on the grounds of ethics, limited advertising claims and
competition among their members. The FTC even sought to strike
down as antitrust violations some formal agreements among firms not
to advertise in a given market. By 1995, longtime FTC veteran and
now Chairman Robert Pitofsky would say, "Advertising is a key source
of price and other information and when competitors band together
to restrict it, consumers lose."[38]

Another simultaneous development that served to weaken support for stricter, command-and-control regulation of advertising claims was the formation of industry-led organizations such as the national Council of Better Business Bureaus to serve as an umbrella organization for local groups that received complaints from dissatisfied consumers and promulgated instances of deceptive advertising and other questionable business practices.[39] Its National Advertising Division became a way for industry essentially to improve its own reputation by identifying egregious cases without having to use government regulations or lawsuits to require some kind of conforming action. Again, it became clear that while it is possible to fool some consumers some of the time, one of the best weapons against fraudulent claims was publicity—and counterclaims by rival companies.

## WHAT MAKES AN ADVERTISEMENT EFFECTIVE?

While controversy certainly continues about the effects of advertising and other kinds of promotion on market outcomes and consumer welfare, I think it would be fair to say that the discussion has come a long way from the time of Galbraith asserting to popular acclaim in the 1950s—with the assent of much of the academic establishment of his day—that advertising was inherently wasteful and monopolistic. A new economics of advertising has taken hold, a body of theories and empirical data that demonstrates how advertising can lower the full cost of goods to shoppers and communicate useful information to them about what they are buying—as well as introducing them to the existence of goods and services that they might want to buy.

Still, there remain some challenging questions. First of all, what makes any particular ad or advertising campaign effective? It is not a contradiction to say that advertising expenditures appear to correlate with particular outcomes (positive or negative) *and* that it is unclear how advertising generates those outcomes. To adopt a somewhat strained metaphor, this is akin to saying that physicists know gravitation exists, they can measure its effects, and they can predict its influence on physical bodies and electromagnetic radiation—and yet they cannot say with any certainty exactly what gravitation consists of and how and why it operates. That gravity exists is obviously valuable information. It influences the decisions we make every day, particularly if we live or work in a high-rise building. But it would also be extremely valuable to know how and why it works, which is why physicists continue to study and contemplate the workings of gravity.

With advertising and the marketing mix in general, there is no shortage of theories. Some emphasize basic consumer recall of brand names and related information. Others point to the signaling effect of quality claims about brands, as described above. Most find it useful to distinguish forms of advertising on the basis of their chief functions. *Direct-response advertising* seeks to motivate consumers to do something immediately, such as calling a toll-free number, returning a response card, visiting a website, or going out to purchase a car before the sale ends on Sunday. *Delayed-response advertising*, on the other hand, is designed to build awareness and preference for a particular brand over time. *Institutional* or *corporate advertising* focuses not on particular brands but on building a favorable impression of a company, either for the purposes of leveraging product advertising or perhaps to improve the company's public image in the face of adverse publicity or the risk of governmental regulation.

Given the great diversity of industries, products, fashions, fads, and consumers in America alone, it should not be surprising that no consensus is evident in the marketing literature about what consistently "works" in advertising or why it does. There is a consistent pattern, however. Whenever marketing, sales, and advertising professionals feel threatened by internal or external events—be it recessionary drops in marketing expenditures, declining viewership of popular advertising media, or scandals and legal squabbles—many engage in a great deal of hand-wringing about what they do not know or cannot prove about advertising. And there is evidence to back up some of their self-doubts.

In 1989, for example, just as the advertising business was entering another slump, two professors published a comprehensive examination of advertising effectiveness for more than 300 common consumer products. They concluded that slightly fewer than half of the ads studied resulted in increased sales (a finding that is strikingly reminiscent of John Wanamaker's old complaint that he knew about half of what he spent on advertising was wasted, but didn't know which half). Even when researchers can find links between particular ad campaigns and sales gains, they often find the improvements to be short-lived. By 2000, a piece in *Harvard Business Review* sought to confront readers bluntly. "Research indicates that only about a third of all ad campaigns have a significant immediate impact on sales, and fewer than a quarter have any prolonged effect," the author asserted. "That's a shocking record."[40]

But, as University of Southern California business professor David Stewart wrote, such studies contain a measurement problem and thus contribute to undue skepticism about the effectiveness of advertising. The problem is that within a market of rivalrous competition, advertising often acts as a defense mechanism. Responding to an aggressive marketing effort by a competitor, a well-established firm might spend lots of money on advertising and yet see no increase in sales or market share. That does not mean, however, that the dollars have been poorly spent. Without them, the firm might well have experienced *declines* in sales and market share. A related problem is that marketing researchers know more about how to attract consumers' attention initially but far less about what can retain them as repeat customers. And in the new media marketplace of the twenty-first century, still another question is how different kinds of marketing compete for the attention of an audience with an unprecedented capability to choose how and when they consume news, entertainment, and consumer information.[41]

An interesting 1995 paper by Marnik Dekimpe of Catholic University and Dominique Hanssens of University of California, Los Angeles, offered a new look at some of these old problems. Using statistical techniques to measure how sales trends evolve over time, they studied home improvement stores and found that much of their sales and media spending had strong but delayed effects on sales trends. "Traditional modeling approaches would not pick up these effects and, therefore, seriously underestimate the long-term effectiveness of advertising," they found. Essentially the same error had plagued earlier generations of studies by critics who asserted that firms used advertising to establish monopoly positions and thus boosted their profits at the expense of consumers. As uncovered by Harold Demsetz in an influential 1979 paper, the measurement problem here was that the studies treated advertising dollars as an immediate expense and deducted them in full rather than depreciating them over time, which would be the proper method if advertising were thought of as a capital good intended to generate returns (increased sales) over time. When he made the accounting adjustment and reexamined the same data, Demsetz found no evidence for the proposition that advertising established or promoted monopoly power.[42]

The old, Persuasive View of top-down manipulation and brainwashed masses may have faded from the mainstream of economic analysis, but many advertising and marketing specialists have not gotten the memo. Thus they are not spending enough time examining how advertising is actually used by real people in their personal and cultural contexts, Stewart concluded. Research based on a one-way flow of advertising as an independent variable and consumer responses as the dependent variable will not capture what is going on. To a larger degree, he wrote, "The focus of research should be the ways in which consumers control advertising, and other marketing stimuli, rather than how advertising controls consumer behavior."[43] Another survey of the literature about marketing research put it this way: "Unfortunately, theory development in consumer behavior has fallen far short of expectations. . . . There is still little agreement among researchers, creatives, and clients about what makes consumers tick."[44]

Interestingly, some of the latest work in this area, in seeking to measure and understand advertising effectiveness more broadly, offers perspective on another question that even the modern economics of advertising does not adequately address. That is, what is the value of so-called noninformational advertising? There is an unmistakable defensiveness on the part of many free market economists on this matter. They defend advertising as an important means of reducing consumer ignorance. But they are not sure what to do with popular advertising icons such as Ronald McDonald and the Energizer Bunny, with celebrity spokesmen such as Michael Jordan and Tiger Woods, or with "experiential" ads that seem to associate a product with pictures, sounds, and feelings rather than pure information about prices, quality, and availability.

In Stigler's case, for example, the noninformational content in advertising was treated as either a sort of memory-enhancement device or a way to make the search process less tedious or strenuous. "The assimilation of information is not an easy or pleasant task for most people, and they may well be willing to pay more for the information when supplied in an enjoyable form," he wrote in his "Economics of Information" paper. "In principle, this complementary demand for information and entertainment is exactly analogous to the complementary demand of consumers for commodities and delivery service or air-conditioned stores."[45] Even among Austrian economists, who have a more expansive view of the role of advertising in the competitive process, commercial imagery that does not convey prices or other hard information is typically viewed as playing an indirect role. First you get the consumers' attention with the imagery. Then you convince them to purchase—or repurchase—the good or service in question. Advertising professionals call these processes *brand imagery* (attracting consumers' attention and making them increasingly favorable to the product) and *brand salience* (reminding them that the product is available and will address an immediate need).[46] But do these concepts really capture the entirety of how pictures, jingles, colors, celebrities, and dramatic or comedic stories within advertising messages serve to affect consumers?

Certainly many analysts of advertising who are not economists—cultural scholars, authors, satirists, historians, and political activists—do not think that it does. They resist the interpretation of advertising and other forms of marketing according to the principles of modern economics, if in fact these critics are even aware of such principles. They wonder why so many resources are devoted particularly to broadcast advertising that conveys little specific information to consumers, and more to the point they worry about such issues as the substitution of product placement for segregated advertising breaks, the commercialization of art and cultural transmission, and the role that heavily advertised brand names play in the rearing of children and the socioeconomic ordering of adults.

But their concerns are not really so far removed from those of researchers who study the marketing process within a modern economic or business context. About how advertising works, the title of a recent article queried, "Do You Really Want to Know?" While the author cast a lot of cold water on traditional claims of advertising effectiveness, he pointed to new studies that look at how subjects retain information. "Effective messages are likely to make the consumer interact with those messages to involve them," he wrote. "Indeed, when consumers 'try on' ideas in a commercial, when they wonder about how those ideas might fit in their lives, or even when they question some of the messages, active processing is at work."[47] The next chapter examines this revelation at some length, and considers not just its economic but also its aesthetic and ethical implications.

# CHAPTER 5

# Living the Commercial Life

Americans are drowning in commercial messages. Everyone knows that. The only open questions, it seems, are the depth of the water and the strength of the undertow. "The average American sees about 400 advertisements a day," stated a university-based feminist organization in 2003. Its members were upset about the effects of ads on the self-image of American women.[1] But this statistic was limited to visual messages. "The average American sees *or hears* 560 advertisements a day" (emphasis added), according to a commonly used Internet reference as well as an August 2004 report by a West Coast television station.[2] No, say many other critics and commentators—these numbers are way, way too low. No less a reputable source than PBS, warning teenagers of the "negative effects of media," stated in 2003 that "the average American sees 3,000 advertisements a day."[3] Not to be outdone, well-known authors and marketing consultants Tom Collins and Stan Rapp, chairman of McCann-Erickson Worldgroup, asserted that on a typical day, "an average American sees over 5,000 advertisements."[4]

The leap from 400 ads a day to more than 5,000 is a gigantic one and begs for an explanation. As is the case for many such factoids—statements or statistics that sound authoritative but lack appropriate documentation—it was difficult to track down where these various estimates came from. But after some digging, a timeline began to form. I tracked the estimate of 560 ads per day to a 1965 book by Charles F. Adams, then an executive at an advertising firm in New York. Adams said it was based on the following assumptions about a typical consumer's media habits: watching 3.8 hours of television a day, listening to 2.3 hours of radio, reading an average of 1.5 newspapers and half a magazine, and seeing one direct-mail piece. Even when Adams wrote, in the mid-1960s, many advertising analysts and critics were using much higher estimates of 1,500–1,600 a day. Adams viewed his statistic as a necessary corrective to what he saw as advertising hyperbole. Assuming that (as yet) advertisers have no access to our dreams, a waking day of 17 hours or so would yield an estimate of 33 ad messages per hour if employing Adams's 560 estimate, or about 1 ad every 2 minutes. Could average exposure to advertising really be three times that? "The estimate of 100 exposures per hour per individual has . . . never been validated by competent research techniques," Adams wrote.[5] He speculated as to one source of the error: a General Foods executive had hypothesized in a 1958 speech that a typical family of four in suburban New York might be exposed to 1,500 ads per day. It was entirely erroneous, of course, to extrapolate that such a household was representative of the United States as a whole, and then to mix up ads *per household* with ads *per individual*.

In 1970, futurist Alvin Toffler popularized Adams's 560-ads-per-day statistic by mentioning it prominently in his book *Future Shock*.[6] Many media accounts then not unreasonably rounded 560 up to 600, a statistic that was cited well into the 1980s along with the higher, exaggerated numbers of 1,500 to 1,600. Then commentators began quoting a well-known source of media statistics, Jupiter Research, as generating an estimate of 3,000 exposures to advertising per day for the average American. By 2001, some claimed, Jupiter had bumped its annual estimate up to nearly 4,000.[7] Jupiter is the only named source I could find for the high-end estimate (Rapp and Collins appear to have extrapolated from it). It is also highly dubious on its face—reflecting gross exaggeration of media consumption, errors such as confusing households and individuals, or defining ad exposures to include multiple viewings of simple brand names (such as a Nike swoosh on one's own T-shirt or the Apple on one's own laptop). Wondering how a reputable company such as Jupiter could have come up with such an estimate, I called the company's press staff, who in turn asked around among Jupiter researchers. None of them could tell me where the 3,000 or 3,838 ads-per-day statistics came from.[8]

As marketing analyst Jim Rosenfield explained in a September 2001 article, the (apparently orphan) 3,838-per-day estimate assumes that the average American is (given 17 waking hours) exposed to about 230 ads per hour, or nearly 4 per minute. The problem is that during the largest single period of media consumption per day, watching television, *there are many fewer than 4 ads per minute* even if one is generous with the definition. Is television actually a *haven* from advertising? Seems unlikely. It would require that advertising be truly a constant presence, at 4–5 exposures per minute, during the average American's everyday activities—"when they're working, chatting, seeing dentists, eating, gazing out the window, walking the dog, and going about their business," Rosenfield wrote.[9]

## OUR LOVE-HATE RELATIONSHIP WITH THE PITCH

Why would such extravagant claims as 3,000 to 5,000 ad exposures per day be so readily accepted without thinking through the basic math? Because many Americans, "experts" and regular folks alike, exhibit a seemingly curious love-hate relationship with advertising, marketing, and salesmanship. We want and need these things—and they also annoy, confuse, and worry us. There is nothing new about this observation. In the midst of the Depression-era assault on advertising and big business, an industry trade journal called *Sales Management* commissioned a series of consumer surveys. Advertising scholar John Calfee later observed that the 1930s-era surveys probably constituted the first serious attempt to gauge public sentiment about the industry, but the findings have been confirmed repeatedly since then. "The surveys revealed a paradox," Calfee wrote. "People did not believe what advertising said, but they used it all the time to get information." The proportions have been remarkably similar over the years, from the 1930s to the 1970s and into the early twenty-first century. About

70 percent of Americans say that, as a whole, advertising claims must be viewed skeptically and cannot simply be accepted at face value. But about 70 percent simultaneously believe that advertising is a useful source of information, and that without it consumers would be harmed and competition lessened. The 70-70 rule is not just an American one; as Calfee notes, surveys in some forty countries have found similar proportions embracing the view of advertising as not generally trustworthy *and* the view of advertising as useful and helpful.[10]

Upon reflection, these views expose some tensions and complexities in how consumers interact with advertising, but they are not really contradictory. For one thing, individuals have diverse preferences and buying behaviors, yet they are being asked about advertising in general. Obviously, for any given advertising message, there can be many viewers or listeners for whom the message is entirely irrelevant and unwanted. Although the media marketplace of the early twenty-first century is much more segmented than it used to be, older tv viewers still see ads for music they would never buy, younger radio listeners hear ads for cars they cannot afford, confirmed nonsmokers see the Marlboro Man on billboards, and vegetarians get coupons for meat-lovers' pizza in their mailboxes.

Even for goods and services that a consumer might make use of at some point, she will often receive numerous solicitations on occasions when she is uninterested in responding, such as the ubiquitous direct-mail pieces promoting mortgage refinancing or new credit cards. If she then expresses annoyance at the amount of advertising she is receiving, that does not mean that she does not appreciate the advertisements that *do* give her useful information at the time she needs it, or that let her know about a new product she may later come to value highly. But such selective interest in buying could well contribute to a perception of being bombarded by advertising. As one advertising veteran put it in 1980, "People I meet at parties, once they discover how I make my living, feel compelled to tell me about the low regard in which they hold advertising. But in return for my listening to their complaints, they have to answer some questions too. I ask them what they think of Hallmark's advertising, or Kraft's, or the Raid advertising with those cute bugs. 'Oh, well, that's different.' "[11] Pollsters have long discovered similar tensions in how people rate other institutions, such as the economy (pessimistic overall but sanguine about their own financial situation) or public schools (mediocre overall, but the local school is just fine).

Second, that consumers are skeptical about advertising claims is hardly an indictment of the machinery of modern marketing. It is more an indictment of the old Veblen-Galbraith-Toynbee school of critics who viewed mass market consumers as mindlessly keeping up with the Joneses or spinning the proverbial squirrel wheel. On the other hand, the phenomenon of the skeptical, mercurial, and footloose consumer has never been an unfamiliar one to those actually in the selling profession. "Anyone who thinks that people can be fooled or pushed around has an inaccurate and pretty low estimate of people— and he won't do very well in advertising," the famous adman Leo Burnett once remarked.[12] Or, as the legendary David Ogilvy put it, "The consumer isn't a moron. She is your wife."[13]

Is this just a comforting façade meant to distract from the mechanism of manipulation behind it? Hardly. Experience teaches that most new business enterprises, products, and brands do not pan out. Of the 85,000 new products advertised in America during the 1980s, one economist estimated, only about 15 percent were still around by 1991.[14] Advertising professionals have *tried* to market the equivalent of Edsels and New Coke. They have failed. That is why their assessments of advertising's role in the buying process are more guarded than those of many outside critics. Faced with intense competition from other claims on consumers' attention, with rapidly changing consumer preferences and media habits, and with the need to generate not just an initial sale but also repeat sales to have real success, marketing pros often view suggestions of their nefarious power over others with a mixture of confusion and derision.

Finally, the hyperbolic claims of those who see advertising as a pervasive and dangerous force in our lives fail to consider how all kinds of marketing efforts occur within a context that is shaped by prior and competing marketing and by consumers themselves. The latter are not a passive group (yes, even while watching television). They are always receiving new images and interpreting new information within personal frames of reference that elevate some things, relegate others, subject still others to immediate skepticism, and seek frequently to change the subject. "Individual ads are best understood as being a sort of freeze-frame from a long-running dialogue between sellers and consumers," Calfee put it. "Almost always, the meaning of what an advertisement says is profoundly shaped by what is happening elsewhere. To a much greater extent than most people realize, advertisers are pawns of the evolving information environment in which they must communicate."[15]

Dispelling the notion of consumers as passive recipients of marketing cues can help to uncover one of the remaining mysteries about the craft of advertising: why so much of it seems to be so far removed from the kind of time, place, and price messages that traditional-minded economists and other analysts have found it easier to explain and defend. If the use of vibrant colors, catchy jingles, power words, mood music, jarring or rapturous pictures, celebrity endorsers, dramatic or comedic storylines, and other images are not the tools of the hidden persuaders—intended to make us buy what we do not need or ignore "real" attributes of products such as price and quality—then what legitimate function do they serve? Are they just mnemonic devices, just tricks to aid our memory? I think that they often do something much more. And so do many modern-day analysts of advertising and marketing, though they are not as comfortable with the social and cultural implications as I am. But first, we must backtrack a bit to examine another economic perspective on the role that advertising plays in the market process.

## THE THIRD VIEW: ADVERTISING AS COMPLEMENTARY GOOD

Recall that in the previous chapter, I adopted as a useful tool economist Kyle Bagwell's delineation of three schools of economic thought about advertising. The first, the Persuasive View, contends that advertising and other forms of marketing and salesmanship serve to change consumer tastes and preferences. Some economists see the effect as manipulative, others as benign. The second approach is the

Informational View, as articulated by George Stigler and other free-market economists. They emphasize the role that commercial communication plays in informing consumers about the availability, price, and quality of goods, thus advancing their interest by reducing search costs and facilitating robust competition. The third body of thought on the economics of advertising, the Complementary View, is associated primarily with the writings of Stigler's fellow Chicago school economist Gary Becker and several collaborators and like-minded thinkers. As an outgrowth of the informational tradition, the Complementary View rejects the idea that advertising is fundamentally an act of persuasion, but it also seeks to push beyond the model of advertising as a conveyer of practical information. "Most economists and other intellectuals have not liked advertisements that provide little information," Becker wrote in a widely cited 1993 paper with colleague Kevin Murphy. "Noninformative advertising is claimed to create wants and to change and distort tastes. Although we agree that many ads create wants without producing information, we do not agree that they change tastes."[16]

Becker and Murphy admitted that their approach might "at first blush appear strange," and explained that what they called noninformative advertising could be thought of as a *separate consumer good*, a product that consumers demand and purchase as a complement to the subject of the advertising. Economists used the term *complementary* to describe goods that are often purchased and consumed together, indeed that are worth more to consumers together than the sum of the two goods purchased and consumed separately. The presence of one enhances the consumption of the other. Examples would include DVDs and DVD players, bread and butter, or automobiles and gasoline. Not all ads are complementary goods, Becker and Murphy wrote. Ads are "goods" if people are willing to pay for them, directly or indirectly, and are "bads" if people must be paid to accept them. In the latter category should be placed most radio and television advertising, they argued, because consumers do not really demand it in and of itself but are willing to be "paid"—in the form of radio and tv programs—to hear or watch the advertising. Print ads do not work the same way, they wrote, because it is easier for readers to ignore or evade unwanted advertising when it is printed as opposed to when it is broadcast.[17]

The Complementary View proposed by Becker and others was a welcome attempt by economists to grapple with what had been a long-time complaint among critics of mass marketing: that it relied excessively on messages and images far removed from the textbook version of commercial communication as a means of transmitting hard information. Unfortunately, by seeking to deny the seemingly obvious—that selling involves persuasion—these scholars ironically limited their own persuasiveness. Ads that contain no practical information, Becker and Murphy wrote, can nevertheless "entertain, create favorable associations between sexual allure and the products advertised, instill discomfort in people not consuming products popular with athletes, beauties, and other elites, and in other ways induce people to want the products."[18] If one can "induce" another to want a product, isn't that persuasion? Doesn't that constitute a shift of consumer taste? Unless one employs definitions removed from the common usage of these terms, the answer must be yes.

Furthermore, the notion that advertising might play a role in the *act* of consumption, not merely a purchase that precedes it, was a critically important one. Yet because of the esoteric and counterintuitive aspect of the Complementary View as expressed by Becker and other economists, many intellectuals who denigrated advertising as wasteful, devious, and subversive of consumer welfare did not find it necessary to grapple with their economic insights. The precise language economists used to describe consumption had led them to label advertising as a good separate from, but perhaps complementary to, the product being advertised. Back in the 1930s, Edward Chamberlin had argued strongly for a distinction between *production costs* and *selling costs*. He thought that advertising, as a prime example of a selling cost, helped firms establish monopoly power by creating artificial barriers between competing products—in other words, by creating brands. But even those subsequent economists who drew more favorable conclusions about advertising had nevertheless maintained this distinction between production costs and selling costs or, in Becker and Murphy's case, between a production good and a complementary advertising good.

# THE NEW CRITICS AND THE SOURCE OF VALUE

As previously discussed in Chapter 2, the assault on advertising has never been limited to economists asserting its anticompetitive or wasteful properties. Other critics—theologians, philosophers, historians, social scientists, literary scholars, journalists, and politicians among them—have emphasized social, cultural, and moral concerns. Perhaps, many argued, advertising does play a useful role in informing consumers, facilitating competition, or even pleasantly surprising them with new products they would not otherwise have demanded. But it also encourages materialism, conformity, and envy while destroying independence and authenticity. As the economics-based critique of Veblen and Galbraith failed to age well during the latter decades of the twentieth century (being undercut by new theories and empirical evidence about how the modern mass market actually functioned), a new generation of critics began to return to these broader social and cultural themes. Such writers as Daniel Boorstin, Gary Cross, Gary Ruskin, Daniel Horowitz, Richard Lippke, Ben Fine, Ellen Leopold, Roland Marchand, Jackson Lears, and Michael Schudson offered a somewhat more nuanced critique of advertising, often admitting to its critical role within a capitalist economy and listing both positive and negative social implications before (usually) drawing an anticonsumerism conclusion.

It would be impossible to summarize each analyst's unique contribution to the literature here, so at the risk of some oversimplification let me describe some common themes and propositions contained in their works. All of them, in one way or another, portray advertising as *a source of value*. Advertising influences, and is influenced by, the act of consuming. Such themes represent the intellectuals' attempt to fill in a gap left by much of formal economic analysis, which has typically shied away from describing how consumers form and change preferences and how they come to value what they buy (or do not buy). If economists such as Becker and Murphy assert that "there is no reason to claim that advertisements change tastes just because they affect the demand for other goods," others will gladly step in to answer the question the economists are not willing to frame. As Fine and Leopold argued in their 1990 book, *The World of Consumption*, "Of all the fields of social science, only economics ignores the social construction of a commodity's use value. In any broader social theory, it is clear that advertising addresses the perception of what is consumed."[19] Here are some of the most common claims made within these broader social theories:

**Advertising Is Mechanistic** With a nod to Emerson and other Romantic seekers of the authentic and personal, many modern critics have seen mass marketing practices as supplanting older means of making and exchanging things that preserved individuality and eschewed artifice. "To put the matter abruptly, the advertising industry is a crude attempt to extend the principles of automation to every aspect of society," Marshall McLuhan wrote in 1964. He added that "the simple faith of the salesman in the irresistibility of his line (both talk and goods) now yields to the complex togetherness of the corporate posture, the process and the organization," while advertising tricks its audience into "deserting the individual consumer-product."[20] More recently, Jackson Lears's lengthy tome *Fables of Abundance* offered a cultural history of advertising in America in which he favorably contrasted the carnival atmosphere of advertising's nineteenth-century antecedents with the corporate advertising industry of the twentieth century. If the reader can make his way through a rather dense thicket of turgid and pretentious prose and a clumsy ascribing of sexual and racial innuendo to virtually every advertising image examined—who knew that the black man holding the scythe on an early ad for Cream of Wheat was really a projection of white male fears of emasculation?—he will find in *Fables of Abundance* a critique rather different from the antimaterialist sentiments of Veblen and Galbraith. Lears mourned the loss of the P. T. Barnum side of advertising: the magical, the animistic, the garish, the bizarre. Instead of preserving advertising imagery as a "rhetoric of hedonistic release," he wrote, the corporate takeover of advertising by "managerial elites" in the twentieth century reflected their "therapeutic ethos" and instigated a "rhetoric of control" that put too much emphasis on personal efficiency and utility. Modern ads "continue to construct a separate self in a world of fascinating but forgettable goods."[21]

**Advertising Is Diluting** In a well-known essay called "The Thinner Life of Things," the distinguished historian Daniel Boorstin argued that the arrival of mass consumer culture was extinguishing all those wonderful differences of time and space that in the past had brought meaning to everyday life. No longer having to experience different places, different seasons, and different kinds of people to transact business and acquire things, Americans were becoming more affluent in a materialist sense but less wealthy in other ways. "Advertising . . . has played an important role in attenuating, thinning out, and diluting all our experience," he said. Here the invocation of Emerson is explicit; just as the older writer suggested that "an institution is the length and shadow of a man," Boostin wrote, we can now say that "a commodity is the length and shadow of an ad."[22]

**Advertising Is Antisocial** Critics from traditions such as communitarianism argue, in contravention of the notion that advertising breeds too much consensus and conformity, that modern marketing actually breeds excessive individualism and atomism. Reacting to the transition in consumption patterns that Virginia Postrel and other analysts have described—from the old model of mass marketing to a new model of mass customization—these analysts worry that Americans are rapidly losing whatever shared experiences and values that used to bind the country together. "While earlier forms of consumerism often balanced appeals to individual freedom with the opportunity to join 'consumption communities,' and thus create social bonds through goods, the new consumerism has tipped the scale toward the self," wrote Gary Cross in his 2000 book, *An All-Consuming Century*. Like Lears, Cross offered a complaint strikingly different from those of past critics. The "problem of consumer culture was not that it threatened the cultivated individual," he wrote. "This essential assumption of the jeremiad from Veblen to Packard was wrong. Rather, the dilemma was that consumerism worked so well in meeting immediate needs that Americans found it difficult to want or even to conceive of ultimately more satisfying options," of ways of valuing and consuming products that "balanced the personal and the social."[23]

**Advertising Is Vulgar** If Cross worried that modern marketing allowed individual preferences and experiences to squeeze out social ones, other analysts continued to echo their forebears' distaste for the asserted tendency of advertising to pull cultural and aesthetic standards down to the lowest common denominator. Often, the language used to describe the process is consciously invocative of the vulgar. For example, "There is something of a parasitic quality about advertising," wrote two legal scholars in 1993. "It feeds on the organisms of noncommercial culture—the culture's past and present, ideology and myths, politics and customs, art and architecture, literature and music, and even its religions. . . . For example, women are commodified to sell everything from cars to colognes. . . . Advertising thus pimps its products."[24]

**Advertising Is Intrusive** An argument that originates from elements of both the political left and right is that modern forms of mass marketing no longer stay within their proper societal bounds. Rather than remaining within a clearly demarcated sphere of commerce, they say, advertising intrudes and subverts. "Advertising helps infuse market values into non-market activities, and to displace non-market practices with corporatized alternatives," wrote Gary Ruskin and Robert Weissman. "In doing so, it expands the reach of corporations into personal lives and families." They offer the example of music, which in previous times might be played live in homes and communities but is now a commodity to be purchased and consumed impersonally.[25] On the right, critics such as Michael Medved and Dana Mack have agreed with left-wing writers that commercialism subverts family life and privacy, interfering with the ability of parents, friends, neighborhoods, and congregations to define and honor their own virtues and traditions.[26]

**Advertising Is Frustrating** The consumer culture's greatest sin, some writers contend, was to promise wish fulfillment and then not be able to deliver. "Advertisers in general bear a large part of the responsibility for the deep feelings of inadequacy that drive women to psychiatrists, pills, or the bill," one critic wrote. "You keep telling us over and over that if we could use that or have this or look like that, we would be forever desirable, forever happy. So we spend our time worrying over the gray streak or the extra pound or the dry skin instead of our minds, our hearts, and our fellow men."[27] Similar arguments are made on behalf of slight or balding men, the elderly, racial minorities, the obese, and the poor. In each case, consumers are being set up for a fall. "Living in an age of advertisement, we are perpetually disillusioned," said the author and playwright J. B. Priestley. "The perfect life is spread before us every day, but it changes and withers at a touch."[28] The fundamental problem is, again, that modern society has lost a valuable link to a preferable past, it is argued. In preindustrial societies, tradition guided personal consumption. It offered a set of norms to assist consumers in deciding what scarce goods to purchase to satisfy a limited set of wants. But today's advertising encourages an unrealistic ethic of abundance. "The consumer society does not set up its own fixed models of behavior to replace traditional ones," wrote three like-minded scholars in 1986, "but rather constructs through marketing and advertising successive waves of associations between persons, products, and images of well-being in an endless series of suggestions about the possible routes to happiness and success."[29]

The modern social critics of advertising and consumer culture obviously retain some strongly negative views. But the more discerning and widely respected among them—such as Roland Marchand, Daniel Horowitz, and Michael Schudson—demonstrate a more level-headed approach that eschews wild-eyed rhetoric, the demonization of advertising professionals and clients, and any pretense of utopianism. They may be deeply uncomfortable with mass market capitalism and its implications, but they are also uncomfortable with the elitist and counterfactual attacks on advertising made in the past. They often see no clear alternative in the modern world.

Horowitz, for example, is the author of interesting books such as *The Morality of Spending* and *The Anxieties of Affluence* that trace the history of moralist attacks on advertising and consumption from the late nineteenth century into the 1970s. While Horowitz exhibits sympathy for many past critics, and clearly approaches the subject of advertising with a skeptical eye, he also observes the critics' shortcomings and defeats. Horowitz said that his work was "a critique of a view of consumption that I still hold to a considerable extent" and, seeing it undermined by time and events, he awaited the arrival of a new and "coherent counterargument."[30] Perhaps the most intellectually honest position taken by modern-day critics is to admit that their concerns are not really about advertising as an often-abused capitalist tool, but about the persistence of capitalism itself.[31] Lears made a similar point in a review of Marchand's pathbreaking work, *Advertising the American Dream*. While Marchand had described the mass marketing practices of the 1920s and 1930s as "easing the transition to modernity," Lears complained that such language was imprecise and misleading. "Here, as elsewhere in recent scholarship," he wrote, "the idiom of 'modernity' provides a convenient framework for avoiding the dread word 'capitalism.' "[32]

## IDENTITY, BRAND, AND THE DREAM

It is telling how often today's critics of advertising reference the past. While most of them hail from the political left, they are astoundingly conservative in their outlook. They see the rise of mass marketing in the twentieth century as overturning traditional norms and values that, in their view, protected consumers from deception and disappointment while ensuring societal equality and harmony. The more realistic of these analysts do not believe that there is any alternative immediately available. They do not think that the advertising genie can be stuffed back in the bottle. But they sit on the beach, mournful, watching with disgust the genie dispensing magic tricks and pretending to conjure things out of thin air.

Are they right about the revolutionary nature of advertising? Well, there is no doubt that the rise of the penny press and the department store in the mid-nineteenth century, truly national print media in the late nineteenth century, and broadcasting in the mid-twentieth century transformed the way we bought and sold goods to each other. The peddler, the frontier store, and the small-town merchant gave way to catalogs, supermarkets, and shopping malls. Trade signs and simple text advertisements in early newspapers yielded to glossy magazines, full-page spreads, inserts, radio, tv, and the Internet. But a case can be made that these changes were ones of degree and scale, not of kind.

As discussed in Chapter 1, the practice of salesmanship has been remarkably consistent over time. Ancient Roman merchants and medieval tradesmen used slogans, jingles, attractive or even salacious images, sounds, colors, celebrity endorsements, and merchandising to the extent they could. What limited that extent? At least two considerations were important: technology and the size of the consumer market. The latter was perhaps the most significant limiting factor, in that until relatively recent times only a minority of citizens of any community enjoyed enough discretionary income to be regular shoppers for anything other than the basic staples of life. For those with the wherewithal, consumption has always been an activity associated with personal identity and aesthetic values. Part of the attraction of eating food spiced with pepper or cinnamon and dressing in garments of fur and silk was that these acts of consumption were associated with faraway lands, with rare and exotic delights, and with a desired self-image as one who could acquire and appreciate the finer things of life.

There is no evidence to suggest that human beings, having achieved unprecedented technological prowess and productive capacity in the twentieth century, suddenly became fascinated with self-image, group identity, and luxury. Human beings have always tended to tribal and totemistic behavior. It is part of our nature. Surely it is better that we seek to group ourselves on the basis of personal computer interface (PC or Mac?) or infuse our choice of automobile with totemistic qualities (am I the automobile equivalent of a sports car or a minivan?) rather than with the older tribes of ethnicity, religion, or rigidly stratified and hereditary social castes. "Advertising gives meaning to goods and ultimately to ourselves," as mass communications professor Jeffrey Goldstein put it. "Indirectly, this identity rubs off on the consumer. In a world where one's identity is no longer determined solely by class or race, advertising helps us create and maintain a self image and communicate who we are to others."[33]

While economists have done a great deal to explicate how advertising facilitates the market process, much of their work has also served to erect artificial boundaries within consumer culture that obscure rather than elucidate. Specifically, the notion that advertising as a good should always be considered separable from the good being consumed is a faulty one (though it is hardly limited to economists, of course). Advertising messages and symbols are often best understood as *part of the product itself.*

Economists of the Austrian school never fell into the trap of rigidly dividing the advertised and the advertising, as they understood that a "product" was whatever a consumer thought it was, and that consumers assigned value to that product in subjective ways that were difficult to aggregate or universalize. As Israel Kirzner has observed, the distinguished Austrian economist Ludwig von Mises provided an illustration of this insight long ago that retains it explanatory power. A man has a choice of two restaurants, serving identical meals, identical food. But in one restaurant the owners have not swept the floor in six weeks. The meals are the same. So would the other restaurant's regular sweeping properly be considered a "selling cost," a marketing expense for vending food? Chamberlin would probably think so. So would many critics of advertising who see it as merely a way of inducing a purchase. But this is nonsense, according to Kirzner:

> What you buy when you enter a restaurant is not the food alone. What you buy is a meal, served in certain surroundings. If the surroundings are desirable, it's a different meal, it's a different package. That which has been spent to change the package is as much a production cost as the salary paid to the cook; no difference.[34]

One might make a similar point about the appearance of all sorts of familiar consumer products. What difference does it make whether a car is painted red or gray? Its color will have no effect on whether it gets you where you want to go. But the paint job is irrelevant only if you believe that the sole value a consumer might derive from owning a car is mobility. Based on the actual behavior of millions of consumers since the invention of the automobile, such a belief is fallacious. A car is a package of amenities and experiences—some tactile, some auditory, some visual, some conceptual. How many owners of sport-utility vehicles have actually taken them four-wheeling? Probably not very many. So why do so many tv ads for SUVs show them tromping through the mud and climbing to the top of mountains? In part, it is because prospective car buyers appreciate the feeling of freedom and autonomy that comes with owning a vehicle *capable* of off-road travel. And, in part, it is because four-wheeling looks like fun, just as red cars often look like they would be more fun to drive than gray ones.

Perhaps some intellectuals do not want to admit it, but the truth is that human beings are emotional and aesthetic creatures. We are unlikely ever to be clothed in the monochrome unitards that show up in science fiction shows purporting to predict the future. Fashion is a constant in every human society, ancient and modern, primitive and sophisticated. So is the tendency to identify ourselves with the goods we acquire, to invest value in material possessions. Like it or not, we enjoy the sizzle along with the steak. We enjoy unwrapping the foil before eating the candy bar. We like the banter *and* the haircut, the feel of a knit shirt *and* the symbolism of its logo, and the smell and feel of a new book *and* what is written within it. Indeed, sometimes we *do* judge a book by its cover, or at least appreciate the story more because of it (the wonderfully illustrated jackets of the *Harry Potter* novels alone make that point undeniable). These facts do not mean that materialism, overconsumption, superficiality, and envy are not excesses worth worrying about. Just because a behavior is natural, even healthy to some degree, does not mean that it cannot become pointless, debilitating, and destructive at some higher degree. But the existence of obesity does not suggest that we should not enjoy a good meal. The existence of drunkenness, licentiousness, and promiscuity does not mean that the life of a cloistered monk or nun is the only moral one.

That advertising can act as part of a product, a part that enhances the value of the product to consumers, may not fit most academic definitions of the subject. But it is a commonly accepted view within the marketing profession. As far back as 1925, an advertising copywriter explained that "you do not sell a man the tea, but the magical spell which is brewed nowhere else but in the teapot."[35] More recently, a longtime advertising executive wrote that "advertisers and marketers are in the business of creating an experience," and that "advertising is being asked to keep the product or service out of the 'commodity trap'"—a state in which consumers place no value on it other than physical utility.[36] A related point, appreciated by many in the profession, is that this identification process makes the other functions of advertising more successful. Ads that employ images to communicate abstract ideas prompt consumers to "figure it out," to picture themselves using or owning the product and the benefits that would bestow. This response, called *elaboration*, appears to increase consumers' attention and positive feelings toward an ad as well as their memory of its contents.[37]

Nor has the historical connection between brand identity and tribal identity gone unnoticed by the industry. "In strong brands, the brand becomes part of the consumers' cultural existence," said one consultant who specializes in the conjunction of marketing and storytelling, "and gains strength by the formation of brand communities or tribes that share an affiliation with the sacred beliefs of the brand."[38] In his 2004 book, *The Culting of Brands*, Douglas Atkins picked up on this theme of brand identification as analogous to religious belief by analyzing the way that corporations as diverse as the Body Shop, Harley-Davidson, eBay, Saturn, and jetBlue sought to sell not just physical products but also a set of beliefs and feelings to their customers. There is no doubt, Atkins observed, that people "hunger" to belong to larger groups with shared values or characteristics.[39] Juliet Schor, author of *The Overspent American* and other fretful books, observed the same phenomenon but did not like it very much: "The collection of brands we choose to assemble around us have become among the most direct expressions of our individuality—or more precisely our deep sociological need to identify ourselves with others."[40]

Advertising plays a key role in the identification process. Soft drink ads serve as an instructive example. At various times, we have been invited to "Be a Pepper," "Do the Dew," and join the "Pepsi Generation." Or consider the evolution of automobile brands and marketing. When Ford introduced the Mustang in the mid-1960s, an early series of tv spots portrayed people as transforming themselves by driving the new car (the ads were actually referred to as the "Walter Mitty" series). One spot featured a quiet antique dealer who leaves his shop, flips the sign to "Out to lunch," exchanges his glasses for sports goggles and his jacket for a red vest, and then takes off down the highway to pick up his date. "Why don't you change your life?" the voice-over asked. A few years earlier, the Volkswagen Beetle had established a different brand identify, and cultivated a different "consumer tribe," by emphasizing its unique size, style, and economy. These and other marketing campaigns from the automobile industry, observed *Advertising Age*, have made "consumers feel they aren't just buying four wheels and a chassis, but a chance to be remade into a reflection of the car's image."[41]

One might suggest that all this talk of the emotional and aesthetic aspects of advertising is just another way of saying that it is detached from reality, that it is fundamentally artificial and deceitful. But this reflects a very cramped view of reality. In the real world—as opposed to the abstract, fictional world of "perfect competition" and "social engineering" devised by economists and other theorists—consumers want more that just to acquire and use physical objects. They seek enjoyment, excitement, surprise, comfort, and belonging. Charles Revson of Revlon once explained that "in the factory we make cosmetics; in the store we sell hope."[42]

Whether it is von Mises's restaurant, where food is only a part of the product, or the bewildering diversity of automobile brands developed over the past 100 years, a search for the "realism" of consumption divorced from emotions and aesthetics will be fruitless. Theodore Levitt, a professor of business administration at Harvard University, once drew an explicit connection between advertising and art. He noted that John Keats's "Ode to a Grecian Urn" did not offer a realistic, engineering description of a vessel to carry water in. Instead, he wrote a poem that used meter, rhyme, allusion, illusion, metaphor, and sound to elicit an emotional response. "Neither the poet nor the ad man celebrates the literal functionality of what he produces," Levitt wrote, because they are engaged in "symbolic communication." Their job is not necessarily to "tell it exactly 'like it is' to the naked eye, as do the classified ads." Instead, they speak to a deeper human impulse:

> Few, if any, of us accept the natural state in which God created us. We scrupulously select our clothes to suit a multiplicity of simultaneous purposes, not only for warmth, but manifestly for such other purposes as propriety, status, and seduction. Women modify, embellish, and amplify themselves with colored paste for the lips and powders and lotions for the face; men as well as women use devices to take hair off the face and others to put it on the head. Like the inhabitants of isolated African regions, where not a single whiff of advertising has ever intruded, we all encrust ourselves with rings, pendants, bracelets,

neckties, clips, chains, and snaps. . . . Everywhere man rejects nature's uneven blessings. He molds and repackages to his own civilizing specifications an otherwise crude, drab, and generally oppressive reality.[43]

# RELIGION AND THE COMMERCIAL LIFE

The notion that advertising helps to feed a human longing to "reject nature's uneven blessings" and "the natural state in which God created us" obviously invites a return to one of the themes discussed in Chapter 2: the centuries-long debate among theologians, the clergy, and believers about the morality of advertising. Some scriptural interpretations and religious teachings have suggested that business practices that indulge human temptations for material things, that lead people to desire things or qualities that they do not already possess, run afoul of God's laws. If human beings are created in a certain natural state, the argument goes, it must be wrong to encourage them to aspire to a different state—and this can be true *regardless of whether such a state is actually obtainable*. While the harmful consequences would seem clearly to be more pronounced when advertising promises something it cannot deliver (the harms being not only envy but also deception and despair), the argument also applies to situations in which consumers really do derive personal satisfaction or pleasure from buying the advertised item. In such a case, then, the assumption is that consumers cannot be trusted to assess accurately their own well-being. Consumers may feel happy when they purchase advertised dreams from those who sell them, but would be happier still if they would just wake up and learn to live in the "real world."

Before one reflexively rushes to the defense of the absolute moral freedom and sovereignty of the individual consumer, however, this religious second-guessing of consumer choice should be taken seriously. After all, if all choices made by consumers, including all responses to commercial messages, are to be considered inherently outside the bounds of moral questioning, the result is to reduce morality down to little more than personal taste. This is not only inconsistent with most religious teaching, but also incoherent as a guide for moral behavior. Whether one examines Christian, Jewish, Muslim, Hindu, or other major faith traditions, one commonality is the notion that moral rules are designed to protect individuals from adverse consequences they cannot initially foresee—or, alternatively, to afford them beneficial consequences that they cannot initially foresee. For example, one seemingly universal characteristic of "the natural state in which God created us" is that we enjoy eating food and having sex. In both instances, morality typically teaches us not to say "yes" to every opportunity to eat or have sex, though our immediate natural impulses may tell us otherwise. Without moderation, eating becomes gluttony. Without the confining bonds of marriage and love, sex becomes promiscuity or adultery. Moreover, at the time of decision we may not fully comprehend how happy we will be in the future if we moderated our consumption or maintained healthy and faithful sexual relationships. If religion can have nothing legitimate to say about consumption—because whatever a consumer chooses to do is inherently deserving of moral respect—then religion can have nothing legitimate to say about personal behaviors other than those aggressively harming others, such as murder or theft.

The real question is a process question. It concerns how individuals who seek to follow God's laws, or honor other deeply held moral convictions, should seek to distinguish between moral and immoral acts of consumption. It is not hard to place some choices in one or the other category. Few mainstream religious teachings would condemn the act of buying and drinking a soda. And few religions would fail to condemn the purchase of child pornography. But what if, in the first case, a consumer purchases the particular soda because she identifies it with her favorite basketball player? There are some religious institutions that would condemn her choice—and thus, by extension, the morality of advertising messages featuring the basketball player—because there is no "real need" to identify a beverage with sports. You drink, they say, solely to quench your thirst.

The Pontifical Council for Social Communications of the Roman Catholic Church is a prime example. Its much-debated 1997 report, *Ethics in Advertising*, repeated and clarified the church's previous teachings about marketing practices: that moral problems exist far beyond the obvious, and essentially uncontroversial, command that Christians not engage in false advertising. In particular, the Pontifical

Council worried that "the practice of 'brand'-related advertising can raise serious problems," because there are often "only negligible differences among similar products of different brands, and advertising may attempt to move people to act on the basis of irrational motives ("brand loyalty," status, fashion, "sex appeal," etc.) instead of presenting differences in product quality and prices as bases for rational choice."[44] Obviously, if this view of Catholic teaching on advertising is well founded, then any advertising messages beyond the purely informational should be highly suspect. Actually, the council's position is even more sweeping, in that it would seem to indict marketing uses of brand names that use signaling and other means of associating perceptions of quality with particular products. "Almost everything that an advertiser does is aimed at building loyalty to the brand," wrote Michael Prewitt, an advertising executive who is also ordained by the Presbyterian Church. "If, in the process, factual information is conveyed that helps the consumer make a reasoned choice, fine. But that is simply not what the advertising is trying to do."[45]

There are two problems with the way the council, and other like-minded religious critics of advertising, frame this issue. Both are issues of agency. First, what is the basis for asserting that "negligible differences" existing among similar products of different brands? Consumers place varying values on the attributes of the products they purchase and use. It could be said that whether one's car is painted red or gray is a "negligible difference" if the car is thought of merely as a means of transportation. Perhaps according to some radically antimaterialist reading of religious scripture, it would be sinful to prefer one color to another. But most believers would reject such a reading as unsound, bizarre, and in contradiction to human beings' God-given ability to appreciate the sights, sounds, smells, and tastes of God's creation. Because these kinds of preferences are often tied to matters of experience or affinity—examples would include the association of a color with a cherished possession, memories of a loved one, or one's identity as a member of a religious or social community—it is difficult to sustain the argument that a legitimate concern for materialism must result in a blanket condemnation of the aesthetic, emotional, and abstract functions of brands.

Surely materialism, as a matter of serious moral concern, must be defined as a lack of balance or moderation. It reflects willingness to sacrifice important human values and priorities in order to possess material goods. Materialism cannot reasonably be defined as placing *any* value on goods beyond their basic ability to keep one fed, clothed, sheltered, and safe. This would be an overly broad and unworkable definition—setting a standard of human asceticism that few would meet, and not many more would think to aspire to. But once consumers are morally authorized to go beyond the satisfaction of such primitive needs, they are inevitably entering a world of tastes, experiences, expectations, and dreams that is in part shaped by brand names and marketing messages—and has been since at least the days of ancient Pompeii.

Second, religious critiques of advertising that fail to place consumers at the center of the consumption process, but instead treat them as passive recipients of marketing messages, fail to explain how moral choices are to be made. The Pontifical Council says that advertisers should avoid marketing goods that do not satisfy "the imperatives of authentic human fulfillment," and that human beings can tell true needs from false ones because the former are "written on their hearts." These statements are, unfortunately, little more than question-begging exercises. Are the "imperatives of authentic human fulfillment" inherently the same for every human being? How do consumers, and prospectively advertisers, know whether a given desire they seek to satisfy is "written on their hearts" or the product of artificial commercial persuasion?

It would seem that the only practical way for human beings to answer these questions is to engage in a process of offering goods for sale, marketing them, and then buying or not buying them, using or not using them. Over time, consumers will learn which goods they appreciate and benefit from and which ones they do not. They will learn this not only by personal experience but also by observing what others buy and use. Debra Jones Ringold, a marketing professor at Willamette University, argued that advertising must be an integral part of a consumption process whose goal is moral choice. "Advertising gives consumers more choices, which sometimes involve 'good or evil,' at lower costs," she wrote. "Thus, as advertising enhances freedom, it puts morality to the test."[46] This argument is not hedonistic. It is not that all personal choices have equal moral worth. Rather, it is an argument for using a "push-and-pull" process to learn how best to apply moral principles about consumption.

Consumers seeking enjoyment, surprise, balance, and fulfillment are unlikely to make uniform choices. To return to my previous examples, there are some people who can eat more than others without endangering their health, making themselves obese and unhappy, and thus falling into a destructive cycle of gluttony. For many, an appreciation of fine foods and unique cuisines—perhaps developed from and heightened by advertising messages and imagery—constitutes a celebration of aesthetic excellence, the hard work of talented farmers and chefs, and a broader experience of fellowship, group identity, and human achievement. Similarly, if advertising plays a role in the decision of a wife to purchase some new perfume or lingerie to take on a holiday trip with her husband, the result may be to enhance the experience and strengthen the marital bond. Surely these values are consistent with what most religions teach us about how to live a moral life and follow the dictates of conscience and the divine. The assertion that some goods are "unneeded" and their purchase "wasteful and materialistic" is one that recognizes few of the specific conditions and contexts that shape the real behavior of many individuals who are, as they understand it, seeking to live a moral life.

Branding, imagery, and other tools for selling the dream help to facilitate what the Pontifical Council elsewhere states is a legitimate worldly pursuit: "the growth of man's productive capacity and . . . the ever-widening network of relationships and exchanges between persons and social groups." Prewitt, the advertising executive and seminary graduate, put it this way:

> Brands have increased in importance because they are the most important way a product or service connects with a group of consumers to develop an ongoing relationship rather than just a single transaction. . . . Advertising is one means for a company or a not-for-profit organization to initiate and sustain the interaction with customers in a commercial community. As the relationship is sustained, the customer is free to grow more or less loyal to the community. Through

the network of these relationships, the economy and society are sustained.[47]

There are, of course, tensions between advertising and morality other than the general issue of whether advertising is consistent with observing religious teachings about envy, consumption, and materialism. The use of sexual images to sell products and the marketing of products that facilitate sinful behavior are two good examples, and are discussed at some length in Chapter 8. It is important to remember, however, that these are issues of application. They concern whether advertisers, the media, and consumers are making proper moral choices in specific cases—not whether advertising as an institution accommodates moral choices in the first place.

A final irony about the relationship of advertising and religion is that it has so often been symbiotic, not antagonistic. For example, during much of the latter half of the nineteenth century, religious publications financed by advertising were a major player in the American media market. Weekly circulation of religious newspapers and magazines in 1870 was estimated at about 5 million, compared with 2.6 million for secular dailies and 10 million for secular weeklies. Publications such as the *Independent*, the *Churchman*, the *Congregationalist*, the *Evangelist*, and the *Advocate* (published by the Methodists) were read by leading citizens and average folks alike. "The influence was great," wrote historian Frank Presbey, "and advertisers used them liberally."[48] The same is true today. There are dozens of major religious publishers and broadcasters, plus hundreds if not thousands of smaller ones, serving millions of Americans and sustaining themselves in whole or in part through advertising. They include television and radio networks and broadcasts, local newspapers published by Catholic dioceses, magazines from evangelical and denominational associations, and many newsletters, websites, bulletins, and billboards.

Naturally, many religious institutions express their moral beliefs by limiting what advertising they accept or purchase. But these limitations rarely extend beyond tobacco, alcohol, guns, birth control devices, and the like to ordinary consumer products, services, or even "luxury" goods. More than a few advertising professionals have seen no contradiction between their jobs and a strong faith. In 1925, ad executive Bruce Barton famously released a book entitled *The Man Nobody Knows* that addressed the issue directly. Jesus Christ's parables, he wrote, should be viewed as "the most powerful advertisements of all time. . . . He would be a national advertiser today."[49]

## ETHICS AND THE COMMERCIAL LIFE

Critics of advertising's social and cultural effects do not uniformly approach the issue from a religious perspective. Indeed, most modern critics appear to be secular. They have fashioned an ethical critique of advertising based on the conceptually distinct but often mutually reinforcing propositions discussed earlier in the chapter. At least two themes are evident in this critique: (1) advertising subverts or interferes with natural human satisfactions and aspirations, and (2) advertising weakens autonomy and treats individuals as means rather than as ends in themselves.

In the first case, the philosophical debate is about whether advertising is "natural" or "artificial," whether it helps or hinders human beings as they pursue their innate desires for happiness, satisfaction, achievement, fulfillment, and belonging. This line of inquiry captures Emerson's quest for authenticity, Boorstin's concerns about the modern "thinning" of experience, and various expressions of antimaterialism that have egalitarian, ecological, or other secular roots. The second philosophical debate is about individualism. Does advertising facilitate personal freedom and choice? Or does it weaken real autonomy through manipulation, obfuscation, and false consciousness?

On advertising and human nature, Dr. Jeffrey Maciejewski of Creighton University published a fascinating paper in 2003 entitled "Can Natural Law Defend Advertising?" In it, Maciejewski surveyed the writings of philosophers and ethicists who have considered the broader question of whether market economies reflect or conflict with the natural law, and then sought to apply these principles to actual marketing practices. Again, as has been true across many disciplines, it has proven to be less controversial to defend informational advertising on ethical grounds—as long as it communicates truthful information—than to defend more abstract, aesthetic, or emotional appeals. History and experience suggest that markets arise from a natural human inclination to truck and barter, not from exploitation. Promulgating information on the price and quality of goods is essential to such markets, and is thus essential to the ability of human beings to live according to their nature and pursue their natural goals and aspirations. But so are other kinds of advertising, Maciejewski concluded, which use modern forms and technologies to facilitate an age-old search for meaning. "Although symbols may lack a universally shared meaning, man's propensity to learn vocabularies of symbols, and to deploy these meanings in the varied interpretations of symbols, is clearly part of his nature," he wrote.[50]

On authenticity and "thinness," the inescapable reality is that these qualities are solely in the eye of the beholder. If one person says that a past identification of heroic athleticism with Achilles, King Arthur, or Paul Bunyan is more authentic and "thick" than a modern identification of heroic athleticism with John Wayne, Batman, or Michael Jordan, another person will likely disagree. Thus if one person owns a vase depicting Achilles at Troy and another a collectible plate depicting a scene from *The Searchers*, which is the authentic one? There is obviously nothing new about associating personal possessions or experiences with popular characters, stories, and images. The real philosophical doctrines behind this modern criticism of consumer culture are elitism and intrinsicism, according to philosopher Jerry Kirkpatrick. In the latter case, *intrinsicism* refers to the old idea that certain products possess value "in, by, and of themselves" and cannot be made more valuable by marketing claims.[51] Does everyone really place the same "intrinsic" value on goods? No, the argument goes, but they should—and would, if advertising was not in the way. Not surprisingly, few advertising critics are willing to use such blunt language, as it reveals the circular and arbitrary character of their reasoning. One columnist complained in 1991 about General Electric's then-ubiquitous ad campaign celebrating the political and social changes underway in Hungary and employing the slogan "GE, we bring good things to life." What, the philosopher wrote, "does the desire to sell electric bulbs have to do with celebrating Eastern Europe's return to freedom?"[52] He meant this to be a rhetorical question, but he would not like my answer: "Plenty. Should I make a list?" In purely practical terms, for example, one of the immediate consequences of the end of communism and Soviet domination of Eastern Europe was that millions of people could purchase reliable, high-quality consumer goods for the first time. They were no longer forced to endure unreliable automobiles, outdated computers, and, yes, flickering lights. More importantly, the GE spots in question drew an obvious parallel between banks of light bulbs coming on and Eastern Europeans gaining their freedom. One image showed a woman's face brightening at the sight of dazzling theater lights. Only an academic philosopher could miss the import of these images.

Something similarly circular is going on in the second ethical attack on advertising, which blames it for diminishing human autonomy and dignity. Philosopher Richard Lippke wrote that true autonomy is developed within "social conditions" that allow people to know about "alternative belief-systems and lifestyles." Mass market advertising acts to "suppress the development of the abilities, attitudes, and knowledge constitutive of dispositional autonomy," he continued, thus seeming to foster individuality and freedom of choice while actually doing the reverse. If false consciousness is the problem, though, how are we to know if Lippke's proposed consciousness of autonomy is the true one? The answer was, again, revealing. "Critics of my approach may point out that many individuals seem to lack a strong desire for the sort of autonomous life I elucidate," he admitted. "We should not, however, be misled by this appearance." Many persons will assent to the principle that "the choices of individuals ought to be respected" but it actually "makes little sense to urge such respect where peoples' choices do not reflect an autonomous way of living."[53] Essentially, Lippke was arguing, advertising makes people lose their autonomy. But what if people say they value advertising because it helps them make autonomous decisions? That can be discounted, because advertising has caused them to lose their autonomy.

Lippke and other analysts themselves recognize how all this sounds, but it does not appear to deter them. "Any sober look at the goods and services produced in advanced capitalist societies like the United States should lead to the conclusion that there are some that its citizens could do without and not be any worse off for the lack thereof," he wrote. "Many of us suspect this, but are disinclined to admit it publicly for fear of being regarded as elitists or authoritarians." It may be, he allowed, "that the market is wiser than any other authority, but only under conditions where individuals are not relentlessly subject to manipulative advertising." And what advertising is manipulative instead of useful? For starters, he suggested, anything that induces people to buy things with no useful purpose. "There will be disagreements about what goes into this category," he helpfully added, "but here is a partial list: plug-in air fresheners, crock pots, pizza cookers, salad shooters, numerous toys, various automobile-related accessories, and chia pets. It is hard to imagine that individuals are genuinely worse off without such items."[54]

Professor Lippke, thank you for your opinion.

## IS THERE A PARADOX OF CHOICE?

Some critics will still dismiss economic, religious, and ethical justifications on the grounds that even if marketing efforts have a salutary *intention*—to communicate practical information, to facilitate competitive markets, or to enhance the enjoyment and satisfaction of consumer goods—they do not have a salutary *result*. The most recent iteration of this argument is that our consumer culture contains a paradox. As described in recent works such as *The Paradox of Choice: Why More Is Less* by Barry Schwartz and Gregg Easterbrook's *The Progress Paradox: How Life Gets Better while People Feel Worse*, the contradiction is that as individual consumers gain access to a wider variety of economic options, they go into a sort of information overload. Schwartz suggested that they become overwhelmed by the time it takes to make these choices and later feel more remorse about the "bad" ones than they feel satisfaction with the "good" ones. "As a culture, we are enamored of freedom, self-determination, and variety, and we are reluctant to give up any of our options," Schwartz wrote. "But clinging tenaciously to all the choices available to us contributes to bad decisions, to anxiety, stress, and dissatisfaction—even to clinical depression."[55] Easterbrook made the related point that rising average levels of affluence can make individuals feel worse off—because they become increasingly likely to see others with luxury goods they still cannot afford—while failing to address their heartfelt needs for deeper and richer experiences, for such things as love, friendship, respect, and awe. Both authors pointed to trend lines over time to buttress their otherwise anecdotal and impressionistic case. Schwartz cited a 2003 report showing a threefold increase in diagnosed cases of clinical depression over the past twenty-five years. Easterbrook reported that while only 3 percent of Americans in 1957 said they were "lonely," the rate is now 13 percent.[56]

Actually linking such trends to the effects of our advertising-driven consumer culture is a difficult task, at best. Many factors likely influenced the changes in survey findings and medical diagnoses the authors cite, not the least of which being the growing willingness of Americans to talk about their personal anxieties and to seek professional help for depression, in part because there are more drugs and other treatments available for the condition than in the past. Moreover, in neither case do the vast majority of Americans seem to be suffering from loneliness or depression despite being oppressed seemingly from all sides by the tyranny of consumer freedom. A more straightforward approach to testing the paradox hypothesis would be to examine the available evidence for overall happiness and life satisfaction. The problem is that it does *not* support the idea of a paradox of choice.

The two oldest polling organizations in the United States, Gallup and Harris, offer the most useful data. In December 2003, Gallup released what was then the latest in a series of surveys going back nearly fifty years regarding American perceptions of well-being. The 2003 survey found that 55 percent of Americans described themselves as "very happy" and another 40 percent as "fairly happy"—the highest levels of happiness that Gallup had ever recorded. Asked a different question, to describe "the way things are going in their personal life," 58 percent of Americans said they were "very satisfied" and 30 percent said "fairly satisfied"—again, the highest levels of satisfaction ever. High levels of happiness and satisfaction were present across all sexes, races, and ages. No statistically significant differences were apparent. However, there was a correlation with marriage (single people are less happy) and especially with income. The percentage saying they were very satisfied with their personal lives was 41 percent among those earning less than $30,000 a year, 53 percent among middle-income people, and an astounding 75 percent among those making more than $75,000.[57] Since it is virtually axiomatic that affluence correlates with consumer choice, Gallup's findings seem entirely inconsistent with the paradox theory and more generally with the supposition of critics who think that modern-day advertising and consumer culture interfere with our ability to find happiness, satisfaction, authenticity, and fulfillment. So do the findings of the Harris organization, which regularly compares American attitudes with those in European countries where advertising is more restricted and the consumer culture somewhat less pervasive. In its 2003 survey, Harris found that 57 percent of Americans said they were "very satisfied with their lives" (strikingly similar to the 58 percent found by Gallup) compared to an average of only 21 percent in Europe. Americans were also more likely than most Europeans to say that their lives have improved in the past five years and will continue to improve.[58]

Perhaps there are Americans who hate living the commercial life. Certainly there seem to be many professors, journalists, and social commentators who feel that way. But most Americans do not share their sentiments. Now, there are many things about advertising and marketing practices that Americans do not like. They especially do not like to have their time wasted looking at or listening to advertisements for products they have no interest in buying, and often seek ways to consume advertising on their own terms rather than on the marketers' terms. It is obvious that one of the sources of the growing popularity of media alternatives such as premium cable channels, video games, Internet sites, and now satellite radio is the promise of fewer or no commercial interruptions. This simply underlines the point that consumers are active participants in a market process, not mindless automatons and passive recipients of whatever Madison Avenue tries to implant in their heads. It does *not* mean that most Americans place little value on advertising or hate mass marketing. To understand the more complex and conflicted view of advertising held by many Americans, it will be helpful to consider some difficult cases in which advertising claims are difficult to evaluate or prove, aimed at vulnerable populations other than responsible adults, and clash with the social views and moral sentiments of many in the listening and viewing audience.

# CHAPTER 6

# Health Claims and the Problem of Fraud

In Chapter 1, I discussed the nineteenth-century debut of the American "penny press" as an important turning point in the history of journalism. Beginning with Benjamin Day's *New York Sun* in 1833, and quickly emulated by James Gordon Bennett's *New York Herald*, the penny-press model reflected the insight that publishers would be more successful by reducing their newspapers' prices, maximizing circulation, and then seeking to earn profits through advertising revenue. Almost overnight, the *Sun* and *Herald* became the most widely circulated newspapers in the world, and the concept quickly spread to other American and European cities. But now, as Paul Harvey might say, it will be revealing to hear the rest of the story.

In 1835, just as Bennett began preparations to transform the *Herald* into an effective New York City competitor to Day's *Sun*, a young English immigrant named Benjamin Brandreth arrived in the city with his wife and three children, a small nest egg, and a "secret formula" handed down to him by his grandfather. Dr. William Brandreth, a physician in Liverpool, had spent much of his life experimenting with a combination of herbs to treat patients suffering from fatigue and a variety of specific ailments. Benjamin, inheriting the formula and an interest in medicine from his grandfather (and business acumen from his Quaker/merchant father), had come to America to produce and sell his Vegetable Universal Pills to a potential market far larger than he could find in England. Reaching that market, Brandreth realized, would require far more than the word of mouth or handbill advertising used by many of his contemporary apothecaries, druggists, and nostrum makers—a group that was already known to many as *quacks* (a shorter version of *quacksalver*, or "seller of salves," and possibly also related to an old term for mercury, *quicksilver*, which was a common ingredient in early medicines).[1]

Brandreth decided that mass circulation newspapers were the answer. His New York plant began production of Vegetable Universal Pills in the same month that Bennett's new *Herald* debuted, and the two began a long and fascinating business relationship. Indeed, just months into the new venture, Bennett's printing plant for the *Herald* was destroyed by fire. A major contract with Brandreth gave Bennett the capital needed to rebuild and resume publication.[2] For years, Brandreth spent massive sums advertising in the *Herald*, the *Sun*, and other periodicals. So did his escalating number of patent medicine competitors. But the relationships were not always cordial. Two years after Brandreth began advertising in the *Herald*, Bennett suddenly revoked the contract, returned all advance payments, and then launched an editorial attack against Brandreth. "For many months past," the *Herald* darkly commented, "this city has been flooded with medical pills from a certain laboratory, which appear to have spread over the face of the earth with the rapidity and virulence of the ten plagues of Egypt." Brandreth, Bennett claimed, had convinced "his dupes to swallow his pills as fast and as rapidly as they would their dinner" by employing "the merest twaddle of medical language that ever made the ignorant gape, or the educated cry 'bah!' " Then Bennett lay down his marker: "This is the age of Brandreth pills. No—this has been the age of Brandreth pills; but a revolution has begun and they will sink more rapidly into oblivion than they ever rose in consequence."[3]

Those who thought it odd that a newspaper publisher would turn so swiftly and vociferously on one of his largest advertisers were in for an even bigger surprise. Yes, the war of words escalated for a time. In the pages of the rival *Sun*, Brandreth with a knowing wink called Bennett "an old bachelor," and Bennett then responded with further attacks on Brandreth's ethics, medical expertise, and grammar. But the feud soon ended. Eventually, Brandreth's pills again became a major advertiser in the *Herald*, which during the schism had continued without shame to advertise far more disreputable and dangerous products such as Madam Gardion's Specific for Leucorrhoea and Dr. Goodman's American Anti-Gonorrhoea Pills. Actually, it was not at all uncommon for American newspapers of the nineteenth century to run, simultaneously and even side by side, advertisements for miracle cures *and* exposés of useless or dangerous medicines. The self-styled journalistic reformer Horace Greeley was a case in point. Referring to the *Sun*, the *Herald*, and other competitors, Greeley's *New York Tribune* thundered against "puffing" and wondered whether advertising revenue from abortionists and venereal cures would prove to be "blood money" that would be a "curse to its receivers," who were called "vampyres." Yet, Greeley's *Tribune* itself advertised cures for consumption, cancer, painful menstruation, and "falling of the womb." Challenged to defend his newspaper's standards, Greeley deflected the criticism: readers should "complain to our advertisers themselves, who are not responsible to us for the style or language (if decent) of their advertisements, nor have we any control over them."[4]

## DRUG ADVERTISING AND ITS PROGENY

It is no accident that the first major federal legislation targeting false and misleading advertising claims was the Pure Food and Drug Act, enacted in 1906. It is impossible to make sense of the consumerist movement of the early twentieth century, and its nineteenth-century antecedents among secular and religious critics of commerce, without examining the role that health claims of dubious merit played in the history of advertising. Advertising scholar James Twitchell reported that until the Civil War, virtually all of the nationally recognizable brand names in the United States were to be found on bottles, packages, and cartons of patent medicine. As late as 1890, nearly half of all advertising placements and ad agency revenues derived from medicines that promised cures for ailments ranging from headaches and "female troubles" to life-threatening illnesses such as tuberculosis.[5]

But the relationship between health and advertising predates the antebellum transformation of American marketing as exemplified by the New York penny press and the department store. Indeed, ads containing tantalizing health claims are about as old as newspapers themselves. Frank Presbey's classic 1929 history of advertising argued that the first such "puff" ad was probably a piece in a 1591 German newsbook that reported the discovery of a mysterious and wonderful curative herb. In 1652, an English handbill was addressed to those suffering from "sore eyes, headaches, rheums, consumptions, coughs of the lungs, running humours, king's evil, spleens, hypochondriac winds, stone, gout, dropsy, [and] scurvy." It suggested that a visit to Pasqua Rossee's London establishment, to consume a new beverage made from "a berry called coffee" from "little trees only in the desert of Arabia," might just do the trick. Similarly, one of the earliest display ads in an English newspaper urged sufferers to see comfort from drinking "that excellent and by all Physicians approved Chia drink called by the Chineans Tcha, by other nations Tay alias Tee."[6]

In early America, health claims were commonplace in advertising for products as varied as furnaces, beverages, clothes, and foods along with formal medical preparations. Just a few years after Brandreth's plant was founded in New York City, an apothecary in Lowell, Massachusetts, named J. C. Ayer patented his Cherry Pectoral in 1844 and later followed with Ayer's Cathartic Pills in 1854, Ayer's Ague Cure in 1857, Ayer's Sarsaparilla in 1859, and Ayer's Hair Vigor in 1864. His company became one of the most successful and longlasting firms in the industry. Ayer products were advertised widely, sold copiously, and used regularly well into the 1940s. The company issued trade cards, wartime postage stamps, pamphlets, and testimonials while purchasing plenty of newspaper and magazine space. As Ayer and other early patent medicine makers were starting to make use of mass advertising in the 1840s and 1850s, other manufacturers began to experiment with making health claims on behalf of their wares as well. In 1851, Benjamin Babbitt became the first to manufacture and market soap in bar form. Previously, soap had been sold in large quantities directly to grocers who then cut smaller bars to sell to customers. Babbitt saw an opportunity to sell directly to users, thus creating a valuable brand and using advertising to promote general hygiene—which, in turn, would promote the purchase of soap. Later, as Juliann Sivulka discusses in *Stronger than Dirt: A Cultural History of Advertising Personal Hygiene in America*, Babbitt and other soap manufacturers were to make more explicit claims about cleanliness leading to better health, higher social status, and even better marriages and child rearing. "Nationally advertised, brand-name soap, toiletries, and even bathrooms made their way from seldom-used luxuries to necessities of American life in a remarkably short period of time" during the nineteenth and early twentieth centuries, Sivulka wrote.[7]

While health claims were part of marketing practice before the 1860s, it was really the Civil War that pushed the entire industry up several notches in national exposure and effect. Wars have often been a catalyst for change in health practices, for obvious reasons. Battlefield wounds become lifelong disabilities. They reveal inadequate medical and sanitary practices, or prompt innovators to come up with new medicines, devices, and treatments. Back in the 1840s, the Mexican War had generated far more American casualties from diseases such as malaria than from the musket balls and blades of Mexican soldiers. Returning soldiers had formed a ready customer base for medicines of varying levels of effectiveness against tropical and debilitating diseases. (In response to the problem—and, not coincidentally, the effective lobbying of domestic druggists, manufacturers, and the new American Medical Association—Congress enacted the Import Drugs Act of 1848.)[8]

A similar but far greater dynamic came into play after the end of the Civil War in 1865. Entrepreneurs marketed cures of all sorts to returning soldiers. Brandreth's Pills received a testimonial from "Sixty Voices from [the] Army of the Potomac." A Union officer serving in the Shenandoah Valley campaign called Hostetter's Bitters "the Soldier's Safeguard."[9] After the war, Dr. H. T. Hembold became a household name with his marketing of Buchu, as did Radway's Ready Relief, Drake's Plantation Bitters, and Mrs. Winslow's Soothing Syrup. Then in the 1880s, a new kind of drug ad made its debut: an item printed in the newspaper's own typeface and made to look like a regular news story. Presbey credited an enterprise called Warner's Safe Cure for originating this concept, which is akin to our modern-day advertorial (the "safe," by the way, had a double meaning: it was a reference to not only the benign nature of the product but also the fact that its originator had been a safe salesman who paid for his ads by giving strong boxes to newspapers).[10]

By the turn of the century, the industry had spawned dozens of well-known national brand names and hundreds of products purporting to treat or cure a bewildering variety of ailments. Lydia Pinkham's Female Compound sported her picture—and hers became one of the most recognized faces in America for generations. By 1897, the Sears Roebuck catalog was advertising scores of medical preparations, including Female Pills for Weak Women, Dr. Rose's Arsenic Complexion Wafers, and Electricating Liniment for Man or Beast. Cynthia Crossen reported in the *Wall Street Journal* that the patent medicine business had by 1904 become a $1.6 billion industry,[11] representing an astounding 1400 percent increase over the 1860s estimate even after adjusting for changes in the country's population and average prices.[12]

What made the marketing of patent medicines so successful—and, in the eyes of many, so despicable? Critics of advertising offer ready answers. They argue that the nostrum charlatans were under no effective system of regulation, either administrative or through fraud claims in court, and so were able to make the wildest and most expansive promises imaginable to cure disease and relieve plan. By employing medical jargon and titles, testimonials of questionable provenance, scary or salacious headlines, visually arresting images, and memorable or alliterative brands and slogans, these advertisements are said to represent a classic, even paradigmatic, case of consumer manipulation. The anticonsumerism literature of the late nineteenth and early twentieth centuries is full of excoriation of advertising and patent medicine, which to many critics' minds were roughly the same industry. Writing in 1904, Thorstein Veblen argued that in a market economy many businesses might well succeed without actually contributing much of real value to the economy or society. The example he offered was "many well-known and prosperous enterprises which advertise and sell patent medicines."[13] The following year, 1905, saw the publication in *Collier's* magazine of a ten-part investigation of the industry, entitled "The Great American Fraud," which went further than ever before in arguing that the most popular medicines were largely made from alcohol, opiates, common herbs, and fillers that ranged from the merely inert, such as flour and sawdust, to lice, not always deceased. As the medical advances of the nineteenth century began to take hold, spread, and provoke experiment and innovation, Crossen wrote, "the split between science and patent medicines widened. Warner's Safe Cure for Diabetes cured nothing but its maker's finances, and the active ingredient in Mrs. Winslow's Soothing Syrup for fussy babies was morphine sulfate."[14]

According to this explanation and chronology of events, it was the political force of Progressivism and the investigative journalism of muckrakers that finally won out over the forces of predatory capitalism and ghoulish manipulation with the beginnings of federal regulation in 1906. The Pure Food and Drug Act got its first test with the prosecution of Robert Harper, the purveyor of a widely advertised product with the memorable if tacky name of Cuforhedake Brane-Fude. Yes, it was sold as a headache remedy. During Harper's sixteen-day trial, the defense offered the testimony of many prominent patients and expert witnesses claiming that Cuforhedake Brane-Fude did, in fact, alleviate headache pain. But the jury returned a guilty verdict, and Harper was fined $700.[15] While prominent Progressives, including President Teddy Roosevelt, were displeased with Harper's punishment (they wanted jail time) and quickly became disillusioned with the 1906 act's relatively limited application, the achievement of a federal law was still widely perceived as a promising opening battle of what would become a major campaign against advertising's excesses and abuses.

It did not happen. Instead, Congress in 1912 clarified that while the act prohibited false advertising claims about the health benefits of medicines, the federal government had the burden to prove that medicine manufacturers knew their claims were false and made them anyway. Otherwise, while presumably manufacturers could be "informed" of the government's own research on the matter, they could not be criminally prosecuted. The activists fumed that this proviso kept the Department of Agriculture's Bureau of Chemistry, and later the Food and Drug Administration, from using the Pure Food and Drug Act to eliminate the advertising, and thus effectively the selling, of what they still considered to be large numbers of useless medicines. The *Nation* magazine snorted that the failure to regulate more effectively had essentially enshrined "the sacred right of freeborn Americans to advertise and sell horse liniment as a remedy for tuberculosis" and "his God-given right to advertise and sell extract of horsetail weed as a cure for diabetes."[16] It took until 1938, after many years of agitation, for the like-minded Roosevelt administration to push the Federal Food, Drug, and Cosmetic Act through Congress. It shifted the burden of proof to require that drug manufacturers submit scientific proof that new products could be safely used before putting them on the market, and removed the requirement that prosecutors prove actual fraud. Now they only had to prevail in court on the issue of whether the advertising claims were true or false.[17]

Finally, in 1962, the burden of proof shifted yet again against manufacturers and their advertising claims. Already required to submit evidence that their product was safe for human consumption, and to avoid making specific claims about effectiveness that could not be substantiated if challenged in court, manufacturers were now subjected to a new hurdle: they would have to prove both the safety and the effectiveness of a drug *before* it could be marketed to the general public. In effect, pharmaceuticals (and later medical devices) would have to be sold first to federal regulators as safe and effective before they could be sold to consumers.[18]

## INTRODUCING CONTEXT AND COMPLEXITY

This is the way the story of federal regulation of health claims is usually told. First, there is a jungle out there, where unwitting consumers are swallowed up by predatory beasts. Then public-spirited activists and regulators come along as askaris (guards) to protect the consumer safari. Finally, the federal government solves the problem by clear-cutting the jungle, clearing out the underbrush, and allowing only strictly licensed professionals to introduce a limited number of new trees and animal varieties to what has become a tidy, carefully tended garden.

Unfortunately, this version of events is about as accurate a depiction of how and why the regulations came about as an 1880s advertorial for Warner's Safe Cure was an accurate depiction of how to cure diabetes. In reality, the onset of government regulation of health claims for drugs, foods, and other substances reflected a host of conflicting facts, demands, and interests. For one thing, to assume that the dramatic expansion of the patent medicine industry in the last half of the nineteenth century was made possible only by fraudulent and abusive advertising practices is to treat millions of American consumers as entirely passive and incompetent. As we have seen, advertising a useless vial of liquid as a cure for headaches or rheumatism will "work" for many consumers only once. If no relief is perceived, a repeat sale becomes unlikely—and few products can make their purveyors really prosperous if marketed to each consumer only once.

So what held the key to the appeal of patent medicines? For many longtime customers, it was precisely the ingredients that had so many activists up in arms against the industry: alcohol, cocaine, caffeine, and morphine and other opiates. Until well into the twentieth century, physicians could offer a surprisingly limited range of effective treatments for disease. Hospitals were not sanitary and often presented more danger to patients from infection than simply staying home and suffering through a malady (perhaps with the assistance of whatever beer, wine, grain alcohol, or other pain-numbing drug might be available). When physicians "prescribed" medications for their patients, the preparations were often quite dangerous themselves, consisting of ingredients such as mercury, arsenic, and strychnine. Even into the late nineteenth century, some doctors treated their patients with bleeding, purging, vomiting, blistering, and other therapies of questionable safety and efficacy.[19] And what valuable medical care that was available was relatively expensive.

No doubt there were many physicians active in the campaign to regulate patent medicines who truly believed that many of them were useless, dangerous, and fraudulently advertised. But there were also doubtless many physicians who recognized that self-medication, facilitated by national advertising claims and brand names, offered an effective form of competition against their profession, which had already begun to form state-regulated cartels to maintain their pricing power and ability to exclude "unqualified" competitors. Shortly after its founding in the 1840s, the American Medical Association (AMA) was surprisingly candid about the problem of too many doctors chasing too few patients. In an 1847 report, an AMA committee noted that because of an "army of doctors" and a "long list of irregular practitioners who swarm like locusts," the profession of medicine no longer enjoyed an "exalted position," and "the merest pittance in the way of remuneration is scantily dole[d] out even to the most industrious in our ranks."[20] Keep in mind that this was written at a time when many if not most ailing patients would actually have been better off to sip a bottle of "medicine" laced with alcohol or morphine to dull their pain rather than to visit a doctor and be bled or blistered, or visit a hospital and risk catching a far more serious, if not deadly, disease.

Physicians, organized into the new state cartels, developed a strong aversion to advertising. They often adopted ethical guidelines forbidding the advertising of medical services, arguing that the practice was unseemly, led to unwarranted health claims, and associated the practice of medicine with professions of ill repute such as, well, patent medicine purveyors. The guidelines extended beyond just the use of newspaper ads or handbills to regulate even the size of the letters on a doctor's office sign.[21] Interestingly, medical societies did make exceptions in cases where advertising would serve to promote, rather than erode, their members' market power. For example, during the 1930s and 1940s hospitals formed Blue Cross plans and doctors formed Blue Shield plans. In both cases, they were responding to the prospect of for-profit life insurers getting into the business of offering commercial health insurance policies. Early experience with such policies revealed that health providers were forced to compete strenuously on price and quality, either when commercial insurers negotiated payments with providers or when they paid reimbursements directly to patients, who first had to see and pay their own hospital and physician bills. Far better, hospital and medical associations believed, would be a system of prepaid care within "nonprofit" health plans owned or at least controlled by the providers themselves, who would then be exempt from pesky and potentially costly oversight by consumers and their agents. By 1950, Blue Cross and Blue Shield plans controlled about half of the health insurance market—in part because of favorable governmental regulation and tax treatment, but also because doctors allowed the "Blues" to advertise in their offices and sometimes advertised their own participation in them—which stood in stark contrast to the ethical (and some legal) restrictions barring health providers from advertising offerings and prices directly to consumers. The creation of Medicare and Medicaid in 1965 on the Blue Cross model and increases in tax rates on income (which made the tax exemption for workplace-based insurance more valuable) further accentuated the trend.[22]

Two other groups worked diligently throughout the nineteenth and early twentieth centuries to impose federal regulation on medical advertising. The first comprised the staff and affiliated scientists and activists of the Department of Agriculture's Bureau of Chemistry, which later became the Food and Drug Administration. In 1883, the state chemist of Indiana, Harvey Wiley, became head of the Bureau of Chemistry. He then spent more than two decades actively lobbying for federal regulation of food and drugs, regulation that his own office would enforce. The campaign was wide-ranging. Wiley fanned out across the country to speak to legislatures, universities, civic clubs, agricultural organizations, business groups, and other audiences. His team of scientists uncovered instances where foods or drugs were adulterated or tainted, and then offered them to newspapers and magazines to form the basis for muckraking exposés. In 1902, Wiley—who clearly had a flair for the dramatic—created a "poison squad" of young volunteers who ate foods containing various chemicals to demonstrate their health effects over time. It became a national media sensation, even inspiring popular songs.[23]

It must be said, of course, that while Wiley may have been lobbying for what was essentially more power and staff for himself, he also had a point. There *was* a case to be made for more disclosure to consumers of what went into prepared foods and drugs. And fraudulent promotional claims *were* difficult to prosecute in state courts given existing law and precedent. Some established food processors and medicine manufacturers actually favored a disclosure bill because they thought it would reward honesty and best practices in the industry. But what really clinched it, according to Wiley at least, was the decision by American women's clubs to adopt pure food and drugs as a national political cause. They were motivated in part by the discovery of who had become the obvious and vocal opponents of the measure: whiskey distillers and patent medicine companies that used alcohol or opiates as ingredients.[24] Politically active women's organizations, it should be recalled, formed the core of support in many communities not only for suffrage and so-called family issues but also for prohibition. In effect, the temperance movement had its first success in federal policy not with the later passage of the Eighteenth Amendment to the U.S. Constitution but with the 1906 Pure Food and Drug Act, which offered the prospect of hampering one means of selling intoxicants to the general public.

There is another element left out of the usual story of how federal drug regulation arose during the twentieth century. My account relies to a large degree on the official history of the Food and Drug Administration, but this does not even mention the case of Dr. O. A. Johnson, which reached the U.S. Supreme Court several years after the more celebrated case of Cuforhedake Brane-Fude. Johnson was charged with a violation of the 1906 act in his marketing of a combination of pills to treat the symptoms of cancer. He chose to fight— and won. Writing for the Court, Justice Oliver Wendell Holmes argued that the law was not intended to criminalize medical claims that contrasted with the conclusions of government scientists. Congress had sought "to regulate commerce in food and drugs with reference to plain matter of fact, so that food and drugs should be what they professed to be," he wrote, not to "distort the uses of its constitutional power to establishing criteria in regions where opinions are far apart."[25] It was this legal finding that enraged activists and led them to push for new legislation, eventually accomplished in 1938 (and after President Roosevelt had intimidated a Supreme Court suspicious of expanded federal regulatory authority with his threat to pack it with his political supporters).

## THE CURRENT CONTROVERSY OVER ADVERTISING HEALTH CLAIMS

The issues surrounding health claims in American advertising are no less salient and controversial today than they were decades ago. Many politicians, academics, and activists continue to believe that the advertising of medical devices, drugs, and services is excessive, abusive, dangerous, and frequently fraudulent. They continue to associate today's medical advertising with the dubious claims of nineteenth-century quacks and medicine shows. And while a modern understanding of advertising allows some of their claims of economic and social harm to be dismissed out of hand, other issues remain complex, controversial, and deserving of more serious consideration.

First, the dismissals. As demonstrated in previous chapters, some of the most persuasive evidence of advertising's value to consumers concerns health care professions and industries. A crucial 1972 study looked at state regulation of advertising within the ranks of optometrists and opticians. Eyeglasses cost 25 percent more in states with ad bans compared to those without them. In 1976, a different study found negative, albeit much smaller, price consequences for consumers from state bans on prescription drug advertising.[26] Still later, the Federal Trade Commission (FTC) found in 1983 that optometrists who advertised themselves on price and quality tended to do a better job of fitting contact lenses—measured objectively on the basis of prescription and injury to the cornea—than those who did not advertise. More generally, economists point out that health care fields such as eye care, orthodontics, and plastic surgery in which there is significant and aggressive competition, fueled by specific and widely circulated advertising claims and facilitated by consumers paying cash rather than swiping insurance cards, are also the fields in which price inflation is among the lowest, innovation among the greatest, and customer satisfaction among the highest in the entire health care sector.[27]

American physicians have given up their resistance to advertising only grudgingly, when forced to do so, and many have still not adjusted to the concept. In 1975, the FTC concluded that the American Medical Association's ethical guidelines against physician advertising were an illegal attempt to limit competition, a decision later enforced by FTC actions and upheld by U.S. Supreme Court decisions in 1976 and 1982. As late as 1991, however, an AMA representative said that "lots of physicians still associate advertising with quackery. Some doctors don't want to even list their names in the Yellow Pages." A survey by scholar Gene Burton demonstrated that attitudes were changing, albeit slowly: while only about 8 percent of AMA members in 1978 said they approved of advertising, Burton's 1988 study found that 22 percent of physicians surveyed had advertised and another 45 percent said they planned to advertise in the future.[28]

Perhaps the most contentious issue that remains in this area is the practice of direct-to-consumer (DTC) advertising, both on behalf of prescription drugs and for foods, herbs, and vitamin supplements that may confer some kind of health benefit on consumers. After federal regulators and courts struck down advertising bans as restraints of trade in the early 1980s, firms began to experiment with various ways of marketing their products directly to newspaper and magazine readers, radio listeners, and television viewers. Such ads continued to be closely regulated by the FDA—that is one reason why they include so many specific cautions and provisos, albeit in small type—and use language that has usually been carefully vetted to avoid making unsustainable claims. Still, their use has invited vociferous objection. From a miniscule level in the mid-1980s, expenditures for DTC advertising for prescription drugs approached $4 billion in 2004. Critics argue that these ads induce excess demand from patients who do not really need or cannot benefit from the drugs, thus helping to fuel the nation's problem of health care inflation. John Abramson, a physician and the author of *Overdosed America*, blames such advertising for many medical and social ills. The intention of drug advertising "is no more to improve our health than it is the fast-food industry's mission to improve our diet," Abramson said in 2004.[29]

The debate over DTC advertising would benefit from fewer strained, hyperbolic analogies and more careful consideration of the available evidence. Naturally, the ads are designed to induce consumers with particular maladies or risk factors to purchase the drugs being marketed. But for prescription medicines, the purchase is impossible without conferring with physicians. Critics argue that harried doctors, pressed for time and loathe to anger their patients, simply sign off on costly new medications that really confer few benefits and may bring dangers of abuse or adverse reactions. But a 2004 study in the prestigious journal *Health Affairs* relied on a survey of physicians to explore how DTC advertising affects physician decision making. It found that they were just as likely to respond to patient requests about a drug by recommending a lifestyle change (39 percent) as they were

to prescribe the drug (39 percent), and in 12 percent of the cases they actually recommended an over-the-counter drug. In only 6 percent of cases did physicians prescribe the drug to placate patients even though another drug or treatment would be better. Perhaps more important than the physicians' reaction to a patient request, however, was the existence of the patient request in the first place. The advertising might well induce higher consumption for name-brand drugs, wrote study author Joel Weissman, but it also has positive effects for patients, such as new nonpharmaceutical treatments, "that transcend merely prescribing a DTC drug."[30]

## HEALTH CLAIMS AND THE INFORMED CONSUMER

There are many such potential side benefits of advertising. One is the wide dissemination of new medical discoveries and innovations, including among physicians. Many do not have time to read every important journal article or industry press release. Another is the possibility that patients are prompted by advertising to seek medical attention in the first place. In other words, what may be more important than a physician's reaction to a patient request is the very existence of that patient request, which may lead to the diagnosis of a previously unrecognized disease or patient involvement in preventive care, diet, and exercise for the first time. Surveys show that the vast majority of patients see DTC advertising as a prompt to seek additional information, not only from their own doctors but also from pharmacists, medical texts, and websites. One FDA survey found that nearly 30 percent of viewers of DTC advertising had subsequently asked their doctors about a medical condition they had not previously discussed.[31] Bans on such advertising, wrote Emory University professor Paul H. Rubin, would endanger the lives of thousands of Americans who might otherwise never hear that taking aspirin can reduce the risk of heart attack, or that using certain prescription drugs can reduce the risk of cancer. Regulation of drug advertising "often does more harm than good," he concluded.[32]

What about prices? Critics of drug advertising use the same essential proof of consumer harm that previous generations of critics have employed against advertising in general: since it costs something to produce and distribute, it must necessarily result in a higher selling cost that is passed along to consumers (or, in this case, to third-party payers such as insurers or the federal government). But today's critics are making the same mistake that the previous generations did, by treating the question as a simple accounting problem rather than as one of describing how dynamic, competitive markets operate. In fact, patented drugs still compete with other treatments for the same injuries or illnesses. Brand-name advertising facilitates effective competition and thus tends to reduce, not increase, consumer prices. A 2004 paper in the *New England Journal of Medicine* concluded that the introduction and advertisement of competing brand-new drugs do not simply result in "me-too" drug purchases that constitute wasteful expenditures. Instead, they drive down prices.[33] And a 1997 paper found that the gross retail margins for advertised prescription drugs were lower than for other drugs. "If drug manufacturers adopt DTC advertising on a broader scale, the potential savings at the consumer level brought on by increased competition at the retail level could be substantial," the authors wrote.[34]

Advertising scholar John Calfee offered another example of the way consumers can benefit from health claims: the advertising of healthful foods. During the 1970s, he reported, public health officials began to describe compelling evidence of the health benefits of eating a diet high in fiber. Among them was a reduction in the risk of colon cancer, the second deadliest form of cancer in the United States. But a few official statements and some public service announcements were insufficient to spread the word about this. It took the Kellogg Corporation to come up with the idea in 1984 of seeking an endorsement from the National Cancer Institute for an advertising campaign emphasizing the potential health benefits of its high-fiber All-Bran cereal. "At last some news about cancer you can live with," the ad copy began, before describing the new research on fiber and colon cancer. Quickly, the Food and Drug Administration protested that All-Bran cereal was being marketing as a drug, and thus was subject to its regulation—and blocked from making such claims. The Federal Trade Commission, however, successfully retained its jurisdiction and allowed the campaign to continue. So many other food manufacturers emulated the All-Bran campaign, touting the potential health benefits of myriad products as low in cholesterol, fat, calories, sugar, and carbs or as high in fiber, protein, vitamins, and minerals. The trend has continued to the present day; in 2003, about 16 percent of new foods introduced in the U.S. market made some kind of health claim, up from 13 percent in 2001. Ad executives said that such claims can actually be easier to explain and substantiate than claims about how foods taste.[35]

Calfee summarized the resulting benefits for consumers. Not only did many began to purchase and consume more healthful foods, but also secondary benefits included a greater degree of media coverage of diet and health in the major media, new incentives for industry to invest in research about links between diet and disease prevention, and a higher awareness of these issues among the general public. "The health claims advertising phenomenon achieved what years of effort by government agencies had failed to achieve," he wrote. "With its mastery of the art of brevity, its ability to command attention, and its use of television, brand advertising touched precisely the people the public health community was most desperate to reach."[36] Other researchers have found compelling evidence that previous bans on advertising health claims for food had resulted in less knowledge about diet among consumers and fewer healthful products brought to market by manufacturers, who did not believe they could make them profitable without advertising their potential health benefits.[37]

## RESPONDING TO FRAUDULENT CLAIMS

Still, there remains the issue of fraud. Most advocates of free markets and a free flow of economic information via advertising also believe that one of the proper functions of government is to enforce laws against fraud in business transactions. It is too facile to say that freedom requires a regime of full caveat emptor ("buyer beware") in which consumers should have no legal recourse, and government no legitimate regulatory role, when demonstrably false or misleading claims are made on behalf of products. Todd Seavey, an editor at the American Council on Science and Health and a free market advocate, wrote in the libertarian *Reason* magazine that the preregulation days of drug ads and medicine shows had indeed featured a great deal of flimflammery and fraudulent claims that caused consumers real harm. "It is not unreasonable to argue that companies making scientific claims ought to have scientific evidence to back them up," he wrote, "and clinical trials are the best means we have yet devised for getting that evidence. It is no coincidence that many of the FDA's harshest critics—aside from those who object to regulation on principle—are adherents of 'alternative' medical methods that would never withstand the scrutiny of carefully constructed clinical trials, such as most herbal remedies and virtually all 'homeopathic' ones."[38]

Seavey's choice of words offers one useful distinction that might conceivably be used to differentiate health claims: if an advertising claim implies the mantle of a scientifically proven treatment, then the advertiser should be prepared to substantiate the claim. On the other hand, if an herb is advertised as an "ancient Chinese remedy," then most consumers can be expected to interpret the claim accordingly. Rather than relying on prior restraint, in other words, regulators would simply be in a position to investigate charges of fraudulent advertising and, if specific medical claims lack medical substantiation, would then be in a position to levy a fine sufficient to deter future abuses.[39] Economist Donald J. Boudreaux made a broader point when he warned against regulations that trivialize the real problem of fraudulent advertising by equating it with lighthearted efforts at humor, satire, or making brand names memorable. "If firms are discouraged from placing in their ads all but the most dry factual claims," he wrote, "consumers will be forced to spend more of their own time and resources discovering which products are available."[40] Remember that one function of advertising is to attract attention from consumers with many demands on their time.

Unfortunately, such careful distinctions are hard to make in some practical situations. Nor am I persuaded, as are some limited-government advocates, that access to the courts alone is a sufficient recourse for consumers who believe themselves wronged by fraudulent advertising. One idea might be to reform current regulations requiring the advertising, promotions, and labeling of prescription drugs to disclose details about efficacy, usage, interactions, and risks. Interestingly, many critics of drug ads believe that the regulations require both too much and too little—too much small print, spread over large swaths of newspaper or magazine pages, with too little information imparted effectively to readers using concise, straightforward language. This may well be the case where less is more. A related idea, similar to current labeling requirements for the ingredients and nutritional value of products, would be to require disclosures to be in the form of tables or graphs that would be both more arresting to the eye and more effective in communicating relative benefits and risks with numerical values.[41] The preponderance of the evidence suggests that, if properly designed, product warnings are an effective way of ensuring consumer safety and satisfaction and are thus an attractive alternative to restricting or banning the use of a product.[42]

At the very least, all involved in the debate about health claims in advertising should be willing to agree to this proposition: if a claim is true, it is not fraudulent and is unlikely to harm consumers. At present, this proposition is not universally shared by regulators. The so-called hollow health claim is a case in point. The FDA long argued that using a slogan such as "cholesterol free" to promote a food product is misleading if competing brands are also free of cholesterol.[43] But it is hard to see the real harm to consumers. If the competing brands are, indeed, free of cholesterol and respond by saying so, consumers get more truthful information and can choose a brand by other criteria. If all the brands are free of cholesterol but for some reason most choose not to tout that fact, then the company that chooses to do so is aiding consumers by informing them that the product has that attractive quality. Why shouldn't the advertiser be rewarded for providing such useful information by making more sales of its own brand?

The only policy alternatives appear to be for regulators to require that all brands advertise prominently their lack of cholesterol, which may crowd out other valuable messages they would prefer to accentuate, or that no brand do so, which keeps consumers in the dark about something that might well be in their interest to know. As attorney Jonathan Emord, who successful sued the FDA to inhibit its ability to forbid health claims for dietary supplements, put it in a 2000 article, federal regulators have long operated under the assumption that "deprivation of health claims (the true with the false) protected consumers from fraud and reduced the incidence of fraud. Shrouding consumers in a veil of ignorance, however, leaves them defenseless to those who would make false therapeutic claims"—such as firms that use spam e-mails and are clearly seeking to operate outside the scope of law.[44]

For advertisers, the ethical constraint is not, of course, simply to stay within the parameters of the law at a particular point in time. Rather, they should avoid false or misleading claims because, in the long run, they weaken the effectiveness, credibility, and public support of both their industry and often their own firm. "For advertising to become corrupt and ineffective could be a crippling blow to a free-market economy," wrote marketing consultant and ethicist Wroe Alderson. "This type of economy feeds on innovation and the sponsor must communicate with consumers to induce acceptance of innovation."[45] Fortunately, private institutions such as Better Business Bureaus already perform the valuable service of articulating standards of truth in advertising claims and then using publicity to ensure compliance with them (though it should be noted that advertisers also know there is a risk that if they do not comply with a Better Business Bureau finding, regulators might choose to get involved). Typically, bureau cases begin with complaints from competitors who doubt an advertising claim and demand that it be tested or substantiated.[46]

Whatever steps need to be taken to combat truly harmful fraud in the use of health claims in advertising, it would be risky to let self-imposed industry standards or government-imposed regulations serve to limit the extent of communication between producers and consumers. The best remedy for bad information is usually to combat it with good information, which is why firms should be encouraged, not discouraged, to challenge competitors' claims in their advertising. FDA regulations allow pharmaceutical companies, for example, to contrast their products with rivals' in advertising as long as any claims are based on at least two head-to-head trials that generate meaningful clinical results. But such advertising is still relatively rare in part because of industry fears of political backlash.[47] A clearer statement of policy from regulators, that making such medical claims is perfectly legal as long as there is documentation to back them up, would help to facilitate the practice. That is worth doing. The potential economic and social benefits of "less bad" claims—saying that a product may be risky, but the alternatives are riskier—will be discussed at some length in Chapter 8.

# CHAPTER 7

# Advertising and the Consuming Child

Imagine what it would be like to be a child growing up in a society that did not allow anyone to advertise products to you. When you turned on the television to watch your favorite cartoon show, there would be no commercials urging you to purchase the latest action figures, video games, or building sets. When you went to school, you would see no signs advertising soft drinks or sneakers. When you listened to your favorite radio station, there would be no promotions in between the songs telling you about the special toys you could get with your kid's meal at the fast-food joint.

What would this experience be like? Well, there is nothing imaginary about it and therefore no need to speculate. In 1980, the Canadian province of Quebec enacted a law that banned advertising toys, sweets, and other products to children under the age of 13. A toy company immediately sued the government for violating its free speech rights, but nine years later the Canadian high court upheld it. So for more than a generation, children in Quebec have grown up without, for the most part, seeing or hearing the advertising aimed at their peers in other Canadian provinces or the United States. And, also for the most part, there do not appear to be substantial differences in how many toys they have, how much food they eat, or how happy or healthy they are.

Both proponents and opponents of advertising bans saw the outcome in Quebec as proving their point. By 1985, toy retailers reported that their sales were about the same in Quebec as in other provinces and comparable to sales before the ban. Fast-food chains also reported little appreciable change in revenues. Sweetened cereals seemed to be declining a bit as a percentage of total cereal sales, though it was not obvious what factors were responsible for the trend.[1] See, said advocates of the ban, it is proven that advertising restrictions will not hurt industry and may help families deal with commercial pressures. No, said critics, the outcome demonstrates that advertising does not really increase the amount of consumption but just changes brand preferences. When supporters of the ban saw evidence that Quebec's children recognized fewer brands of toys, they saw success. When opponents of the ban saw the same evidence, they read it as reducing competition and choice and, consequently, resulting in a higher price for toys.

In some ways, the controversy about advertising to children is a microcosm of the larger debate about commercialism and the mass media. Both sides see this kind of advertising as a case that offers particularly compelling evidence for their points of view. Those who worry that advertising bamboozles its intended audience argue that whatever one thinks of adults' ability to separate truth from fiction, certainly children cannot be expected to do so. Boston College sociologist Juliet Schor, one of the leaders of a new anticorporate consumerist movement, wrote that children had "become the ground zero of consumer culture" whose inability to distinguish advertising from content led to unreasonable and excessive desires, dissatisfaction, and depression.[2] On the other hand, defenders of advertising see children's products as a clear case in which the introduction of mass marketing in the 1950s to businesses such as toys and fast food resulted in fundamental changes and measurable benefits for consumers. "Advertising to children, so often believed to be an exception to the rule that advertising makes markets work better, actually provides one of the more compelling examples of the benefits of advertising," former FTC official John Calfee wrote.[3]

# YOUNG INNOCENTS OR
# CONSUMERS-IN-TRAINING?

The argument for treating advertising to children as a special case, deserving of unique consideration and treatment, seems immediately persuasive. We make distinctions all the time between adults and children. The two groups have different capabilities and interests. Even if young teenagers are large and dexterous enough, states do not let them drive. States do not let children make legally binding contracts or, in general, large purchases without adult involvement. Using both law and custom, we shield children from violent or sexually explicit movies, programs, and games. In short, most of us do not see children simply as little adults. We limit what they are exposed to, gradually changing the degree and kind of exposure as their mental and emotional capacities develop.

Why shouldn't we adopt the same approach to advertising and other marketing efforts? Obviously, officials in Quebec decided to do so a generation ago. Other countries have similar policies. Australia, Greece, and several Western and Northern European countries have adopted policies designed to limit children's exposure to advertisements for toys, clothes, fast food, and other products. Sweden's regulations are perhaps the most stringent. A 1991 law prohibited all television and radio ads aimed at children under age 12. A few years later, Swedish politicians tried to get the entire European Union to regulate the marketing of products to children, in part because of concerns that its rules might run afoul of continental free trade policies. They and other advocates of advertising restrictions cited the moral imperative to protect children from exploitation as well as economic and social concerns such as higher consumer prices and rising childhood obesity rates that they linked to fast-food advertising.[4] Most recently, health authorities in Great Britain decided in 2004 to urge a ban on "junk food" tv advertising until 9:00 P.M. each night. The new rules would apply not just to fast-food restaurants but also to many foods sold for home consumption such as salty soup, breakfast cereal, and fish sticks. "We believe there's a strong evidence-based case for action to restrict the advertising and promotion to children of food and drink that are high in fat, salt, and sugar," said one government official.[5]

In the United States, the debate over advertising to children appears to be rekindling after a thirty-year period of smoldering anxiety and resentment. During a burst of consumerist agitation in the early 1970s, many advocacy groups argued that neither Congress nor federal agencies such as the Federal Communications Commission (FCC) and Federal Trade Commission (FTC) had been doing enough to protect American children from the encroaching mass market. A leader of the fight for regulation was an organization called Action for Children's Television (ACT). Its lobbying efforts resulted in a 1974 FCC decision to impose rules on children's television. Advertising was limited to 12 minutes per hour of children's programming on weekdays and 9.5 minutes per hour on the weekend. Broadcasters were also required clearly to separate program content from advertising. That meant that live hosts or cartoon characters could not be used to promote specific products and that there had to be a clean break—such as "We'll be right back after these commercial messages"—clueing young viewers into the fact that the programming and the advertising were not a seamless whole.[6]

ACT, the like-minded Center for Science in the Public Interest, and other activists were not satisfied. They became convinced that only a blanket prohibition, such as the one later passed in Sweden, would protect children from harm. The FTC, whose purview was not child welfare per se but unfair and deceptive trade practices, telegraphed its intentions clearly in 1978. FTC analysts released a summary of research that in their minds showed it was impossible for advertising messages aimed at children to be anything but unfair and deceptive. It then proposed a rule that would ban all television advertising to children under the age of 8 and the advertising of sugared cereals and other sweets to all preteens. The reaction was immediate and vociferous. The toy, food, and advertising industries attacked the proposal as radical, unwarranted, and unconstitutional. Within two years, Congress had enacted legislature to strip the FTC of any authority to restrict television advertising and, just in case it did not get the message, forbade the FTC from moving ahead with any prohibition of marketing legal products to children.[7]

However, as already discussed in previous chapters, by 1980 the FTC had begun to internalize the new economics of advertising articulated by Stigler, Becker, and other scholars and would shortly afterward begin to see advertising *bans*, not advertising, as truly harmful to consumers and in potential violation of federal law. Congressional action probably was not needed to head off the original proposal. In fact, Congress turned out to be the savior of federal regulation of children's programming after the FCC in 1984 lifted its original rules segregating content and advertising. The ensuing proliferation of programs such *He Man and the Masters of the Universe* that mixed stories with thinly veiled marketing of action figures led ACT and other activist groups to lobby Capitol Hill to intervene. The resulting 1990 legislation reimposed time limits on children's advertising (12 minutes per weekday hour and 10 minutes per weekend hour), required stations to broadcast educational programs, and prompted the FCC to bring back content/advertising segmentation. Claiming an ultimate victory, the leader of ACT, Peggy Charen, closed down the organization in 1992.[8]

It was not long, however, before it became obvious that the debate over children's television—and in particular the role of advertising within it—was far from over. Although broadcast stations now appeared to be under more stringent regulation about programming and commercial content, the reality was that they now found it easier to cancel locally produced educational programs. Previously, they had run talk shows, quiz-bowl programs, and other fare to increase their likelihood of receiving license renewal by demonstrating their commitment to public service. Now, with a national minimum established by Congress, they saw the opportunity to meet the standard with less expensive programs supplied by networks and of modestly educational value (the unctuous *Saved by the Bell* being one example).[9] As far as advertising was concerned, there was no appreciable reduction in the commercial content of children's television; indeed, the period after implementation of the regulations in the mid-1990s saw a burst of toy and marketing blitzes arising from imported Japanese fare and shows based around popular Marvel and DC superheroes. Most importantly, the concept of protecting children from commercialization by regulated broadcast television rapidly became quaint as millions of viewers transferred their allegiance to Nickelodeon, the Cartoon Network, the Disney Channel, and a host of other cable channels. If parents wanted their kids to stick to educational fare, they had up to 24 hours' worth of material on such channels as PBS Kids, Noggin, Discovery Kids, and Animal Planet. Many of the options had little or no commercial content, while others freely mixed new and recycled programming with advertising and cross-promotions.

By the end of the 1990s, a social and political movement against marketing to children had reconstituted itself. Reacting partly to the 24/7 availability of kid's programming on cable, the creation of Channel One as an advertising vehicle in the nation's classrooms, and exclusive marketing contracts for soft drinks, computers, and sportswear in colleges and high schools, various groups emerged to argue that government action was needed to protect children from sex, violence, exploitation, and social ills such as drinking, smoking, and obesity. A leading voice was Commercial Alert, founded in 1998 by Gary Ruskin and Ralph Nader. Its proposed nine-part "Parents' Bill of Rights" includes a Sweden-like ban on all tv ads aimed at preteens, ejecting all commercial contracts and content from school, a "Fairness Doctrine" allowing parents and activist groups with response time on broadcast outlets allowing children's advertising, and disclosure rules for any commercial messages imbedded in video games, movies, and books. Several of Commercial Alert's proposed bills have already been introduced in Congress.[10]

By 2004, the movement consisted of a broad array of commentators, authors, scholars, public officials, and private organizations. In addition to Commercial Alert, other interest groups lobbying for more regulation of children's advertising included the Motherhood Project, the Citizen's Campaign for Commercial-Free Schools, and the Coalition to Stop Commercial Exploitation of Children. The Kaiser Family Foundation and World Health Organization each released reports attemping to link fast-food advertising to rising rates of childhood obesity. The American Psychological Association and the American Academy of Pediatrics joined the call for advertising restrictions or bans, the latter stating that "advertising directed toward children is inherently deceptive and exploits children under age 8."[11] The seemingly omnipresent Schor, author of the 2004 book *Born to*

*Buy* and a Commercial Alert board member, appeared in a host of mainstream news outlets to argue that children's advertising led to family stress and childhood depression.[12] Another author, Susan Linn, wrote in *Consuming Kids* that the magnitude of the onslaught had grown far beyond the ability of parents to manage. "Comparing the advertising of two or three decades ago to the commercialism that permeates our children's world is like comparing a BB gun to a smart bomb."[13]

## THE EMERGENCE OF THE CHILDREN'S MARKET

Until the late nineteenth century, few American children spent their days playing with a manufactured toy, chewing on manufactured candy, or eating food prepared by anyone other than a parent (or, in a few cases, a domestic servant). Indeed, the concepts of play as a main activity of childhood, and its facilitation as a business opportunity for manufacturers and retailers, are both modern creations. For most of human history, children of all but elite families were expected to spend much of their waking days working—on the farm, in the rearing of siblings, or as part of a domestic trade. That is not to say that virtually all children everywhere have not engaged in play when they had a chance. It appears to be a universal impulse. Archaeologists have found toy animals, dolls, wheeled toys, hobbyhorses, and children's games in the remains of cultures as disparate as ancient Egypt and Greece, the Harappa culture of ancient India, and the Aztecs, Mayas, and Incas of pre-Columbian America. But many of these playthings appear to have been made as much for adults as for children, and for the most part were fashioned from scraps and items found around the house.

Gary Cross, author of the fascinating 1997 book *Kids' Stuff: Toys and the Changing World of American Childhood*, warned that it is tempting but misleading to assume that the discovery of toys among cultures of the past means that they were used the same way then that they are now. For example, "the worlds of children and adults were far closer in medieval Europe than they are today," Cross wrote. "In part, this meant that playthings initiated children into the adults' world. Medieval children played with miniatures representing their parents' lives." Moreover, adults were closely involved in such play, whether it be games and sports, puppet shows, or setting up toy soldiers and doll houses. Mechanical toys such as tops, clockworks, pecking birds, and windups were originally made for the amusement of adults, not children. Although most toys were crafted crudely at home or by street peddlers out of simple materials, even the items made by skilled craftsmen (most frequently German) for widespread sale across Europe were often purchased by adults for their own enjoyment and then later passed down to their children or sold secondhand to others.[14]

Tellingly, among the first toys that were truly designed and made exclusively for children were educational ones. The seventeenth-century English philosopher John Locke, as if he did not already have enough claims to fame, is often credited as one of the early proponents of toys designed to enhance learning. An experienced teacher of the children of his wealthy patron, Locke rejected the idea that play and leisure were harmful frivolities and that education should be accomplished primarily through rote. "Recreation is as necessary as labor or food," he wrote. "But because there can be no recreation without delight, which depends not always on reason, but oftener fancy, it must be permitted children not only to divert themselves, but do it after their own fashion, provided it be innocently and without prejudice to their health."[15] Locke suggested that parents supply their children with educational toys (but not too many, or all at once) and designed alphabet blocks for the children under his charge. His advice about play, and his colorful blocks, became popular among many upper-crust English parents. In the nineteenth century, his ideas became more broadly known and appreciated due to the publication of child-rearing guides purchased and read across England, Europe, and America.

Just like toys, children's candy also has a long history but was until relatively recently the product mainly of home kitchens and indistinguishable from sweets meant for adults. Once again, archaeology tells us that the ancient Egyptians made candy more than 3,500 years ago. Medieval Arabs and Chinese made confections out of fruits, nuts, sugar, and honey. In Europe, the importation of sugar was so expensive that candies were rare delicacies of the wealthy. Exploration of the New World led to Europe's sixteenth-century discovery of cacao, from which chocolate was made, and later to widespread cultivation of sugarcane and beets from which sugar could be more economically recovered. In the English-speaking world, boiled sweets were popular in the seventeenth and eighteenth centuries, and homemade candies such as peppermints and lemon drops were widely consumed by the early nineteenth century.[16]

The Industrial Revolution transformed the production of toys, candy, and other goods such as children's clothing, but it did not dramatically change how these products were marketed. Mass-produced sweets were sold loose as "penny candy" in the glass cases of general stores. The large department stores of the mid-nineteenth century added toy departments and experimented with seasonal displays, but they catered primarily to an urban population. Until the turn of the century, if American families bought manufactured toys at all, they likely got them at a general store and, as with candy, picked them out of a case or barrel. Montgomery Ward and Sears catalogs listed toys and other children's amusements, but advertised them primarily to adults with simple listings that emphasized price and durability. Sometimes they were listed on the same pages with other "gadgets" such as mousetraps. To the extent that toy advertisements did try to show how they could be used for fun, the target audience usually remained adults rather than children, as was the case with fashion dolls for women and toy guns for men. Cross explained that even in the late nineteenth century, toys were not thought of as part of imaginative play and of a child-generated world separate from adult reality:

> Manufacturers had not yet discovered the possibilities of selling personalities and imagination. Even if they had, few late-19th-century parents would have approved of such toys. Toymakers sold objects whose purpose was conventional and well understood by the parents who purchased them. They were to be used by children to imitate adult roles, not to reenact the fantasy lives of heroes who had little to do with their own worlds.[17]

An inflection point came in the early twentieth century with the retail revolution. The development of national chain stores in America by F. W. Woolworth, J.C. Penney, Sears, and other retailers brought the colorful and enticing toy displays of the big city to other cities and towns across the country. Toy manufacturing exploded during the period, in Germany and increasingly in the United States. Companies such as Fisher-Price and Playskool emphasized educational toys and began to advertise directly to educators.[18] The national consumer catalogs suddenly had many more types and brands of toys to offer and vastly expanded its listings; the Sears catalog had only one page of toy listings in 1914 but forty-six pages by 1931. Starting in the 1910s and 1920s, toymakers advertised directly to parents in mass circulation magazines, and some even began to target children directly in such publications as *Child's Life*. An early ad for Lionel trains urged boys to "take your Dad into partnership" and "make him your pal" in assembling a train set.[19]

Perhaps the first true toy fad of the mass market age occurred in the late 1920s. It was the yo-yo. There was nothing really new about it (our old friends the ancient Egyptians apparently played with an early version), but through advertising, promotions, and other marketing it became a worldwide sensation. The advent of commercial radio in the 1920s and 1930s offered another revenue for marketing toys, games, breakfast cereal, buttons, and other products directly to children during popular programs such as *Jack Armstrong: The All-American Boy* and *The Adventures of Superman*. Still, because of the nature of media consumption, most advertising of children's products continued to be directed at parents. And while toymakers did employ various kinds of national advertising, it did not constitute a significant percentage of their marketing efforts, which continued to focus on selling their wares to retailers, who in turn relied on some newspaper ads and circulars, local promotions such as parades and contests, and in-store displays to entice parents to buy. Louis Marx of Marx Toys famously argued that his products did not really need to be advertised, because children had no disposable income and the demand for playthings was fixed and inherent. Many of his colleagues agreed. As late as the early 1950s, advertising expenditures on toys and games only came to about $1 million a year.[20]

True mass marketing to children, according to many analysts, has a specific birthdate: October 3, 1955. That was the date of the first national broadcast of the *Mickey Mouse Club* on ABC. Ten years earlier, Elliot and Ruth Handler had created a toy company out of their garage. It was called Mattel (a combination of the first names of a partner, Matt Matson, and Elliot). Initially, they specialized in musical toys. Then they branched out to other lines, including a new "Burp Gun" (the term referred to the sound the cap gun made when fired). At first sales were lean. Then ABC approached Mattel with the idea of an exclusive yearlong sponsorship of its new Disney-themed children's show. Although the price of $500,000 was the Handlers' entire net worth, they decided to take a chance. While a few toymakers had dabbled with local tv ads (Hasbro's Mr. Potato Head may have been first on the tube in 1951), a nationwide buy was a new and risky idea. But it paid off: within a month of the first broadcast of the Mickey Mouse Club, Mattel was swamped with orders for its Burp Gun. By Christmas 1955, it had shipped more than a million units and grossed over $4 million. The Handlers had hit pay dirt—as they would a year later when, vacationing in Switzerland, Ruth purchased a "Lilli doll" (originally designed for men and based on a prostitute character from a German adult cartoon) and was inspired to create Barbie, named after her daughter.[21]

Mattel's success in advertising directly to children was quickly emulated. While companies such as Disney and what became DC Comics had since the 1930s enjoyed significant success in marketing tie-ins to their film, print, and broadcasting properties—licensing characters such as Mickey Mouse and Superman to makers of toys, games, clothes, and other consumer products—the late 1950s saw a dramatic upsurge in the sale of licensed products because they could now be advertised directly to a large national audience of children and families. The pump was already primed: rising disposable incomes meant that families could spend a growing percentage on toys, eating out, and other recreational and leisure activities. At the same time, the way that toys and other child-oriented products were retailed in the United States began to change dramatically. Robert Steiner, a former president of Kenner, described these changes in 1973. Before the 1950s, Steiner said, "the American toy industry was essentially an unadvertised business." There was little discounting, and retail sales were rare. Until about 1958, consumers paid on average about 96 cents of every dollar of the list price for toys, while manufacturers actually sold the toys to distributors for about 49 cents on the dollar.[22] In other words, wholesalers and retailers were earning substantial margins in a business that did not advertise much and enjoyed steady if unspectacular demand.

But in the television ad boom that followed the debut of the *Mickey Mouse Club*, the *Howdy Doody Show*, and other children's programming, the toy business went through a rapid and thorough transformation. The change in family buying habits did not, as some theorists might have asserted, result in higher prices due to higher and less elastic demand for toys. Instead, retailers found themselves in a much more competitive industry, attempting to serve the needs of parents looking for the toys they wanted at the most competitive price available. Retail discounting became common. Toy sales at discount stores went from $2 billion in 1960 to $27 billion in 1971. By advertising significant price breaks on the advertised toys, retailers found that they could generate large crowds of shoppers who might then buy many other items. At first, they tried to maintain higher markups on the nonadvertised toys, but that did not work because they had to compete for shopping dollars with the advertised ones. Over time, average toy prices fell substantially while the number of toys purchased per child rose significantly faster than the rate of growth of other consumer goods.

Steiner's research showed that mass advertising via television had reduced toy distribution margins (by about one-third over fifteen years), and that the effect on toy prices and availability had clearly been stronger in the countries that allowed the most tv ads directed at younger viewers. Higher volumes had allowed manufacturers to take advantage of economies of scale in production—and the highly competitive market that developed for toys had pushed most of these savings out to consumers. Interestingly, he found that only in sectors of the toy business where advertising had subsequently declined or been restricted—as was the case with toy gun marketing in the aftermath of the Vietnam War—did prices go up and product innovation dwindle. The moral of the story, Steiner wrote, was that "a relatively small expenditure (about 3.5 percent of manufacturers' sales) on television advertising has a very large multiplier effect on the level of consumer toy prices."[23]

There is a striking parallel between the rise of mass marketing in toys and the similar trend begun in the fast-food industry by Ray Kroc, a former milkshake mixer salesman. In 1954, Kroc visited the innovative restaurant run by the McDonald brothers in San Bernardino, California, and proposed to open additional restaurants as a franchisee. His company was founded just months before the debut of the *Mickey Mouse Club* (Kroc actually knew Walt Disney and tried to work a McDonald's restaurant into the plans for Disneyland), and by 1961 Kroc had bought out the McDonald brothers altogether. Seeing the success of direct-to-children advertising of toys and games on television, Kroc sought to re-create the same magic by marketing fast food directly to children and their families. He encouraged local franchises to seek out ways to get the word out. A franchisee in Washington, D.C., sponsored a local tv show called *Bozo's Circus* that generated such a strong customer response that the corporate office hired the same actor that had played Bozo, future NBC weatherman Willard Scott, to play a new character for the McDonald's chain called Ronald McDonald. After tweaking the character and costume, the company took Ronald McDonald national in a massive tv campaign that eventually featured an entire McDonaldland fantasy world populated by characters such as the Hamburglar, Mayor McCheese, Grimace, and the Fry Kids.[24] In part because of heavy advertising, the fast-food sector quickly became highly competitive, popular with families, and a business where prices were moderate and margins small.

## THE CASE AGAINST ADVERTISING
## TO CHILDREN

To many critics of immersing children in a mass media culture of advertising and commercialization, the effects on price and availability are beside the point. Some might even stipulate that advertising serves the narrow consumer interest by spurring price wars and innovation. Their real concern is that what is being marketed is harmful to children, and that children are not sufficiently developed and mature to recognize they are being manipulated.

Of course, one might say that it only matters that children are easy to manipulate if the results of such manipulation are, indeed, harmful. There are three broad categories of arguments designed either to convince industry to change its ways or to persuade government policy makers to step in and regulate or prohibit advertising aimed at children. Two involve asserted harms inflicted on children themselves, and the third on families and society as a whole.

## Health and Safety

A common theme in the literature and rhetoric of anti-advertising activists is that marketing directly to children results in quantifiable harms such as injuries from unsafe toys and the health consequences of high-fat, high-sugar diets. Since the early 1990s, most new efforts at the regulation of children's advertising have implicated it in rising obesity rates. Most recent was a 2004 proposal for an ad ban in Britain. In the same year, a coalition of health and social activist groups began to lobby for similar action in the United States, offering several studies that asserted a link between advertising and poor diet. They also argued that ads for breakfast cereals, snacks, and other products explicitly urged children to lobby recalcitrant parents to change the family diet or, if necessary, evade parental control altogether. One example they offered was an ad campaign for Kraft's Lunchables line of prepackaged lunches featuring nachos, hamburgers, sandwiches, and similar items. "You're in Control," promised the product's advertising and packaging. "We think it's time for the government to take a real hard look at the industry's practices," said one activist leading a petition drive that called for federal action.[25]

The argument that advertising causes physical harm among children is, however, not based on much in the way of substantive evidence. With regard for diet, for example, a comprehensive 1997 survey of worldwide research on the topic found that while advertising played a significant role in influencing brand preferences in some highly competitive markets, its role in influencing overall family food consumption was limited. "There is no evidence to suggest that advertising is the principal influence on children's eating behavior," the study concluded. One of the study's authors, Dr. Brian Young of Britain's Exeter University, later provided an analysis of how advertising fits into the broader context of food choices and preferences, many of which are "already in place well before children have any idea of what advertising is about or why it's there." They do not have to see advertising to like the taste of sweets and snacks, of course, and parents and other adults make most of their choices for them anyway. "After a rigorous examination of the research literature," Young continued, "we concluded that there is no serious and methodologically sound evidence that shows that food advertising leads to an increase in the consumption by children of whole categories of foods." Moreover, the assumption of a linear relationship between marketing messages and child response is an unrealistic one, ignoring that children "consume advertising selectively and use it as a cultural resource for many social activities unrelated to purchase behavior—they laugh about it, parody it, and talk about it with friends."[26]

In America, activists frequently cited a 1999 study in the *Journal of the American Medical Association* as providing early evidence of the linkage, but it did not actually conclude that advertising had caused higher weight gains among children. After a seven-month experiment among third and fourth graders in California, the study found that the half of the sample who watched more television and played more video games had a slightly greater weight gain than the other half of the sample. While the study's author did control for exercise levels, he found that the tv-watching group consumed an average of one more of their meals in front of the tv each day than the other group. Exposure to advertising was not the only possible explanation for the difference, he wrote, as it could have been the result of the less portly group "simply spending less time sitting in front of the tv, where some children have a habit of eating."[27]

The fundamental problem with the would-be ad prohibitionists' thesis is that it does not match up well with history. The recent upswing in childhood obesity has not occurred during a time of intensified television advertising to children, which has existed for decades. In fact, by the turn of the twenty-first century American children were gaining weight even as they were watching somewhat *less* commercial television than previous generations did. One study estimated that children saw about 15 percent fewer tv ads in 2003 than their counterparts did in 1994.[28] Alas, that does not mean they were playing outside more, as they simply had many more commercial-free alternatives such as premium cable, tapes and DVDs, and video and computer games.

Furthermore, the line of causality from advertising to obesity must run through the intermediate point of eating more, or at least more calorie-laden, food. But there is surprisingly little agreement about this. Federal data reveal that the average caloric intake of U.S. teenagers rose by only 1 percent from 1980 to 2000, while obesity rose 10 percent. Sedentary lifestyles seem to be the more significant factor. During the same period, average physical activity dropped by 13 percent.[29] As FTC chairman Timothy Muris pointed out, "even our dogs and cats are fat, and it is not because they are watching too much advertising."[30] Like their human owners (indeed, because of their owners' own behavior), they are simply spending too little time outside getting sufficient exercise to burn off the calories they consume.

Simultaneously, the very success of enacting ad bans in other countries during the 1980s and 1990s constituted an experiment in adjusting children's eating behavior via governmental regulation. The result? The obesity problem does not appear to be any less worrisome in countries with advertising bans than it is in places where children's advertising in unrestricted. By 2004, after more than a decade of advertising restriction, Sweden's obesity rate was roughly the same as the United Kingdom's. Obesity in Quebec was roughly comparable to obesity elsewhere in Canada.[31] Obesity in the United States is higher, but the American population differs from Europe and Canada in important respects. Similarly, there is no evidence that childhood injuries from toys or other products aimed at children are higher in countries that allow advertising. Indeed, rates of childhood injury have declined fairly steadily throughout the industrialized world regardless of the extent of governmental regulation or children's advertising.[32]

## Constrained Imagination

A common complaint lodged against the advertising of toys is that it helps to warp childhood play by substituting brands and media-driven storylines for the more authentic and developmentally healthy products of an active imagination. Advertising stresses the "flash and glitz" of today's toys and helps to turn children into passive participants in play, observed the popular family magazine *Highlights for Children*. "Indeed, many mass-marketed toys come with detailed 'stories' that stifle the child's natural imagination and creativity."[33]

There is no question that today's toy marketplace is filled with characters from television, film, music, sports, and now video and computer gaming. While the licensing of characters from the mass media has been an important part of the business since the 1930s, the dividing line between the media and the toy industry became blurry in the 1980s with deregulation and the phenomenal performance of blockbusters such as the *Star Wars* and *Star Trek* franchises and a rejuvenated Disney animation studio. Going forward, toy companies began to bid on the licensing rights for shows and movies still in production, and in the case of television became actively involved in developing new content. Talk about selling the dream: these programs and their advertisements were all part of a process of creating and promulgating fictional characters, settings, and plots that would then be purchased and used by families with children to engage in play. "Although all goods have meaning, toys and games, like other communication media, are cultural goods whose play value is the entertainment they provide," wrote Stephen Kline. "Toy companies, like film and tv producers with whom they competed, had to learn how to capture children's imagination, engage their sense of fun and humor, or elicit a momentary fascination."[34] (As we have seen, however, there was absolutely nothing new about advertisers acting as content producers, a practice that began with the radio dramas and comedies of the 1930s. The difference here was one of degree, not of kind.)

The problem with the constrained imagination argument is, once again, that it fails to comport with history. As Gary Cross and other historians of play have observed, children before the advent of mass marketing may have been forced by the crudity of their toys to be more imaginative about what they were playing with, but the content of their play was more about the emulation of adults than about inventing truly new and varied worlds to explore. Young boys played with child-sized versions of the tools, equipment, and weapons of adult men. Young girls used dolls and other toys to reenact what they saw their mothers, older sisters, and other relatives doing in real life.

When the first popular books, magazines, comics, and motion pictures came out in the late nineteenth and early twentieth centuries, many children found new outlets for their play. Radio in the 1930s and television in the 1950s expanded the universe of play characters and storylines further, as did the licensing booms and proliferating media options of the 1970s, 1980s, and 1990s. The real problem, in Cross's mind, is that parents can no longer relate to today's far more fantastic and imaginative worlds of play and childhood. "Many are no longer comfortable with play as a rehearsal for adult gender roles," he wrote. "But this leaves children with few models of the past or future even as it frees them from old constraints on their imaginations. In place of the traditional models of dolls and trucks, toymakers grew rich by producing magical pseudo-technology of violent conflict for boys and maudlin 'caring' play and fashion fantasy for girls."[35]

Critics of modern toy design and marketing would do well to step out of their academic cloisters and their own nostalgic remembrances of childhoods past and into the toy department of their local discount store—or perhaps onto one of the burgeoning websites specializing in toys. What they would find is a nearly bewildering array of options, running the gamut from traditional themes such as cars and trucks, dress-up, animals, and construction toys to action figures, games, devices, and knickknacks reflecting so many different fictional and real-life settings and characters that categorizing them all would seem to be beyond anyone's capacity. Then they should step into their own children's rooms, or find someone else's to visit, and see how these toys are actually used for play. Many kids will rather quickly tire of simply reenacting what they have seen on television or at the movies. Spider-Man, Darth Vader, Power Rangers, Peter Pan, and Pocahontas will soon find themselves attending a party at Barbie's house. Pirate ships, sailing into uncharted waters across the room, turn out to be at war with grotesque space aliens and giant, furry teddy bears. And observers will also find some branded "leftovers" from tv shows that lasted only a few months trapped in the corner of a far closet, never to rejoin the action, while other remnants of failed shows, apparently inexplicably, become popular characters in the drama.

At their root, worries about how advertising and toys interact to enable childhood play and fantasy often reveal a more fundamental ambivalence among scholars, writers, activists, and even parents about the role that advertising and commerce play in the *adult* world. Toys are, Kline points out, "the first possessions to be called 'mine,' " the "first things that children begin to purchase and collect." As developing consumers in a market economy, children use advertising and marketing to identify, learn about, evaluate, and experience the toys they might choose to ask for or purchase. As a process, this is problematic for children to the extent that its mirror image is problematic for adults.

## Overconsumption and Anxiety

This really is the crux of the matter for critics such as Schor: advertising to children generates acquisitive behavior in them that, in turn, may lead to more household consumption than families really need or can afford—or create tensions within the household as parents find themselves constantly saying "no" to children whose appetites for goods have been stoked by greedy and irresponsible corporations. Because children are not just little adults, they cannot evaluate advertising claims or know when they are being manipulated or duped, the argument goes. Schor's 2004 book, *Born to Buy*, added another specific charge to the indictment: the commercialism and tensions instigated by advertising result in actual psychological and even physical harm. "They are becoming depressed and anxious," she wrote. "They are suffering from headaches and stomach aches, too."[36]

Schor came to this conclusion after surveying 300 children ages 10 to 13 in urban and suburban Boston in 2002 and 2003. She divided the sample into groups based on their level of "involvement" in consumer culture, measured not simply by the extent of exposure to advertising and media but also by their answers to survey questions "about how much they were psychically tuned in to the values and aspirations of consuming, such as how much they cared about having a lot of stuff; how important designer labels and a nice family car were to them; whether they usually were focused on acquiring something new; and how much they wanted to be rich and wanted their parents to be richer." The children scoring higher in Schor's involvement measurement also tended to exhibit other traits such as conflict with parents and physical ailments.

But with few other studies asserting a similar linkage, this one small study appears to be a rather weak basis for advocating a nationwide ban on children's advertising, as Schor did. Indeed, by abandoning a straightforward measurement of children's exposure to advertising in favor of a survey-based approach, Schor may well have committed a basic error in analysis by failing clearly to separate her hypothesized cause and effect. Could children prone to anxious feelings about themselves and their families' economic status also exhibit emotional and physical symptoms of distress? Of course. That corporate advertising and marketing practices are the cause of such feelings would seem to be the real question at issue. Unfortunately for Schor and other like-minded analysts, however, there appears to be little evidence for this proposition.

For example, one of the mechanisms by which advertising creates tensions and anxieties within families is said to be "pester power." Any parent knows what this means: the repeated, often spirited attempt by children to get their parents to buy something. That this can be a nuisance is undeniable (though children asking for something they cannot or shouldnot have is likely to be a behavior that long predates modern family life and television culture), but does it rise to the level of a major cultural crisis?

One of the few attempts to answer this question rigorously was published in 1999 by a European team of researchers. They used surveys to determine the extent of pester power in Sweden, which had banned children's advertising, and in Spain, which had not. They found that few parents in either country considered "children pestering" to be a particularly significant problem, at least as compared to other shopping challenges such as long lines, staff assistance, and finding a parking space. If the pester power thesis was correct, Swedish parents should have been less likely than Spanish parents to complain about pestering, but they were in fact more likely to do so. Moreover, even for the small percentages identifying pestering as a problem, fewer than one-fifth of Swedish parents and one-tenth of Spanish parents thought the proper response was to ban advertising aimed at kids (which, of course, the Swedish government had already previously done). Within the entire sample, support for ad bans was minuscule in both countries. "The findings of this study question the effectiveness of the Swedish ban on advertising to children and, in general, present a serious challenge to the argument that television advertising increases children's pestering," the study concluded.[37]

More generally, it turns out that there is little actual research support for the proposition that children are particularly vulnerable to manipulative advertising, that it plays a significant role in harming their physical or emotional health, or that government-imposed limits or bans truly advance a public purpose. Dr. Jeffrey Goldstein, a professor of mass communications at the University of Utrecht, summarized the available research in 1998.[38] Here are some of his main points:

- Children are more influenced by parents and playmates than by mass media in forming and expressing consumer preferences. Youth fads such as in-line skating, pogs, music, jewelry, games, and websites often precede rather than follow widespread advertising, which tends primarily to facilitate entry by competing firms into the new market and thus to serve the interest of consumers by driving quality up and prices down. In Greece, for example, a ban on toy ads did not reduce toy consumption, but what it did do was reduce significantly the market share of non-Greek toy companies in the country,[39] with adverse consequences for consumers such as higher prices and fewer choices.

- The vast majority of new products advertised in the media, including those targeted at younger consumers, fail to survive in the market for more than a few years. This is hard to square with the thesis that advertisers impose their will on vulnerable consumers. To the extent that advertising raises brand awareness and encourages children to ask for specific types of toys, it makes it easier for parents to make purchases that do not end up shoved back into a closet later and ignored. Indeed, it is difficult to sustain the assertion that American parents are as upset about children's advertising as are the political activists speaking in their name. A 1992 study of parental attitudes about television programs based around advertised toys found that while many parents expressed some concern, "parental perceptions and attitudes do not mirror, in magnitude or pervasiveness, the extremely negative views that have been expressed by advocacy groups. . . . Our findings also do not support the notion that parents typically are ardently opposed to these programs."[40] No

doubt many believe the appropriate response to a brazenly commercial and insubstantial tv show is to change the channel or give
their children something else to do besides watching a half-hour
advertisement.

- Efforts to establish ages at which children comprehend advertising's
  purposes and motives are misguided, since the diversity among both
  children and researchers' definitions has generated widely divergent
  findings.[41] Nor is there an apparent link between understanding advertising's motives and being influenced by it. "Indeed, children who
  do not understand advertising may be less influenced by it than
  youngsters who know that it is intended to make them want something," Goldstein wrote. Other research has shown that teenagers
  and even preteens exhibit significant levels of skepticism about advertising claims.[42]

- Exposure to advertising is part of the way children learn about consumption, about making choices and evaluating goods and services.
  It is part of the process of developing into an adult consumer. In his
  1987 book, *Children as Consumers*, Texas A&M scholar James
  McNeal argued that thinking about children's advertising as a learning process should lead both advertisers and parents to exercise
  judgment about what kinds of commercial messages are appropriate for children. "Children have a right to be consumers in spite of
  some inadequacies," he wrote.[43]

- Some advertising directed at children is false and misleading, but
  the same is true of other advertising. Remedies already exist—and
  should exist—to address the problem. Moreover, banning TV ads
  will not end marketing to children and may actually reduce ac-
  countability and parental supervision over it. "At least television is
  within a parent's sphere of influence," wrote Guy Abrahams, a
  British marketing director, unlike what happens among peers at the
  playground.[44] Attributing undue power to television commercials
  reflects a lack of appreciation for how young people interpret media
  within a broader social context of peers, parents, school, and even
  faith. A 2004 study by NOP World Consumer, a New York–based
  market research firm, found that half or more of children aged 8 to
  17 consult their parents before purchasing movies, CDs, and video
  games. The percentage is far higher for preteens.[45] And careful con-

tent analysis of children's advertising shows that prosocial and positive behavior—including friendship, teaching, and helping others—is more common than negative, antisocial images and messages.[46]

Of course, there *are* negative, antisocial images and messages in the mass media that youngsters see and are influenced by, including some advertising (as discussed in the next chapter). But these messages are mostly found in the programming itself—in idiotic and sleazy television shows, in violent and salacious films, in the mindless violence of some video games, and in the nihilist, misogynistic, or pornographic lyrics of some pop songs. Much of the content is made for adults but consumed by children, though not all: a distressing amount of it is targeted directly at youngsters for whom it is entirely inappropriate and potentially harmful.[47] Those who seek to protect children and help them develop into mature, responsible, moral, and healthy adults are looking in the wrong direction if they believe that commercials themselves are the major problem—and that regulation, rather than parental oversight, is the solution. By all means, parents should exercise more discretion in controlling how much and what kind of television their children watch, how much time they spend playing video games or surfing the Internet, and what kind of music they listen to. There is good reason to believe, for example, that American children are too sedentary and that this contributes to obesity and other physical, mental, and emotional harms. But what is really harming these children is the behavior, not the commercials.

# CHAPTER 8

# The Economics and Ethics of Selling Sin

Can advertising be good for fostering competition, reducing prices, expanding choice, stimulating innovation, and adding value to consumer products—and also bad for us?

For many critics, the answer is a clear, resolute, perhaps even loudly shouted, "Yes!" They see modern advertising as a sort of moral sewer, a steady stream of problematic pitches urging us to drink and eat too much, dirty our lungs, or escape reality through mood-altering chemicals while debasing our culture with sexually explicit images that verge on pornography. To escape advertising's assault on our physical, mental, and moral health would require a willingness to withdraw from modern life that most of us do not have, the argument goes. Consequently, we are stuck with advertiser-driven mass media that are, in the end, bad for us. And if that was not bad enough, along comes a new, boundless shopping mall of filth and frivolity called the Internet.

For those who defend advertising on legal, economic, or even aesthetic grounds, this critique of commercial culture is probably the most difficult one to discuss and rebut. I do not mean to suggest that there are no possible rebuttals to it, only that they are less likely to persuade disgruntled critics. Regarding issues of legality or economic efficiency, both sides share some common frames of reference and common goals. If one asserts that the use of advertising makes it easier for a firm to establish a monopoly to subvert consumer welfare, it is possible for another to employ empirical evidence and cogent reasoning to rebut that assertion. But if a scholar, politician, or average citizen states his or her belief that there are too many raunchy ads on television, it is difficult to challenge such a belief by offering empirical evidence (who decides how many is too many?) or arguing that advertising helps consumers conceptualize and obtain what they want (perhaps what consumers want is something they should not have).

I should also say that it is, in fact, quite possible to believe that advertising is a valuable and useful aid to consumers *and* that there are too many raunchy ads on television. I happen to believe both propositions myself. That does not mean that I agree with cultural critics of advertising about all of their descriptions of the problem, or about their recommended remedies. For example, one version of the argument that does not comport with reality is that the intersection between advertising, commerce, media, and "sin" is an inherently modern one, a post-1960s artifact of generalized moral decay. It is impossible to deny that the social movements and changes beginning in the 1960s did, indeed, result in more explicit sexuality in the media and popular depictions of the drug culture. But during the same period, there have also been countervailing trends, such as the end of most positive portrayals of tobacco use and the rise of advertising campaigns urging more responsible use of alcohol. More importantly, there is absolutely nothing new about advertising mood-altering drugs or using sex to sell products. Recall the sometimes ribald commercial culture of ancient Rome as revealed by the archaeological treasure trove of Pompeii. Pictures of voluptuous women and muscular men were commonly used to promote a variety of goods and services. Taverns, inns, and brothels used explicit imagery, including nudes and phalluses, to attract customers. Some of the most intriguing evidence of early attempts to define brands and make persuasive appeals about consumer satisfaction involved a competitive market for wine—and competing claims for how quickly and easily one might get pleasantly, stupidly drunk.

More recent innovations in advertising and marketing are also difficult to disentangle from products and behaviors that many find morally troubling. Some of the most popular trade cards of the nineteenth century, bundled with goods and exchanged as valuable commodities themselves, promoted cigarettes or alcohol and featured beautiful, often buxom and scantily clad women, such as the American Tobacco Company's series of collectible "Women of the Stage" cards in the 1880s.[1] In the 1897 Sears, Roebuck & Co. catalog, readers could see ads not only for clothes, watches, jewelry, and other standard fare but also for "Dr. Chaise's Nerve and Brain Pills," to cure "overworked sexual excesses." Nearby was a pitch for two related products: the "Princess Bust Cream Food," designed by "an eminent French chemist" to help women develop a "plump, full, rounded bosom," and the "Princess Bust Developer," essentially a form-fitted plunger offered for use "if nature has not favored you."[2]

Interestingly, scholars who have studied the content of advertising through the late 1800s and into the 1900s have noted the lack of a straight-line trend. The use of sexually alluring images seems to have waxed and waned depending on the target audience and economic conditions of the day. The definition of sexually alluring has also varied. As women became the dominant audience for mass market advertising in the early twentieth century—making an estimated 85 percent of household purchases as families moved from the farm to cities and began to buy rather than produce many basic necessities of life—the earlier images of scantily clad women gave way to newspaper and magazine display ads featuring demure girls, professional women, or seasoned mothers. Thin was in during the flapper era of the 1920s, followed by curvaceous women in the 1930s, solidly built working women in the 1940s, attractive but prim wives and mothers in the 1950s, shorter skirts and longer hair in the 1960s, natural and playful images in the 1970s, curves again by the 1980s, and so on.[3] The point is that evaluating the role of advertising in defining sexual roles is a complex task and does not lend itself to easy generalizations or description with a single, upward-sloping line on a graph.

Judging from history, there appears to be a widespread—though certainly not universal—human demand for products that are at least arguably not in our medical, psychological, or moral interest to consume, particularly to excess. There also appears to be a basic human interest in beauty and even sexual suggestiveness, an interest seized upon by vendors throughout recorded history to attract consumer attention to their wares. It would be impossible, in other words, to find or even to imagine a culture of advertising and commerce that does not to some degree contain these elements. A simple conclusion one could immediately draw from these facts is that concerns about "selling sin" are irrelevant and unwarranted. Don't like the use of advertising to encourage smoking, promote inebriation, or sell shampoo or automobiles with sex? Too bad. That is just the way the world is made.

But such a conclusion is not merely simple and immediate. It is also simplistic and premature. Ethical considerations do not end at Nature's door. Most human beings, despite the inevitable feelings of conflict and guilt that result, have believed in the past and continue to believe that ethics is rooted in proscriptive morality, which is in turn grounded in religious authority. They do not accept that what is natural is necessarily good; some are guided by their theology to accept the reverse, that human beings are naturally tempted to self-indulgence or inherently predisposed to sin. Even for the secularly minded utilitarian, the issue cannot be so easily dismissed, for it is a fallacy to suggest that any choice or action that "comes naturally" to individuals—or, to put it another way, that immediately induces pleasure or avoids pain—is necessarily in their interest. What may feel good or reduce pain in the short run could well bring great suffering and distress in the long run, just as a heavy helping of chocolate cake might have instant appeal but, upon reflection, too many deleterious consequences to accept. Some would argue that ethical guidelines or moral constraints are needed precisely *because* human beings are easily tempted by immediate gratification to pursue self-destructive actions—that people often find it difficult to foresee the long-term consequences of each of their individual decisions and so would be wise to let general rules or proscriptions guide their behavior.

Thus it is impossible, in the end, to dismiss the deeply felt concerns of those who recoil from what they see in our modern, commercialized culture. But what should they do about such concerns? A common impulse has been to invite the public sector to intervene. During the movement for alcohol prohibition, many activists demanded at the very least that governments restrict or abolish the advertising of alcoholic beverages. More recently, foes of the tobacco industry have sought and largely obtained restrictions on the marketing of cigarettes and other tobacco products. Less frequent are calls for direct government regulation of the sexual content of advertising messages, with the important exception of those on broadcast television, which are assumed to be within the proper scope of governmental oversight because of federal licensing and the scarcity of the airwaves.

However, the impulse to pass a law or regulation to stop the selling of sin might itself be considered a sort of "natural temptation" that critics should be urged to resist. Just as one can consistently defend advertising as a boon for consumers *and* criticize particular advertising images or trends as morally problematic, one can simultaneously worry about immoral content in advertising *and* believe that responding with regulations or bans is unwarranted, unhelpful, and counterproductive. Again, the latter is a fair characterization of my own view, and its validation can be found by a closer examination of three main areas of concern for moral critics of advertising: tobacco, alcohol, and sex.

## CIGARETTE ADVERTISING AND THE PROBLEM OF "LESS BAD" CLAIMS

Western observers of smoking have associated tobacco with poor health for at least four centuries. It was in 1604 that King James I of Britain issued his "Counterblaste to Tobacco," in which he famously referred to smoking as "a custom loathsome to the eye, hateful to the nose, harmful to the brain, dangerous to the lungs, and in the black stinking fume thereof nearest resembling the horrible stygian smoke of the pit that is bottomless."[4] Long before careful epidemiological research established a link between tobacco use and deadly ailments such as lung cancer and heart disease, purveyors of tobacco products had to cope with the widespread testimony of smokers and former smokers about shortness of breath, coughing, fatigue, and other easily perceptible signs that the inhalation of tobacco smoke had adverse consequences for one's health.

It is beyond the scope of this book to discuss whether a product with such potentially harmful effects should have been prohibited. My own view is that prohibitions typically cause more problems than they solve, and that living in a free society means being free to make not only wise choices but also unwise ones. Others see the issue differently, arguing that government should step in to protect people from such poor choices in situations where (1) physical or psychological addiction diminishes or removes a true freedom to choose, (2) adverse consequences are too far in the future for most consumers to realize or take into consideration, or (3) the adverse consequences are so great, both to consumers and their families and associates, that it is worth sacrificing some freedom to avoid such consequences.

For the purposes of considering the ethical aspects of advertising, however, it does not really matter whether prohibition is a permissible or prudent policy. For whatever reason, few public authorities have ever sought to ban tobacco use entirely, seeking instead to put limits on its sale to minors and on its use in common spaces such as government buildings, workplaces, bars, restaurants, and malls. So, the relevant question is, given that smoking is a legal activity, whether it is ethical to advertise tobacco products at all, and if so what kinds of media and messages are proper to employ to do so.

Applying the evidence and analysis provided in previous chapters, it would be reasonable to predict that cigarette advertising confers some demonstrable benefits to cigarette consumers, in the form of lower prices and greater selection. As it happens, research specific to the industry shows exactly that. During the nineteenth and early twentieth centuries, tobacco manufacturers were among the most aggressive and innovative users of new advertising media as well as emerging techniques such as publicity and public relations. In the 1920s, tobacco companies began to target women as a potential market by associating cigarettes with freedom, independence, and sophistication. Later, they used copious amounts of advertising across various media to segment the market and build loyalty to brands through imagery ranging from the rustic and masculine (e.g., the Marlboro Man) to the exotic (Camel) and sexy (Virginia Slims). The link between advertising, competition, and product innovation became evident after a ban on television advertising of cigarettes in the early 1970s. An average of one new brand of cigarette penetrated the American cigarette market each year before 1970. During the following four years, no new cigarette brands appeared.[5] On price, the available evidence suggests that advertising, by facilitating competition, drove down cigarette prices when other trends were held constant.[6]

Of course, to critics of smoking these consumer "benefits" are anything but. If advertising helps smokers find the cigarettes they enjoy at economical prices, it is enabling their deadly habit. But even in the case of smoking and health, the role of advertising is a complex one that is often caricatured and misunderstood. At about the same time that tobacco companies began their advertising campaigns aimed at women, during the 1920s, the industry began to respond to health concerns about smoking with both advertising and PR campaigns using what some analysts have called "less bad claims." An early campaign for Lucky Strikes, for example, offered testimonials from opera stars who said they preferred the brand because it was "less irritating" to the throat. Competing brands such as Chesterfield then sought to rebut the Lucky Strikes claim via ridicule, in one case hiring legendary PR man Edward Bernays to set up a Tobacco Society for Voice Culture, which would work "to improve the cords of the throat through cigarette smoking" so that the public could "express itself in songs of praise and more easily swallow anything." R.J. Reynolds Co. spent millions of dollars on advertising devoted to "turning the light of truth on false and misleading statements in recent cigarette advertisements," meaning ads making Lucky Strikes appear less injurious to health than RJR's products.[7] Consider the irony: competitors in the cigarette business were spending a great deal of time and money encouraging Americans to think about the health consequences of smoking, and denying that their competitors' cigarettes were any less harmful than their own.

Scholars Carl Scheraga and John Calfee have examined in detail the tobacco industry's continuing wars of words into the 1950s and early 1960s, as public authorities began to intervene not only to warn smokers of health risks but also to prohibit certain claims in cigarette advertising. It was in the early 1950s that the first widely accepted medical studies linked smoking and cancer. During this period, cigarette companies responded to the news in part by advertising that their own brands reduced the risk. Firms with lower shares of the do-

mestic market, such as Brown & Williamson and Lorillard, touted
their filtered cigarettes as reducing the tar and nicotine ingested by
smokers. "Just what the doctor ordered," stated one campaign for a
filtered Liggett & Myers cigarette.[8] There were at least two groups
upset with the advent of such "fear advertising." One was the Federal
Trade Commission, which saw the claims as fraudulent because there
were, they argued, very little practical differences among the brands
in their health effects (interestingly, at first the FTC's position was
that less bad claims about cigarettes were fraud because cigarettes,
used in moderation, were not injurious to health; later, the argument
transformed into the assertion that cigarettes were equally harmful
regardless of differences in design or content). The other group that
disliked the small tobacco companies' health claims consisted of the
large tobacco companies that did not want to give up market share
to them.

In 1955, the FTC formally issued a rule forbidding companies
from making reference "to either the presence or absence of any physical effect of smoking." Scheraga and Calfee's examination of industry performance before and after this ruling revealed that the FTC
action benefited the larger firms in the cigarette market. Similarly,
after a 1960 agreement between the FTC and the industry blocked
the use of advertising claims touting lower tar and nicotine, the two
largest firms—American Tobacco and R.J. Reynolds—prospered to a
far greater degree than the smaller firms that had tried to use such
advertising to expand their market shares.[9] The FTC later reversed
its policy, but it seems likely that its regulatory interventions delayed
the proliferation of somewhat less harmful cigarettes.

More generally, as Calfee has argued in his other work on the subject, bans on cigarette advertising have uncertain benefits and some
underappreciated costs.[10] Because there are many other ways to promote what remains, after all, a legal product, such bans do not appear
to make a major dent in smoking. Some advocates have argued otherwise, citing a decline in the smoking rate after the imposition of advertising bans. This is insufficient evidence for their case. Smoking
has declined in places where advertising was never banned, too.
Countries such as Iceland, Norway, Finland, Italy, and Portugal that

enacted advertising bans in the 1970s and 1980s actually saw cigarette consumption drop more slowly than it did in comparable countries that did not ban cigarette ads.[11] More recent efforts to ban advertising have featured the same kind of regulator–big business collusion that occurred decades ago in the American tobacco market. In China, prominent antismoking activists actually met in 1994 with the largest cigarette manufacturer, a state-owned monopoly, and agreed to support an ad ban to keep Western brands out of the huge Chinese market. Thus Chinese smokers ended up with higher prices, less selection, and less access to filtered brands and those with lower amounts of tar and nicotine.[12]

Perhaps the best health argument for a ban on cigarette advertising is simply that it would hurt consumers by raising prices, which would in turn lead some smokers to quit and some young people not to start. Maybe, although the preponderance of the evidence would suggest that price increases large enough to deal a significant blow to cigarette consumption would be far greater than advertising bans impose. Such a price hike would probably require direct government action in the form of a higher excise tax. That may or may not be a good policy, but it has little to do with advertising and takes the conversation back to issues of prohibition and government regulation of personal choices.

There are, of course, ways that advertising and commercial speech can and have been used to combat tobacco consumption. Companies selling smoking-cessation services, such as nicotine patches, have made substantial use of direct-to-consumer advertising. Public service announcements (PSAs) can also be an effective way to transmit information about the health consequences of smoking, particularly if well designed to convey credible messages to young people. Ironically, the 1971 ban on tv ads for cigarettes probably boosted the fortunes of tobacco companies, as many antismoking activists now admit, because it also meant a near-end to effective PSAs against smoking that had been required under the Fairness Doctrine.[13] Finally, as an ethical matter, advertising professionals who believe that smoking is inherently wrong can and should stay clear of the tobacco industry. So should readers and viewers of media sources that accept tobacco advertising. In a free society, there are many ways to promote health and other social causes that *expand* the flow of information, analysis, and debate rather than restricting it.

## ALCOHOL AND THE PROBLEM OF GENERALIZATION

Like tobacco, alcohol has a long shared history with advertising. Also like tobacco, alcohol has been the subject of much agitation in favor of advertising bans, with supporters asserting that less advertising would mean less alcohol abuse and its tragic consequences (including unemployment, poverty, domestic violence, crime, and injuries and deaths associated with drunk driving). Advocates of prohibition in the late nineteenth and early twentieth centuries saw advertising bans as a useful first step toward their ultimate goal, though rarely as an acceptable substitute for it. Later, after the repeal of the Eighteenth Amendment in the 1930s, activists who worried about the resumption of alcohol sales relied on social and political pressure to limit the marketing practices of beer, wine, and liquor producers. In an attempt to appease its political critics, the hard liquor industry "voluntarily" limited its advertising to the print media. It was only after some fifty years, in 1996, that the Distilled Spirits Council announced an end to its self-imposed ban on radio and television advertising.[14] It began to place ads with some outlets, though as recently as 2002 the industry found it difficult to get broadcast networks to accept its ads and was forced to rely on local stations and cable networks.[15]

Beer and wine had, of course, never been subjected to such limitations. Beer ads became a mainstay on network television, generating some of the most memorable jingles, catchphrases, images, and gimmicks in the history of the medium. Repeated attempts to get federal regulators to intervene against all alcohol advertising—most recently in the mid-1980s by the Center for Science in the Public Interest and other activist groups—essentially went nowhere. So critics of alcohol advertising changed their tactics to focus on the issue of underage drinkers. Though the ultimate goal remained more grandiose—a total advertising ban, tightly regulated alcohol sales, and the like—these activists began to push for rules limiting alcohol ads in print or broadcast media with higher-than-average shares of their audience among younger people.[16] This distinction is probably impractical, however, for while truly youth-oriented media under-standably (and properly) do not accept alcohol ads, magazines, radio stations, and tv networks with many teens in the audience—such as those devoted to music, movies, and other facets of popular culture—draw even larger audiences of twenty-somethings and thirty-somethings who are prime (and perfectly legal) targets for such advertising.[17]

To continue the parallel with the case of tobacco ads, an effective argument for restricting or abolishing the advertising of alcoholic bev-erages cannot be based simply on good intentions. Those who down-play the seriousness of alcohol abuse in the United States are either ignorant or disingenuous. But alcohol abuse is not the same as alco-hol *use*, which is not only benign in moderation but also, according to the most recent medical literature, may offer some health benefits by reducing the risk of heart disease, diabetes, stroke, and mental de-terioration in old age.[18] I am a teetotaler, but I nevertheless recognize that curbing overall alcohol consumption is neither a necessary step in the fight against alcohol abuse nor an appropriate test of whether advertising bans might serve the public interest. Unfortunately for ad-vocates of a ban, there seems to be no empirical evidence whatsoever to suggest that alcohol abuse is linked to advertising or would be ame-liorated in its absence. Dr. Morris Chafetz, founding director of the National Institute on Alcohol Abuse and Alcoholism in the U.S. Department of Health and Human Services, wrote in 1996 that "there is not a single study—not one study in the United States or interna-tionally—that credibly connects advertising with an increase" in alco-hol abuse. He called the assertion "fantasy, not fact."[19]

More generally, the notion that advertising bans would reduce overall alcohol consumption seems questionable. Most research on the subject has concluded that there is no statistically significant link.[20] In Sweden, Denmark, and Finland, near-total advertising bans did not result in lower alcohol consumption during the 1980s and 1990s. It stayed the same or rose in those countries, as it did in the United Kingdom, where no such ad ban was in place.[21] In the few cases where bans have been linked to (modest) reductions in consumption, the results suggested that limited bans—say, those aimed at particular age groups or media—would be insufficient to make much of a difference. But since more comprehensive restrictions are infeasible and problematic for many reasons, such research has led even those harboring great concern about alcohol consumption, particularly among the young, to conclude that using advertising itself—in the form of enhanced public service announcements about responsibility, advertising for alternative products, or "counter ads" that aggressively challenge drinking and alcohol companies—would be a far more effective way to advance their goals.[22]

Alcoholic beverages have been an integral part of most human cultures throughout history. In the modern context, there are many familiar, cultural, and social factors in play that create a complex web of traditions, patterns, and experiences influencing how people try their first drink. Advertisers certainly hope to influence brand preferences or to let consumers know about innovative or lower-priced new products. But it is not likely that they play a significant role in inducing people to drink, much less to abuse alcohol and thus endanger themselves or others. One prediction about the effects of an advertising ban can be issued with confidence, however: it would likely help large beverage companies protect their market shares against small upstarts, as previous regulations helped large tobacco companies against smaller ones. "Consumers would clearly be the big losers from a total or partial ban on alcohol advertising," wrote economists Robert Ekelund and David Saurman.[23]

## SEXUALITY AND THE PROBLEM OF CONTEXT

Many people believe two related statements about morality in advertising: sex is widespread in advertising, and sex sells. Both statements have validity but are also fraught with exaggeration. For example, peer-reviewed studies of the extent of sexually explicit images and messages in print and broadcasting advertising certainly do offer support for the common perception that many ads contain such content and that their share of total advertising has risen in recent years. The studies also support the presumption that sex is more likely to be found in advertising aimed at young people and men than in ads aimed at older people and women.

But the actual numbers do hold some surprises. One study of national magazines found that 65 percent of women and 86 percent of men depicted in advertising were *not* dressed in an alluring or sexually revealing manner.[24] More generally, the depiction of people (however clothed) and brands together in magazine ads has actually declined since the 1950s, with visuals becoming more likely to be devoted to the product by itself.[25] In 1998, a different study found, 12 percent of models in prime-time tv commercials were "sexually attired" and 8 percent were involved in "sexual behavior" (though this category included depictions of hand-holding, kissing, and other behavior that many would not necessarily consider improper to show on tv).[26] That means that the vast majority of paid commercial advertising is *not* sexualized (indeed, a 2000 study found that 20 percent of prime-time tv spots that promoted other shows on the network contained sexual content, which goes a long way to show where the greater amount of tv salaciousness is found).[27] While these studies were limited to the content of American advertising, other research suggests that advertising in other countries follows similar patterns.[28]

Even the notion that sex-crazed advertising is a problem related to men and the young deserves a closer look. Tom Reichert, the author of *The Erotic History of Advertising* and a well-known scholar in the field, found in a 2003 study that models were more likely to be dressed sexually in ads for young adults than in ads for mature adults. But the percentages were 28 percent and 24 percent, respectively— hardly a dramatic difference. As for the sex of readers being related to the sexiness of advertising, Reichert's findings might clash with conventional wisdom, though they will not surprise those who frequent supermarket checkout lines: magazines targeting female audiences were significantly more likely to contain ads with sexually dressed models (39 percent) and sexual interactions (38 percent) than were magazines with male audiences (17 percent and 25 percent, respectively) or general interest magazines (21 percent and 27 percent, respectively).[29] On the other hand, women are far more likely to be dressed alluringly in ads than men are, regardless of the target audience, and other research shows that ads offering an implied sexual benefit or promise from consuming a product are more likely to be found in men's magazines (12 percent) than in women's magazines (6 percent).[30]

Consider one of the most controversial uses of sexual suggestiveness in television advertising in recent years, a campaign for Clairol's Herbal Essences shampoo. After an initial setup, each spot showed a woman showering, rubbing the shampoo into her hair, and making sounds and facial expressions clearly intended to mimic orgasm. But while the ads may have stuck in the minds of many young (or not-so-young) male viewers, that fact almost certainly corresponded to wasted ad dollars. Very few men will ever be in a position to select a ladies' shampoo brand. The ad campaign's intended audience was clearly *female viewers*. Obviously, the interaction of attractiveness, sexual imagery, and advertising is more complex that some critics suggest.

Further evidence can be found in a content analysis of the advertising pages in *Ms.* magazine. Founded in 1972 by feminist activists, *Ms.* initially promulgated a strict advertising policy designed to combat sex-based stereotyping and harmful marketing messages: "Obviously, *Ms.* won't solicit or accept ads, whatever the product they're presenting, that are down-right insulting to women. Nor will we accept product categories that might be harmful." But a 1990 study found that during *Ms.* magazine's first fifteen years, ads for cigarettes and alcohol comprised nearly a third of the products advertised. More to the point, the share of depictions of women in *Ms.* ads that were considered "alluring" rose significantly over time. By the end of the period, nearly 40 percent of women in ads were depicted as "sex objects" in a magazine founded by feminists in part to counter precisely such content in other magazines.[31] While some might chalk up the trend to hypocrisy, that would miss the more important point: during the 1970s and 1980s, the magazine found itself competing with a growing number of other publications aimed at women, distinguishing themselves from older women's magazines by mixing substantive and sometimes even politically or ideologically charged journalism with advertising that often contained images of attractive or alluring women. *Ms.* appears to have reacted to the competition. As male readership in this sector is miniscule, it is likely that most female readers do not react to advertising imagery in the visceral way asserted by some of its most vociferous critics. After a change of ownership, *Ms.* magazine decided in 1989 not to accept advertising of any kind. After years of operation as a subscription-only publication, however, *Ms.* resumed accepting advertising in 2002.

But to suggest that complaints about sex in advertising are sometimes simplistic or overblown is not to dismiss the issue as unworthy of concern. Most advertising messages are not sexually charged, yes, but in the course of a given hour of magazine reading or a given night of broadcast television, one certainly will see or hear a number of such messages. Moreover, they are clearly getting raunchier. A study comparing the magazine ads of 1964 with those of 1984, for example, found that while the share containing sexual content changed little, the 1964 ads relied more on verbal innuendo and wordplay and far less on lewd visuals. By 1984, the focus had shifted toward more risqué messages and situations, making use of partially clothed or nude models, mostly women.[32] Since the 1980s, the use of such imagery has surged, particularly in magazines and catalogs aimed at young consumers. The retail chain Abercrombie and Fitch generated a firestorm of controversy with its series of "catalogs" featuring young, attractive models in lewd poses and simulating sex acts—and noticeably wearing little clothing, despite the fact that the goal was presumably to sell Abercrombie and Fitch fashions.[33] On tv, standards have changed in recent years, as well. Reichert pointed out that as late as 1995, CBS refused during prime time to air a commercial for Victoria's Secret in which model Claudia Schiffer danced "seductively" dressed only in underwear. But within a few years, Victoria's Secret ads featuring scantily clad models were commonplace on broadcast tv, as were far more explicitly sexual ads starring the likes of Alyssa Milano and Britney Spears.[34] In 2004, for example, the fast-food chain Hardee's unveiled a series of new tv spots in which attractive women, purportedly to call attention to the size of a new hamburger, stuffed a bundle of straws or a fist into their mouths in what is, even viewed in context, obviously an image designed to resemble pornography.[35] Also that year, a spot for Sirius Satellite Radio showed Pamela Anderson in a wet tank top buffing a car with her body.[36]

One does not have to be a prude to recognize the deleterious consequences of these cultural trends. Sexual identity and relationships are at the core of the human experience, but true romance and sexual allure often derive from what is hidden or implicit, not what is revealed and explicit. To dwell in a media world saturated with lewd images and sexual suggestiveness is ultimately to demystify and devalue the sexual relationship. Contrary to the impression that many young people may get from movies, television, music, or the fleeting images they see in youth-oriented magazines, catalogs, and websites, monogamous Americans typically report far more satisfaction in their sex lives than singles whose sexual behavior is serial or promiscuous.[37] But for many young people dealing with typically adolescent struggles to define themselves in relationship to their peers and parents, media cues inform their judgment of what is "normal" and what kinds of values and behaviors will help them become mature, fulfilled adults. Surveys show that frequent viewers of sexually explicit programming, both youth and adults, are more likely than others to overestimate the extent of infidelity and teen sex. Not surprisingly, there are also survey data to show that such viewers are more likely to engage in premarital, extramarital, or promiscuous sex.[38]

One should not draw a straight-line conclusion about causality here: it is reasonable to assume that individuals who are already sexually active, or predisposed to be for other reasons, are also more likely to be frequent consumers of sexually explicit programming, including pornography. On the other hand, it strains credulity to suggest, as some do, that consuming media awash in sex has no effect on individual attitudes and behaviors. It is not going out too far on a moralistic limb to worry that frequent exposure to explicit sexual imagery—by its very nature depicting little in the way of contraceptive precautions or long-term social and psychological consequences—is bad for these audiences and, in turn, bad for others in society who care about them or must pay the financial and fiscal costs associated with unwise decisions about sex.

The question remains: what should be done about it? As is the case with cigarettes and alcohol, there is actually little stomach for sweeping government prohibitions against sex in the media, whether in the short form of advertising or in the long form of movies, magazines, music, or websites. "Prudence, as well as a decent respect for the in-decent desires of mankind, compels us to accept that the fight against pornography was lost long ago—when Adam fell, and the printing press was invented," wrote Maggie Gallagher, a prominent culturally conservative author and commentator, in the pages of *National Review*. She argued that the goal "ought to be more modest: to find ways to prevent private vice from becoming the prevailing public standard of virtue."[39] I might add that there is nothing to be done about the fact that human beings often prefer to listen to or identify with attractive people, a phenomenon present not just in their media consumption but also in a host of other activities, including politics.

A more reasonable approach, then, is to see that images of physi-cal attractiveness and sexuality are not overused and, when employed, are placed in a context appropriate for the audience. As it happens, in the advertising arena at least the goal of decorum and the ethic of per-sonal responsibility are far more consistent with the business imper-ative to sell products than is commonly appreciated. Although social attitudes about sex have clearly become more permissive over time, and this appears related to depictions of sex in the media, most ad-vertising messages, including those aimed at young adults, are not overly or implicitly sexual. Why? Existing government regulation can-not explain it, since some print and broadcast ads do indeed contain such imagery without legal penalty. Nor can the prospect of future regulation be the major factor in play, though some advertising pro-fessionals worry that too much use of sex in their industry will pro-voke more stringent regulatory responses.[40] The real reason why sex is not more widespread in advertising is that its effectiveness is lim-ited. Simply put, sex sells *sometimes*—but when used too frequently, or too explicitly, it fails to market a brand successfully and can even se-riously damage it.

Advertisers are not just trying to get their audience's attention. They are trying to sell products, either by conveying specific and prac-tical information that consumers did not previously know (such as the availability of a product, how much it costs, and what it does) or by serving as a means by which consumers can identify themselves aes-thetically or psychologically with an emotion, experience, personality, or lifestyle they find congenial (which is my "selling the dream" thesis). Advertising fails at these tasks if consumers do not recall the brand being advertised—or, more ominously, recall it with disdain or disgust rather than fondness or affinity.

There is actually a large and growing body of research suggesting that sexual explicitness, while perhaps attention getting, interferes with effective advertising. One famous 1978 study found that male subjects demonstrated lower recall of brand names from ads showing a nude female model than from ads showing a landscape.[41] Since then, numerous studies have shown how explicit sexuality, especially semi-nude or nude images or those of sexual contact, distracts the intended audience and sometimes even repels consumers, who find the images in poor taste and do not want to identify with them by purchasing the advertised brand.[42] This latter, counterproductive effect appears to be stronger among women than men, but that hardly serves as much of an argument for "beefcake" advertising (featuring sexy men) over "cheesecake" advertising (featuring sexy women). A 1998 paper on the subject concluded that cheesecake boosted men's attitudes toward an ad but not their product recall, while it boosted women's product recall but also negative attitudes. Beefcake had little effect on either group. "Clearly, the nonsexy ads seemed to do the most good with the least harm," the authors wrote. "We found no evidence that attitude toward the brand is helped by a sexy model of either sex with audience members of either sex."[43] There is an important exception worth noting, however: sexiness in advertising does seem to be useful when the product being advertised is itself related to sexual identity or behavior. Using sexy models to promote cosmetics, perfumes, or lingerie allows consumers—again, mostly women—to visualize and to associate brands with their own lives. In general, however, advertising scholar Thomas Whipple has found that "using sex in advertising for a product which has no sexual overtones simple does not work."[44]

As explicit sexuality has become more commonplace in the mass media—in programs targeting both sexes, from adventure and action series to soap operas and daytime talk shows—it can be argued that advertising has been noticeably unwilling to move toward salacity at the same speed. That may reflect the different outcomes they are after. The media want to maximize eyeballs, a goal that may well be advanced with raciness. Advertisers want to maximize sales, which may not. Of course, since print and broadcast media remain dependent on advertisers, it is impossible to rigidly distinguish the interests and behaviors of the two sectors. Advertisers must feel comfortable associating their messages and brands not just with their own ads but also with the content surrounding them. Still, audiences generally understand the difference, allowing for programming to be raunchier than the advertising without those paying the bills raising much of a ruckus about it.

There have been some instances of advertisers or their customers pushing back against the tide of cultural indecency. For example, while sexuality has grown more explicit in consumer advertising, the opposite appears to have been going on within business-to-business advertising. The use of women as "decorative" elements in trade magazine advertising declined significantly during the 1970s and 1980s.[45] By 1993, reported the *Wall Street Journal*, there were about half as many sexy ads in certain trade magazines than there had been just five years before.[46] And after all, in the aforementioned case of Abercrombie and Fitch's soft-porn catalog pitched to young people, a grassroots consumer movement against the company's marketing practices, spearheaded by evangelical leaders such as Dr. James Dobson of Focus on the Family but growing to include a diverse array of individuals and groups, ultimately persuaded Abercrombie and Fitch to withdraw their notorious 2003 "Christmas Field Guide."[47]

Perhaps the most powerful tool that the public has to combat unwelcome, inappropriate, and immoral content—inside or outside the confines of advertising—is the ability to say no, sometimes loudly and forcefully, sometimes silently by a flick of a switch. In a previous age of few local radio and television stations and a relative handful of local or national print publications, audiences might have had good reason to fume about the unhealthful and meager offerings of a media oligopoly. But now, with access to hundreds of cable channels, a panoply of magazines covering every possible interest and niche, and the ability of the Internet to construct a personalized diet of news, information, and entertainment, those who are really motivated to act against the excesses and vulgarities of popular culture are equipped as never before to do so. Marketing is a process, a to-and-fro conversation among buyers and sellers. The best way to shape its ethics for the good, without resorting to costly or counterproductive policy interventions that apply clumsy categories to complex issues, is for advertising professionals and their customers to think critically and act ethically in their own decision making.

# CHAPTER 9

# Conclusion

As long as there has been advertising, there has been change in advertising. As we have seen, the modern marketing mix of the early twenty-first century is the result of an evolutionary process extending back in time not just decades but centuries. Yes, sometimes there have been periods akin to punctuated equilibrium—the introduction of new advertising media or techniques that were clearly noticeable at the time because of either the type or locale of change, such as the 1830s debut of the penny press in New York City or the arrival of national broadcast advertising in the late 1920s and early 1930s. But for every supposed "revolution" in advertising, one can often find an analogue in the past.

Consider a series of events during the 2001–2004 period illustrating what many perceived—and rightly so, for the most part—to be significant changes in the way goods and services were being marketed to consumers in America and around the world:

- In 2003, DaimlerChrysler hired a firm to design a computer game based around its Wrangler Rubicon. The resulting Jeep 4x4: Trail of Life game cost little to produce and was distributed for free on the company's website. Within six months, a quarter of a million people had downloaded the game, providing contact information to the company in exchange and thus helping to build a large database for direct marketing. Other companies began to pay for product placement in popular racing and adventure games.[1]

• Worried that its traditional advertising on television was losing its effectiveness, thanks to a splintering media marketplace and declining viewership of network tv among teens, Coca-Cola began in 2003 to experiment with "experiential" advertising in venues such as red-themed Coca-Cola "teen lounges" located in shopping centers and full of music, movies, videos, and Internet connections. The concept was a tie-in with Coke's prominent ad placement on the top-rated show *American Idol*, which featured a green room for contestants that was actually called the Coke Red Room.[2] Campbell Soup came up with its own twist on the idea: "Soup Sanctuaries" that lure shoppers in with the promise of a comfortable chair and comfort food, as in free soup.[3]

• The American Family Life Assurance Co., or Aflac, saw its "consumer awareness" rating in polls soar to 90 percent in 2004, up from 12 percent in 2001, with a contemporaneous 20 percent increase in its workplace insurance product. What was the company's marketing secret? A series of clever but relatively inexpensive tv ads established its quirky duck character, which quacked "Aflac." The company then followed up with widespread distribution of T-shirts and toys bearing the duck's likeness. Noticing that actor Ben Affleck had joked in public about how his name sounded like the company's, Aflac reps encouraged host Jay Leno to bring up the subject when Affleck visited NBC's *The Tonight Show*, and later sent stuffed Aflac ducks to the *Live with Regis and Kelly* show when Affleck was scheduled to be a guest host. Tv spots perpetuated the gag by pairing the duck character with other celebrities, such as Wayne Newton and Chevy Chase. One marketing consultant told the *Wall Street Journal* that "without [Aflac's] guerilla PR campaign, the advertising campaign wouldn't have been as effective."[4]

• General Motors scored a major marketing coup in 2004 when it arranged for Oprah Winfrey to give away 276 new Pontiac G6 cars on her popular daytime talk show. "This car is so cool!" Winfrey gushed on the program. "It has one of the most powerful engines on the road. And XM satellite radio!"[5]

- In 1999, fast-food giant McDonald's spent two-thirds of its U.S. marketing budget on television ads. By 2004, the proportion had fallen to one-third as the company segmented and extended its marketing budget to include alternatives such as women's magazines, Internet search engines, Spanish-language sports programming, and a special magazine distributed in black barber shops. "We are a big marketer," said a McDonald's executive, but "we are not a mass marketer." Other longtime advertisers such as Procter & Gamble and Unilever also boasted new marketing strategies designed to take advantage of new technologies to identify and satisfy the demands of ever-smaller segments of consumers. In 2003, the pharmaceutical company Pfizer launched for the first time a new drug, a headache treatment, without any television advertising. It used radio, magazines, and the Internet to target young mothers suffering from migraines.[6]
- While major retailers retain top-flight talent agencies in Hollywood to plant their brands in popular movies and television shows, some companies go beyond just product placement to full-fledged mini-productions. Revlon began airing short films during the previews at movie theaters. American Express produced a series of brief buddy movies featuring Jerry Seinfeld and Superman that were teased on tv but aired in their entirety on its website.[7]
- A similar trend became evident in the print media. Toyota hired the advertising agency Saatchi and Saatchi to develop a youth-oriented comic book, *Fuel*, depicting a race between hero Max, driving a Celica GT-S, and antagonist Slam, driving an unidentified car. Meanwhile, articles in consumer magazines seem increasingly to mention brand names of products unrelated to the subject of the piece, leading some media analysts to assume either explicit or implicit product placement. And retailers such as Bloomingdale's begun publication of their own glossy magazines that, in style and content, were virtually indistinguishable from other general interest magazines except for the more narrow range of ads.[8]
- As daytime soap operas have seen their ratings decline in recent years, networks have sought to supplement advertising revenue with more aggressive product placement. The stars of ABC's *All My Children* swigged lots of Florida orange juice. On the NBC soap *Days of Our Lives*, the breakfast product of choice was Frosted Flakes. And

on *The Young and the Restless*, two young lovers got trapped in a snowstorm but decided to wait a bit before pushing the car's OnStar button for help—since the service was so efficient that it promised to cut short their make-out time.[9]

- A summer replacement series for ABC, *The Days*, was cocreated by an advertising agency representing two clients, Unilever and Sears. The rationale advanced was not primarily product placement, though the show may contain advertised brands in the future, but rather a more equitable sharing of costs and revenues.[10]
- In July 2004, a beautiful model strode back and forth along the line of moviegoers waiting to buy tickets at a Boston cinema. She was wearing a flat television screen on her T-shirt that showed trailers for the upcoming science fiction thriller *I, Robot*. "When a beautiful girl walks up to you, and she's wearing the tv commercial on her chest, you just can't get away from it," said the young marketing impresario behind the new promotion.[11] In related developments, a Nebraska man auctioned off his forehead, and a pregnant Florida woman her belly, as space for temporary, tattooed advertising.[12]

What these stories have in common is not just evidence of the influence on marketing of new technologies, media habits, and databases of consumer information. They also reflect seemingly new applications of what turn out to be rather old marketing ideas. Product placement, for example, can be found in ancient times (in the guise of writers paid to promote products in their dramas or poems) as well as in the earliest commercial broadcasting. Recall Jack Benny's shameless and comical plugging of Jell-O on his radio show and the not-at-all-subtle references during 1930s daytime dramas to sponsors such as flour manufacturers and soap flakes.

As for so-called guerilla marketing campaigns using word of mouth, publicity stunts, celebrities, toys, or attractive models to promote brands, such practices date back at least to Edward Bernays's employment of young women to promote cigarette brands in the 1920s and the extensive merchandising of characters such as Mickey Mouse and Superman during the 1930s, and perhaps even earlier to the days of small-town carnivals and medicine shows. Far from being unprecedented, promotional ideas such as companies publishing their own magazines, planting brand names in news stories, or engaging in "experiential marketing" via welcoming public spaces are familiar to students of business history. Big retailers such as John Wanamaker virtually invented many of them during the latter decades of the nineteenth century with their massive department stores and publicity departments. And, of course, to the extent that advertisers and their agents become heavily involved in the generation of television, movies, radio formats, and other entertainment, that represents only the rediscovery of a business model that was the standard for media production for decades before the television networks finally decided to take control of their own content in the late 1950s.

I am not saying that there is "nothing new under the sun" in marketing. Obviously, the technological developments of the past few years have profound implications for how we will buy and sell things to each other in the future. Just the splintering of the television audience by cable and satellite service, made possible by decades-old technology, has led to substantial changes in the marketing mix. A *Wall Street Journal* analysis showed that from 1996 to 2004, the average number of hours of broadcast tv that Americans watched each week dropped by 21 percent. Recorded music also claimed significantly fewer hours of attention, while print media usage was level or slightly declining. Meanwhile, cable and satellite tv soared from eleven hours of viewing in 1996 to nearly nineteen in 2004, with radio also headed upwards (another back-to-the-future trend?) and the Internet and video games rising from very low levels to rival newspapers and books in their claim on the American attention span. Not surprisingly, there have been a great many attempts to integrate paid advertising into the new forms, including product placements in video games, paid-for search results on Google and Yahoo, and ads sent by text message to cell phones.[13] Some of the experiments have shown early promise. Others have bombed. Again, though, that is no different from the multitude of publications, gimmicks, and campaigns that advertisers tried and discarded during the post–Civil War boom, the early twentieth century, the dawn of television, and so on.

If change is a constant in advertising, there is something else that is constant, too. Just as in past periods of punctuated evolution in advertising, the new mass customization movement has its vociferous and embittered critics. "It's across the culture," said left-wing media critic Peter Hart, complaining in 2004 about the blurring of lines between media content and advertising. "You're seeing these tendencies everywhere, whether it's product placement on a sitcom or in the news." Such practices amount to "pulling one on the readers," he added, whatever the fashionable term may be.[14] Gary Ruskin of Commercial Alert reacted angrily in early 2005 when the Federal Trade Commission rejected his organization's demand for a federal investigation into product placement. "The FTC has basically endorsed this epidemic," Ruskin fumed, calling on Congress to requiring copious disclosure of the practice for movies, tv, video games, and books.[15] Paid product placements in motion pictures are particularly objectionable, other critics say, because ads inherently subvert works of art.[16] Also like before, some of the fretful are advertising and marketing professionals themselves, who fear the disruption of cozy business arrangements and struggle to see what will replace what is lost. The proliferation of DVR technology, such as TiVo, that makes it easier for tv viewers to zap through the commercial breaks "has the potential to blow apart the entire network business model," said one former network chairman.[17] Perhaps. But another possibility is that the resulting pressure will force advertisers to become more creative in making their advertising engaging, informative, and entertaining— while the personalized data stored by the DVR devices will allow future messages, including produce placements, to be targeted more effectively to get a better bang for the marketing buck.

As we have seen, many longstanding concerns about advertising stem from longstanding myths and misunderstandings. Ads are tools for enhancing competition and innovation, not propping up stodgy monopolies. Having a wide variety of such tools allows firms to be more effective competitors and innovators, an effect already being demonstrated by the rising productivity of marketing expenditures in the new era of mass customization. At the same time, ads generally reduce prices rather than increase them. The proliferation of advertising platforms and the rediscovery of techniques such as product placement have coincided with one of the longest periods of low inflation in modern history, with real prices (dollars per unit of consumer value) actually dropping substantially for many goods and services such as automobiles, clothes, and electronic equipment.

As for concerns about the reintegration of advertising and entertainment content, whether it occurs within the production process or as brands inserted into the work, there is surprisingly little evidence that most American consumers detest the practice the way their self-appointed guardians do. As previously discussed, during the heyday of product placement on radio in the 1930s, audiences did not necessarily see the practice as manipulative or deceptive. In some cases, they clearly stated a preference *for* product placement over formal advertising spots that, in their minds, interfered with the flow of the story. More recently, a 1993 survey found that only a small minority of young adults objected to product placement on ethical grounds.[18] Consumers can and do insist on boundaries, however, as demonstrated by the abortive attempt to promote the film *Spider-Man 2* by putting a Spider-Man web logo on Major League Baseball bases. Only twenty-four hours after the idea was floated, massive public opposition led the league to disown the idea.[19] It is hard to imagine how best to find the right balance other than through trial and error.

Does advertising make us materialistic and take away our freedom to choice? Such arguments typically oversimplify the issues involved. The formation of personal values and of preferences are both complex processes, reflecting often-subtle interactions over a long period of time with family, friends, professional colleagues, social institutions, the media, and other influences. Certainly it is reasonable to conclude that advertising is one of those factors helping shape what we are interested in, and how much. But it is overstating the case to say that advertising or the media as a whole *determine* these values and preferences, or subvert our freedom to do so. A major study comparing television viewing and survey measurements of materialism, for example, found the link to be "tenuous at best," with the likelihood being that those who for other reasons tended toward acquisitiveness or materialistic values also tended to be more interested in consuming advertiser-driven mass media.[20] Similarly, while advertising obviously enables people to form demand for things they would not otherwise have wanted or even know about, that dynamic is consistent with sovereignty and freedom of choice, not in conflict with them. In 1964, Dr. George Katona of the University of Michigan's Survey Research Center used the example of air conditioning to explain why the notion of "artificially created wants" as articulated by the likes of John Kenneth Galbraith did not comport with reality. While air conditioners had been installed in movie theaters, offices, and other large buildings in the years following World War II, most Americans expressed little or no interest in purchasing air conditioners for their homes—even though many of them spent their summers sweltering in the heat and humidity. Only after the industry began to market the attractiveness of air conditioners to homebuilders and directly to consumers did the amenity come to be demanded with increasing eagerness in the 1950s and 1960s. "Shall it then be said that room air conditioners did not fill a real need or want when they were finally produced and sold by advertising?" Katona asked.[21] The issue becomes clearer still if one remembers that unlike air conditioners, most consumer products are not profitable if purchased seldom or just once. Consumers must repurchase, which means that they presumably must find advertised products to be useful in some way, either in a utilitarian sense or in an aesthetic or aspirational one.

Yes, there certainly remain difficult ethical and moral issues to sort out in situations where enthusiastic commercial behavior intersects with law, family life, the innocence of children, and the temptation to overindulge or embrace self-destructive behaviors. But these conflicts exist because life is complicated, because we must simultaneously carry out distinct roles that reflect the commercial, the charitable, the social, and the moral sides of our personality. These conflicts do not exist because of words and images, and they would not go away if the words and images did. Some products would still disappoint us, and some people would still disappoint us in how they used or abused what they bought.

The greatest fallacy of all to be found in the anti-advertising critique is the notion that much of what we read, hear, and see in our commercial culture has no real value because it fails to convey strictly utilitarian information. This fallacy reflects a poor understanding of what makes information useful (its value is subjective and situational, not objective and transcendent) and applies an interpretative standard to commercial communication that few would think to apply to other ways that humans use symbols to convey meaning—or even to discover it. The more advertising seeks to connect the brand names of tangible products to the intangible, the aesthetic, the social, and the individual, the more it accomplishes its underappreciated role of helping us infuse meaning and aspiration into what would otherwise be little more than the rote acquisition of basic necessities and the pointless accumulation of objects. Those who resent this use of advertising and call it irrational, immoral, wasteful, or pathetic must, in the end, apply the same adjectives to human nature as a whole. There is absolutely no evidence that human cultures have ever thrived without buying and selling, and without the choosy shopping and showy salesmanship that necessarily follow. That leaves such critics with either of two unattractive prospects, it seems to me: they must either set themselves up as superior arbiters of how the rest of us should trade with each other, suggesting that they alone have escaped the surly bonds of human nature that keep the rest of us chained to our couches and charge cards; or they must abandon all hope that commerce can make life at least a bit safer and healthier, its daily routines a bit less predictable and more enjoyable, and its inevitable drudgeries and tragedies a bit more bearable.

One recommendation comes to mind for these curmudgeons: have a Coke and a smile.

# Notes

## INTRODUCTION

1. *Crazy People* (Paramount Studios, 1990).

2. For example, see Jack Hough, "Slogan's Heroes," SmartMoney. com, May 26, 2004, www.smartmoney.com/stockscreen/index.cfm?story= 20040526intro&nav=RSS091; and the Motley Fool investment website, August 10, 2000, www.fool.com/news/foolplate/2000/foolplate000810.htm.

3. Vincent Canby, "Dudley Moore Acts Up in Tony Bill's 'Crazy People,'" *New York Times*, April 11, 1990, p. C16.

4. Maurice Babbis, "Tony Bill Talks about Crazy People," *Latent Image: A Student Journal of Film Criticism*, Emerson College, May 1990, http://pages.emerson.edu/organizations/fas/latent_image/issues/1990-05/crazy.htm.

5. Quotes collected in an online archive by Jef I. Richards, "Advertising Quotes," http://advertising.utexas.edu/research/quotes/Q100.html.

6. Ibid.

7. Ibid.

8. As described on the official website of Fox Home Entertainment, www.foxhome.com/capsule/rockhunt.htm.

9. Stephen Fox, *The Mirror Makers: A History of American Advertising and Its Creators* (New York: William Morrow, 1984), p. 206.

10. Quoted in Lori A. Strauss, "The Anti-Advertising Bias in Twentieth-Century Literature," *Journal of American Culture* 16, no. 1 (Spring 1993): pp. 81–85.

11. Quoted in "Advertising (The Last Word)," *Journal of Business Strategy* 23, no. 4 (July–August 2002): p. 48.

12. Ralph Glasser, *The New High Priesthood: The Social, Ethical, and Political Implications of a Marketing-Orientated Society* (London: Macmillan & Co., 1967), p. 4.

# CHAPTER 1

1. Frank Presbey, *The History and Development of Advertising* (New York: Doubleday, 1929), pp. 4–5.

2. Depicted in "Asiatic Traders in Egypt," in "An Introduction to the History and Culture of Pharaonic Egypt," http://nefertiti.iwebland.com/trade/asiatic_traders.htm.

3. There is more discussion of the history of the trade sign in British Inn Sign Society, "History of the Signboard," www.bjcurtis.force9.co.uk/html/history_of_signs.html.

4. John Rokicki, "Advertising in the Roman Empire," *Whole Earth Review* (Spring 1987): p. 84.

5. Raymond Serafin, "Flourishing Roman Ad Biz Found," *Advertising Age*, June 16, 1986, p. 1.

6. Rokicki, p. 85.

7. Presbey, p. 7.

8. Ibid.

9. Ibid., pp. 11–12.

10. Serafin, p. 93.

11. Jennifer Rooks, "Ancient Pitches," *Archaeology* (March/April 1991): p. 72.

12. Presbey, p. 5.

13. "Acta Diurna," *Columbia Encyclopedia*, 6th ed. (New York: Columbia University Press, 2001).

14. See www.printersmark.com/Pages/Hist1.html for more information.

15. "Newspaper," *Encyclopedia Britannica*, 1998, www.lian.com/TANAKA/comhosei/NPinEB.htm.

16. Ibid.

17. Ibid.

18. Christina Mierau, *Accept No Substitutes: The History of American Advertising* (Minneapolis, MN: Lerner Publications Company, 2000), p. 7.

19. "Advertising," *Microsoft's Encarta Online Encyclopedia*, 1997–2005, http://encarta.msn.com/encyclopedia_761564279_3____21/Advertising.html #s21.

20. Mierau, p. 9.

21. Ibid., pp. 12–13.

22. Ibid., p. 13.

23. Ted Curtis Smythe, "The Diffusion of the Urban Daily, 1850–1990," *Journalism History* 28, no. 2 (Summer 2002): pp. 73–85.

24. Thomas O'Guinn, Chris T. Allen, and Richard J. Semenik, *Advertising* (Cincinnati, OH: South-Western College Publishing, 1998), p. 60.

25. "The Advertising Century," *Advertising Age*, http://adage.com/century/timeline/index.html.

26. Mierau, p. 38.

27. James Twitchell, *Adcult USA: The Triumph of Advertising in American Culture* (New York: Columbia University Press, 1996), pp. 78–79.

28. Mierau, p. 47.

29. Leigh Eric Schmidt, "The Commercialization of the Calendar: American Holidays and the Culture of Consumption, 1870–1930," *Journal of American History* (December 1991): p. 898.

30. James West Davidson and Mark H. Lytle, *The United States: A History of the Republic* (Englewood Cliffs, NJ: Prentice-Hall, 1986), p. 218.

31. U.S. Census Bureau, "Historical Census of Housing Tables: Home-ownership," January 6, 2000, www.census.gov/hhes/www/housing/census/historic/owner.html.

32. Larry Schweikart, *The Entrepreneurial Adventure: A History of Business in the United States* (Ft. Worth, TX: Harcourt College Publishers, 2000), pp. 292–294.

33. Ken W. Parker, "Sign Consumption in the 19th-Century Department Store: An Examination of Visual Merchandising in the Grand Emporiums (1846–1900)," *Journal of Sociology* 39, no. 4 (December 2003): pp. 355–356.

34. Ronald A. Fullerton, "Art of Public Relations: U.S. Department Stores, 1876–1923," *Public Relations Review* 16, no. 3 (Fall 1990): pp. 69–70.

35. Parker, pp. 357–358.

36. Presbey, pp. 303–307.

37. Fullerton, pp. 72–74.

38. Ibid., pp. 76–77.

39. Karen Talaski, "Montgomery Ward Closes after 128 Years," *Detroit News*, December 29, 2000.

40. Lori Liggett, "The Founders of Sears, Roebuck & Company,"

American Culture Studies, Bowling Green State University, www.bgsu.edu/departments/acs/1890s/sears/sears.html.

41. Beth Martens, "Sears, Roebuck and Co. and Its Effect on Retailing in America," *Illinois History* (April 2000): pp. 52–53, www.lib.niu.edu/ipo/ihy000452.html.

42. Twitchell, p. 71.

43. Quoted in Tom McNichol, "Can Minor Strike Gold?" Salon.com, 1998, http://archive.salon.com/21st/feature/1998/03/cov_13feature.html.

44. "History of Curtis Publishing Company," www.scripophily.net/curpubcom.html.

45. "History of *Scribner's*," www.spartacus.schoolnet.co.uk/USAscribners.htm.

46. Twitchell, p. 80.

47. Ibid., p. 73.

48. William G. Gabler, "The Evolution of American Advertising in the Nineteenth Century," *Journal of Popular Culture* 2 (Spring 1978): p. 767.

49. Computed from *Historical Statistics of the United States, Colonial Times to 1970*, bicentennial ed., (Washington, DC: U.S. Census Bureau, 1975), table R 244–257, p. 810.

50. Thomas L. Powers, William K. Koehler, and Warren S. Martin, "Selling from 1900 to 1949: A Historical Perspective," *Journal of Personal Selling & Sales Management* 8 (November 1988): pp. 12–13.

51. Margaret Moore, "Salesmen of the Past," *Contemporary Review* 268, no. 1563 (April 1996): p. 205.

52. Walter A. Friedman, "John H. Patterson and the Sales Strategy of the National Cash Register Company, 1884 to 1922," *Business History Review* 72, no. 4 (Winter 1998): pp. 552–555.

53. "State Expenditures by Function," in Scott Moody, ed., *Facts and Figures on Government Finance*, 3rd ed. (Washington, DC: Tax Foundation, 1999), p. 164.

54. Tamaski.

55. Ronald A. Fullerton, "How Modern Is Modern Marketing? Marketing's Evolution and the Myth of the 'Production Era,'" *Journal of Marketing* 52 (January 1988): pp. 118–120.

56. Gerben Bakker, "Building Knowledge about the Consumer: The Emergence of Market Research in the Motion Picture Industry," *Business History* 45, no. 1 (January 2003): p. 101.

57. Jack Honomichl, "The Man Who Built Market Research," *Advertising Age*, August 20, 1987, pp. 117–118.

58. Raymond Serafin, "A 100-Year Ride Fulfills Advertising's Destiny," *Advertising Age*, January 8, 1996, pp. S1–2.

59. "100 Years of Auto Ads: Gallery 1896–1920," *Advertising Age*, January 8, 1996, pp. S6–7.

60. David Wells, "The Great Innovators: Reinventing the Company," *Business Week*, March 22, 2004, p. 24; see also Serafin, p. S3.

# CHAPTER 2

1. Quoted in Jackson Lears, *Fables of Abundance: A Cultural History of Advertising in America* (New York: Basic Books, 1994), p. 208.

2. Gib Prettyman, "Advertising, Utopia, and Commercial Idealism: The Case of King Gillette," *Prospects* 24 (1999): p. 241.

3. J. Mansfield, "The Razor King," *American Heritage of Invention and Technology* (Spring 1992): pp. 40–46.

4. Paul Lukas, "Gillette: Blade Runner," *Fortune*, April 18, 2003, www.fortune.com/fortune/print/0,15935,433734,00.html.

5. Prettyman, p. 242.

6. Ibid.

7. Ibid., p. 243.

8. Lukas.

9. King Camp Gillette, *The Human Drift* (Boston: New Era Publishing Co., 1894; reprint, Delmar, NY: Scholars' Facsimiles and Reprints, 1976), p. 112.

10. Prettyman, p. 239.

11. Quoted in Michael Prewitt, "The True Worldliness of Advertising: Apologia pro Vita Mea," *Theology Today* 60 (2003): pp. 387–388.

12. Jeremy Benstein, "Advertising and the Tenth Commandment," *The Jerusalem Report*, August 13, 2001.

13. Quoted in David Weissbard, "Coveting," Unitarian Universalist Church, April 27, 1997, p. 2. This is a published sermon, http://members. aol.com/uurockford/S96-18.htm.

14. As discussed favorably in Brian Rosner, *How to Really Get Rich: A Sharp Look at the Religion of Greed* (Leicester, UK: IVP, 1999).

15. Martin Noth, *Exodus: A Commentary* (Philadelphia: Westminster Press, 1962), pp. 152–153.

16. This is the English translation used in several modern versions. The King James Version is, on this point, remarkably similar: "Defraud not."

17. Quoted in Weissbard.

18. Edmund A. Opitz, "Humane Values and the Free Economy," in *Religion: The Foundation of a Free Society* (Irvington-on-Hudson, NY: Foundation for Economic Education, 1994), pp. 198–199.

19. *Catechism of the Catholic Church*, 2nd ed., "Part Three: Life in Christ, Section Two: The Ten Commandments," Saint Charles Borromeo Catholic Church website, www.scborromeo.org/ccc/p3s2c2a0.htm.

20. Robert B. Ekelund, Jr., and Robert F. Hebert, *A History of Economic Theory and Method*, 4th ed. (New York: McGraw-Hill, 1997), pp. 14–20.

21. St. Augustine, *The City of God*, ch. 16, trans. Rev. Marcus Dods, posted online by Calvin College, www.ccel.org/ccel/schaff/npnf102.iv.XI.16.html.

22. Quoted in Ekelund and Hebert, p. 22.

23. Ibid., p. 26.

24. Thomas Aquinas, *Summa Theologica: Selected Questions on Law and Justice*, trans. Fathers of the English Dominican Province (New York: Benziger Brothers, 1947), www.lonang.com/exlibris/aquinas/sum22077.htm.

25. John Moser, "The Origins of the Austrian School of Economics," *Humane Studies Review* 11, no. 1 (Spring 1997): www.gmu.edu/departments/ihs/hsr/s97hsr.html#austrian.

26. Michael Barton, "The Victorian Jeremiad: Critics of Accumulation and Display," in Simon J. Bronner, ed., *Consuming Visions: Accumulation and Display of Goods in America 1880–1920* (New York: Norton, 1989), pp. 61–62.

27. Susan J. Matt, "Children's Envy and the Emergence of the Modern Consumer Ethic, 1890–1930," *Journal of Social History* 36, no. 2 (Winter 2002): p. 283.

28. Matt, *Keeping Up with the Joneses: Envy in American Consumer Society 1890–1930* (Philadelphia: University of Pennsylvania Press, 2003), p. 8.

29. Daniel Pope, "The Morality of Spending: Attitudes toward the Consumer Society in America, 1875–1940" (book review), *Business History Review* 60 (Winter 1986): p. 667.

30. Arthur Hugh Clough, "The Latest Decalogue," in *The Poems of Arthur Hugh Clough* (London: A.L.P. Norrington, 1968), pp. 60–61.

31. "Advertising (The Last Word)," *Journal of Business Strategy* 23, no. 4 (July–August 2002): p. 48.

32. Quoted in Lears, p. 359.

33. Ibid., p. 89.

34. Larry Schweikart, *The Entrepreneurial Adventure: A History of Business in the United States* (Fort Worth, TX: Harcourt College Publishers, 2000), p. 262.

35. Lears, p. 267.

36. Israel M. Kirzner, "The Ugly Market," in Mark W. Hendrickson, ed., *The Morality of Capitalism* (Irvington-on-Hudson, NY: Foundation for Economic Education, 1992), p. 104.

37. Matt, p. 9.

38. Michael Schudson, "Delectable Materialism: Second Thoughts on Consumer Culture," in David A. Crocker and Toby Linden, eds., *Ethics of Consumption: The Good Life, Justice, and Global Stewardship* (Lanham, MD: Rowman & Littlefield, 1997), pp. 345–351.

39. Adam Smith, *The Wealth of Nations*, ed. Edwin Cannan (1776; reprint, New York: Modern Library, 1937), p. 28.

40. Ekelund and Hebert, p. 238.

41. Robert B. Ekelund, Jr., and David S. Saurman, *Advertising and the Market Process* (San Francisco: Pacific Research Institute, 1988), p. 9.

42. Alfred Marshall, *Industry and Trade* (London: MacMillan, 1920), p. 304. Quoted in John Calfee, *Fear of Persuasion: A New Perspective on Advertising and Regulation* (Monnaz, Switzerland: Agora, 1997), p. 5.

43. Quoted in Robert B. Ekelund, Jr., and David S. Saurman, *Advertising and the Market Process* (San Francisco: Pacific Research Institute for Public Policy, 1988), p. 19.

44. Arthur C. Pigou, *The Economics of Welfare* (London: MacMillan, 1920), pt. 2, ch. 21.

45. Thomas C. O'Guinn, Chris T. Allen, and Richard J. Semenik, *Advertising* (Cincinnati, OH: South-Western College Publishing, 1998), p. 63.

46. Ekelund and Hebert, pp. 409–410.

47. Thorstein Veblen, "Why Economics Is Not an Evolutionary Science," *Quarterly Journal of Economics* 12, no. 2 (1898): http://socserv2.mcmaster.ca/~econ/ugcm/3ll3/veblen/econevol.txt.

48. Veblen, *The Theory of the Leisure Class* (New York: Macmillan Company, 1899), pp. 99–100.

49. Veblen, *The Theory of Business Enterprise* (New York: Charles Scribner's Sons, 1904), p. 58.

50. Ibid., pp. 60–61.

51. Lears, p. 240.

52. Daniel Pope, "Advertising as a Consumer Issue: An Historical View," *Journal of Social Issues* 47, no. 1 (1991): p. 47.

# CHAPTER 3

1. Computed from the following sources: advertising expenditures, *Historial Statistics of the United States, Colonial Times to 1970*, bicentennial ed. (Washington, DC: U.S. Census Bureau, 1975), table T 444–471, pp. 855–856, inflation estimates, Eva E. Jacobs, *Handbook of Labor Statistics* (Lanthan, MD: Bernan Associates, 2004), pp. 451–452; and population, U.S. Census Bureau, www.census.gov/population/www/censusdata/hiscendata.html.

2. Ibid.

3. James B. Twitchell, *Adcult USA* (New York: Columbia University Press, 1996), pp. 82–83.

4. Thomas White, *United States Early Radio History*, 2004, http://earlyra diohistory.us/ATTmemos.htm.

5. Ibid., http://earlyradiohistory.us/sec019.htm.

6. From Bulova's official corporate history, www.bulova.com/about/his tory.aspx.

7. Cynthia Blair, "It Happened in New York: First TV Commercial Broadcast from NYC," *Newsday*, July 1, 2004.

8. Frank Presbey, *The History and Development of Advertising* (New York: Doubleday, 1929), p. 579.

9. Raymond Serafin, "A 100-Year Ride Fulfills Advertising's Destiny," *Advertising Age*, January 8, 1996, p. S3.

10. An example would be Evan Morris, author of the syndicated "Word Detective" newspaper column, www.word-detective.com/back-r.html#doozy.

11. John W. Spalding, "1928: Radio Becomes a Mass Advertising Medium," *Journal of Broadcasting* 8 (1964): pp. 31–42.

12. Twitchell, *Adcult USA*, pp. 85–87.

13. Roland Marchand, "The Golden Age of Advertising," *American Heritage* 36, no. 3 (April–May 1985): p. 79.

14. Marilyn Lavin, "Creating Consumers in the 1930s: Irna Phillips and the Radio Soap Opera," *Journal of Consumer Research* (June 1995): p. 75.

15. Ibid., p. 77.

16. More detail about Benny's Jell-O jokes can be found at the delight-ful website OldTimeRadio.com, www.old-time.com/commercials/jello_gets_ ribbing.html.

17. Computed from *Historical Statistics of the United States*, 1975, and Jacobs, 2004.

18. Stuart Chase, *The Tragedy of Waste* (New York: Macmillan Company, 1928), p. 112.

19. Daniel Pope, "Advertising as a Consumer Issue: An Historical View," *Journal of Social Issues* 47, no. 1 (1991): p. 45.

20. Carrie McLaren, "Selling Advertising: The Ad Industry's Battle against the Consumer Movement of the 1930s: An Interview with Inger Stole," *Stay Free*, May 2001, www.stayfreemagazine.org/archives/18/inger .html.

21. Wallace Janssen, "The Story of the Laws behind the Labels," pt. 2, FDACompliance.net, 2002, http://fdacompliance.net/free/overview/history 1a.htm.

22. Marvin Olasky, "The Development of Corporate Public Relations, 1850–1930," *Journalism Monographs* (1987): p. 9.

23. Ibid., p. 18.

24. Marvin Olasky, "Ivy Lee: Minimizing Competition through Public Relations," *Public Relations Quarterly* 32, no. 3 (Fall 1987): pp. 9–16.

25. Alan R. Raucher, "Public Relations in Business: A Business of Public Relations," *Public Relations Review* 16, no. 3 (Fall 1990): p. 24.

26. Elizabeth Fones-Wolf, "Creating a Favorable Business Climate: Corporations and Radio Broadcasting, 1934 to 1954," *Business History Review* 73, no. 2 (Summer 1999): p. 222.

27. Ibid., pp. 221–222.

28. Ibid., p. 222.

29. Lears, p. 243.

30. Thomas L. Powers, William F. Koehler, and Warren S. Martin, "Selling from 1900 to 1949: A Historical Perspective," *Journal of Personal Selling & Sales Management* 8 (November 1988): p. 17.

31. Fones-Wolf, p. 222.

32. Randall Rothenberg, "Advertising Sold the New Deal and World War II Patriotism," *Advertising Age*, March 29, 1999, p. C9.

33. Marchand, p. 89.

34. Pope, p. 46.

35. Lears, p. 249.

36. Harry Matthei, "Inventing the Commercial: The Imperium of Modern Television Advertising Was Born in Desperate Improvisation," *American Heritage* 48, no. 3 (May–June 1997): pp. 62–64.

37. Ibid., p. 66.

38. "Brand Stories: Timex," Emediaplan.com, 2002, www.emediaplan .com/admunch/Brands/timex.asp.

39. Serafin, p. S36.

40. Victor Kenyon, "Ever Vigilant to Present 'the Preferred Angle,'" *Advertising Age*, January 8, 1996, p. S22.

41. Christine Mierau, *Accept No Substitutes: The History of American Advertising* (Minneapolis, MN: Lerner Publications Company, 2000), p. 71.

42. Inger L. Stole, "The Kate Smith Hour and the Struggle for Control of Television Programming in the Early 1950s," *Historical Journal of Film, Radio, and Television* 20, no. 4 (2000): pp. 549–561.

43. Richard W. Pollay, "The Subsiding Sizzle: A Descriptive History of Print Advertising, 1900–1980," *Journal of Marketing* 49 (Summer 1985): pp. 24–37.

44. Lionel Kaufman, "Five-five Years in Print, from 'B.T.' to 'A.T.,'" *Marketing and Media Decisions* 21 (January 1986): pp. 48–54.

45. Mikkelson Barbara and David Mikkelson, "Subliminal Advertising," Snopes.com, August 18, 2002, www.snopes.com/business/hidden/popcorn .asp.

46. Vance Packard, *The Hidden Persuaders* (New York: Random House, 1957), p. 3.

47. "Hidden Persuasion?" ParaScope, 1999, www.parascope.com/articles/ 0397/sublim1.htm.

48. Mikkelson and Mikkelson.

49. Twitchell, pp. 115–116.

# CHAPTER 4

1. John Kenneth Galbraith, *The Affluent Society* (Cambridge, MA: Riverside Press, 1958), p. 159.

2. Ibid., pp. 152–155.

3. Quoted in Jackson Lears, *Fables of Abundance: A Cultural History of Advertising in America* (New York: Basic Books, 1994), pp. 255–256.

4. James S. Duesenberry, *Income, Saving, and the Theory of Consumer Behavior* (Cambridge, MA: Harvard University Press, 1949), p. 31.

5. S. A. Drakopoulos, "Keynes' Economic Thought and the Theory of Consumer Behavior," *Scottish Journal of Political Economy* 39 (August 1992): pp. 318–336.

6. Kyle Bagwell, *The Economics of Advertising* (Cheltenham, UK: Edward Elgar, 2001; updated by author March 2003), pp. 7–8, www.columbia.edu/ ~kwb8/papers.html.

7. Joan Robinson, *Economics of Imperfect Competition* (London: Macmillan and Company, 1933), p. 101.

8. Bagwell, pp. 11–12.

9. Harvey Leibenstein, "Bandwagon, Snob, and Veblen Effects in the Theory of Consumers' Demand," *Quarterly Journal of Economics* 44, no. 2 (1950): pp. 183–207.

10. Quoted in Bagwell, p. 14.

11. Milton Friedman, "Biographical Memoir: George J. Stigler," National Academy of Sciences, www.nap.edu/html/biomems/gstigler.html.

12. George J. Stigler, "The Economics of Information," *Journal of Political Economy* 69 ( June 1961): p. 213.

13. Ibid., 213–225.

14. Thomas C. O'Guinn, Chris T. Allen, and Richard J. Semenik, *Advertising* (Cincinnati, OH: South-Western College Publishing, 1998), p. 26.

15. Friedrich A. Hayek, "The Non Sequitur of the 'Dependence Effect,'" *Southern Economic Journal* 27 (April 1961): p. 347.

16. Bagwell, pp. 6–25.

17. Arnold Toynbee, *America and the World Revolution* (New York: Oxford University Press, 1966), pp. 144–145.

18. Virginia Postrel, *The Substance of Style* (New York: HarperCollins, 2003), p. 32.

19. Edward Maze, "Advertising and Market Power," *Advertising Quarterly*, no. 26 (Winter 1970–1971): p. 32.

20. Jules Backman, "Is Advertising Wasteful?" *Journal of Marketing* (January 1968): pp. 2–8.

21. Robert B. Ekelund, Jr., and David S. Saurman, *Advertising and the Market Process: A Modern Economic View* (San Francisco: Pacific Research Institute for Public Policy, 1988), pp. 113–124.

22. Bagwell, p. 83.

23. Phillip Nelson, "Advertising as Information," *Journal of Political Economy* 82 (1974): pp. 729–754.

24. Benjamin Klein and Keith B. Leffler, "The Role of Market Forces in Assuring Contractual Performance," *Journal of Political Economy* 89, no. 41 (1981): pp. 615–641.

25. Raymond Marquardt and Anthony F. McGann, "Does Advertising Communicate Product Quality to Consumers? Some Evidence from Consumer Reports," *Journal of Advertising* 4, no. 4 (1975): pp. 27–31.

26. Maxwell K. Hsu, Ali F. Darrat, Maosen Zhong, and Salah S. Abosedra, "Does Advertising Stimulate Sales or Mainly Deliver Signals? A Multivariate Analysis," *International Journal of Advertising* 21, no. 2 (2002): pp. 175–188.

27. Amna Kirmani, "Advertising Repetition as a Signal of Quality: If It's Advertised So Much, Something Must be Wrong," *Journal of Advertising* 26, no. 3 (Fall 1997): pp. 77–87.

28. Quoted in Ekelund and Saurman, pp. 82–93.

29. James Ferguson, "Advertising and Liquor," *Journal of Business* 40 (1967): pp. 414–434.

30. Richard Posner, "Advertising and Product Differentiation," in John S. Wright and John E. Mertes, eds., *Advertising's Role in Society* (St. Paul, MN: West Publishing, 1974), pp. 45–45.

31. Israel Kirzner, "Advertising in an Open-Ended Universe," foreword to Ekelund and Saurman, pp. xviii–xx.

32. Galbraith, "Economics and Advertising: Exercise in Denial," *Advertising Age*, November 9, 1988, p. 84.

33. Ian Brailsford, "Madison Avenue Puts on Its Best Hair Shirt: US Advertising & Its Social Critics," *International Journal of Advertising* 17, no. 3 (1998): p. 367.

34. Stanley E. Cohen, "'Protecting' Consumers: The Battle over Truth and Fairness in Advertising Led to Close Government Examination of Business," *Advertising Age*, March 29, 1999, p. C120.

35. Daniel Pope, "Advertising as a Consumer Issue: An Historical View," *Journal of Social Issues* 47, no. 1 (1991): p. 52.

36. John Calfee, *Fear of Persuasion: A New Perspective on Advertising and Regulation* (Monnaz, Switzerland: Agora Association), 1997, p. 12.

37. Ibid., p. 13.

38. Ibid., p. 18.

39. Cohen, p. C120.

40. John Philip Jones, "The Mismanagement of Advertising," *Harvard Business Review* 78, no. 1 (January 2000): p. 22.

41. David W. Stewart, "Speculations on the Future of Advertising Research," *Journal of Advertising* 21, no. 3 (September 1992): pp. 2–7.

42. Harold Demsetz, "Accounting for Advertising as a Barrier to Entry," *Journal of Business* 52, no. 3 (1979): pp. 345–360.

43. Stewart, p. 16.

44. L. McTier Anderson, "Marketing Science: Where's the Beef?" *Business Horizons* 37, no. 1 (January/February 1994): pp. 8–10.

45. Stigler, p. 222.

46. Stephen Miller and Lisette Berry, "Brand Salience vs. Brand Image: Two Theories of Advertising Effectiveness," *Journal of Advertising Research* 38, no. 5, (September/October 1998): p. 77.

47. Alexander L. Biel, "Do You Really Want to Know? (How Advertising Works)," *Journal of Advertising Research* 36, no. 2 (March/April 1999): p. RC2.

# CHAPTER 5

1. Quoted on Feminist Majority Leadership Alliance website, University of North Texas, http://fmla.homeip.net/loveyourbody.php.

2. Reported by KTVL News 10, Medford, Oregon, August 5, 2004, www.ktvl.com/trivia_archive.shtml.

3. Cited by PBS, "Reach Out," www.pbs.org/kcet/senioryear/reachout/do.html.

4. Quoted in Kathlyn Gay, *Caution! This May Be an Advertisement: A Teen Guide to Advertising* (New York: Franklin Watts, 1992).

5. Charles F. Adams, *Common Sense in Advertising* (New York: McGraw-Hill, 1965), pp. 191–192.

6. Alvin Toffler, *Future Shock* (New York: Bantam Books, 1970), pp. 166–167.

7. Cited in, among many others, Bob Houk, "Counter Ads," *Outlook*, October 2000, www.phaster.com/counter-ads/too_many_ads.html.

8. Personal conversation with Warren Sethachutkul, Jupiter Media, February 11, 2005.

9. Jim Rosenfield, "Lies, Damned Lies, and Internet Statistics," September 2001, www.jrosenfield.com/articles/Lies.htm.

10. John E. Calfee, *Fear of Persuasion: A New Perspective on Advertising and Regulation* (Monnaz, Switzerland: Agora, 1997), pp. 37–40.

11. John O'Toole, *The Trouble with Advertising* (New York: Chelsea House, 1981), p. 27.

12. Leo Burnett, *100 Leo's* (New York: McGraw-Hill, 2003), p. 86.

13. David Ogilvy, *Confessions of an Advertising Man* (New York: Ballantine, 1971), p. 84.

14. S. Lebergott, "Pursuing Happiness: American Consumers in the 20th Century," in Jib Fowles, ed., *Advertising and Popular Culture* (Thousand Oaks, CA: Sage Publications, 1996).

15. Calfee, p. 43.

16. Gary S. Becker and Kevin M. Murphy, "A Simple Theory of Advertising as a Good or Bad," *Quarterly Journal of Economics* 108, no. 4 (November 1993): p. 941.

17. Kyle Bagwell, *The Economics of Advertising* (Cheltenham, UK: Edward

Elgar, 2001; updated by author March 2003), pp. 22–23, www.columbia
.edu/~kwb8/papers.html.

18. Becker and Murphy, p. 943.

19. Ben Fine and Ellen Leopold, *The World of Consumption* (London; New
York: Routledge, 1990), p. 214.

20. Marshall McLuhan, "Ads: Keeping Upset with the Joneses," in John
Sherman Wright and John E. Mertes, eds., *Advertising's Role in Society* (New
York: West Publishing, 1974), pp. 5–9.

21. Jackson Lears, *Fables of Abundance: A Cultural History of Advertising in
America* (New York: Basic Books, 1994), p. 11.

22. Daniel J. Boostin, "The Thinner Life of Things," in Wright and
Mertes, pp. 113–114.

23. Gary Cross, *An All-Consuming Century: Why Commercialism Won in
Modern America* (New York: Columbia University Press, 2000), pp. 234, 238.

24. Ronald K. L. Collins and David M. Skover, "Commerce &
Communication," *Texas Law Review* 71 (1993): pp. 709–710.

25. Gary Ruskin and Robert Weissman, "The Cost of Commercialism,"
*Multinational Monitor* 20 (January–February 1999): p. 9.

26. Cross, p. 246.

27. Richard Pollay, "The Distorted Mirror: Reflections on the
Unintended Consequences of Advertising," *Journal of Marketing* 50, no. 2
(April 1986): p. 27.

28. Quoted in Edward F. Murphy, *The Crown Treasury of Relevant
Quotations* (New York: Crown Publishers, 1978), p. 14.

29. William Leiss, Stephen Kline, and Sut Jhally, "Goods as Satisifiers,"
in *Social Communication in Advertising* (London: Methuen, 1986), p. 239.

30. Quoted in Michael Schudson, "Delectable Materialism: Second
Thoughts on Consumer Culture," from David A. Crocker and Toby Linden,
eds., *Ethics of Consumption: The Good Life, Justice, and Global Stewardship* (New
York: Rowman & Littlefield, 1998), p. 353.

31. See, for example, Barbara J. Phillips, "In Defense of Advertising: A
Social Perspective," *Journal of Business Ethics* 16, no. 2 (1997): pp. 109–118.

32. Lears, "Truth, Power, Consequences," *The Nation*, September 13,
1986, p. 223.

33. Jeffrey Goldstein, "Children and Advertising—the Research,"
*Commercial Communications*, July 1998, p. 3.

34. Israel Kirzner, "Advertising," *Freeman*, September 1972, p. 521.

35. Lears, *Fables of Abundance*, p. 226.

36. Michael Prewitt, "The True Worldliness of Advertising: Apologia pro
Vita Mea," *Theology Today* 60 (October 2003): p. 393.

37. Barbara J. Phillips and Edward F. McQuarrie, "The Development, Change, and Transformation of Rhetorical Style in Magazine Advertisements, 1954–1999," *Journal of Advertising* 31, no. 4 (Winter 2002): pp. 1–14.

38. Steve Denning, "Leader's Guide to Storytelling," http://stevedenning .typepad.com/steve_denning/2004/09/use_narrative_t_1.html.

39. Clayton Collins, "The Most Successful Brand Names Inspire Sacred Devotion from Fans," *Christian Science Monitor*, July 6, 2004, p. 16.

40. Juliet B. Schor, *The Overspent American* (New York: Basic Books, 1998), p. 57.

41. Laurie Freeman, "Ultimate in Ad Lore: Buy a Dream, Not a Product," *Advertising Age*, January 8, 1996, p. S28.

42. Theodore Levitt, "The Morality (?) of Advertising," *Harvard Business Review*, July–August 1972, p. 88.

43. Ibid., pp. 88–89.

44. Pontifical Council for Social Communications, *Ethics in Advertising* (Vatican City: Vatican Documents, 1997), p. 16.

45. Prewitt, p. 391.

46. Debra Jones Ringold, "A Comment on the Pontifical Council for Social Communications' Ethics in Advertising," *Journal of Public Policy and Marketing* 17, no. 2 (Fall 1998): p. 335.

47. Prewitt, pp. 394–395.

48. Frank Presbey, *The History and Development of Advertising* (New York: Doubleday, 1929), pp. 281–282.

49. "Advertising in the 1920s," EyeWitness to History, 2000, www.eye witnesstohistory.com.

50. Jerry Maciejewski, "Can Natural Law Defend Advertising?" *Journal of Mass Media Ethics* 18, no. 2 (2003): p. 119.

51. Jerry Kirkpatrick, "A Philosophic Defense of Advertising," in R. Hovland and G. B. Wilcox, eds., *Advertising in Society* (Lincolnwood, IL: NTC Business Books, 1989), p. 513.

52. Konstantin Kolenda, "Honesty in Advertising," *Humanist*, November/December 1991, p. 37.

53. Richard Lippke, "Advertising and the Social Conditions of Autonomy," *Business & Professional Ethics Journal* 8, no. 4 (1989): p. 37.

54. Lippke, "The 'Necessary Evil' Defense of Manipulative Advertising," *Business & Professional Ethics Journal* 18, no. 1 (1999): pp. 7, 12.

55. Barry Schwartz, "Choice Cuts," *New Republic Online*, August 5, 2004, www.tnr.com.

56. Robert J. Samuelson, "The Afflictions of Affluence," *Newsweek*, March 22, 2004, www.msnbc.msn.com/id/4522583/.

57. Jennifer Warner, "Americans Are Happy and They Know It," WebMD Medical News, January 6, 2004, http://content.health.msn.com/content/article/79/96103; see also Andrew Coyne, "We're Happier Now than We've Ever Been," *National Post*, January 10, 2004.

58. "Americans Are Far More Optimistic and Have Much Higher Life Satisfaction than Europeans, Recent Surveys Show," News Release, Harris Interactive, May 21, 2003, www.harrisinteractive.com/news/printerfriend/index.asp?NewsID=624.

# CHAPTER 6

1. James Harvey Young, *The Toadstool Millionaires: A Social History of Patent Medicines in America before Federal Regulation* (Princeton, NJ: Princeton University Press, 1961), reprinted by Quackwatch.com, www.quackwatch.org/13Hx/TM/00.html.

2. Frank Presbey, *The History and Development of Advertising* (New York: Doubleday, 1929), p. 290.

3. Quoted in Young, www.quackwatch.org/13Hx/TM/06.html.

4. Ibid.

5. James B. Twitchell, *Adcult USA: The Triumph of Advertising in American Culture* (New York: Columbia University Press, 1996), p. 69.

6. Presbey, p. 289.

7. Juliann Sivulka, *Stronger than Dirt: A Cultural History of Advertising Personal Hygiene in America* (Amherst, NY: Humanity Books, 2001).

8. Wallace Janssen, "The Story of the Laws behind the Labels," FDACompliance.net, 2002, www.fdacompliance.net/free/overview/history1.htm.

9. Young, www.quackwatch.org/13Hx/TM/07.html.

10. Presbey, pp. 293–294.

11. Cynthia Crossen, "Fraudulent Claims Led U.S. to Take On Drug Makers in 1900s," *Wall Street Journal*, October 6, 2004, p. B1.

12. Author calculation based on available U.S. Census data for population and consumer prices in 1867 and 1900.

13. Thorstein Veblen, *The Theory of Business Enterprise* (New York: Charles Scribner's Sons, 1904), p. 51.

14. Crossen, p. B1.

15. Todd Seavey, "Regulation for Dummies: Is the FDA Necessary?" (book review), *Reason*, April 2004, www.reason.com/0404/cr.ts.regulation.shtml.

16. Quoted in Seavey.

17. Wallace Janssen, "The Story of the Laws behind the Labels," Part 2, FDACompliance.net, 2002, www.fdacompliance.net/free/overview/history1a.htm.

18. "History of Federal Regulation 1902–Present," FDAReview.org, www.fdareview.org/history.shtml#tenth.

19. Elizabeth Burns, "Wizard Oil Patent Medicine Salesman," *Clinician Reviews* 12, no. 7 (July 2002): p. 43.

20. "Proceedings of the National Medical Convention Held in the City of Philadelphia in May 1847," *New York Journal of Medicine* 9 (July 1847): p. 115.

21. Gene Burton, "Doctors and Their Advertising," *Business & Professional Ethics Journal* 10, no. 2 (Summer 1991): p. 33.

22. Dale Steinreich, "Real Medical Freedom," Ludwig von Mises Institute, August 27, 2004, www.mises.org/fullstory.aspx?Id=1588.

23. Janssen, www.fdacompliance.net/free/overview/history1.htm.

24. Ibid.

25. See *U.S. v. Johnson*, 221 U.S. 488 (decided May 29, 1911), http://caselaw.lp.findlaw.com/scripts/getcase.pl?court=us&vol=221&invol=488.

26. Robert B. Ekelund, Jr., and David S. Saurman, *Advertising and the Market Process: A Modern Economic View* (San Francisco: Pacific Research Institute for Public Policy, 1988), pp. 113–124.

27. See Steve Forbes, "Health Care Crisis Cure," *Forbes*, July 26, 2004, www.forbes.com/forbes/2004/0726/029_print.html.

28. Burton, p. 42.

29. Gregory M. Lamb, "Drug Risks Raise Doubt about Ads," *Christian Science Monitor*, December 24, 2004, p. 4.

30. Joel S. Weissman et al., "Physicians Report on Patient Encounters Involving Direct-to-Consumer Advertising," *Health Affairs*, April 28, 2004, http://content.healthaffairs.org/cgi/content/abstract/hlthaff.w4.219v1.

31. John Calfee, "Public Policy Issues in Direct-to-Consumer Advertising of Prescription Drugs," *Journal of Public Policy & Marketing* 21, no. 2 (Fall 2002): pp. 174–193.

32. Paul H. Rubin, "The Health Risks of Censorship: FDA's Advertising Regulations Cost Lives!" Independent Institute, November 7, 1995, www.independent.org/newsroom/article.asp?id=162.

33. Thomas H. Lee, "Me-Too Products: Friend or Foe?" *New England Journal of Medicine*, January 15, 2004, http://content.nejm.org/cgi/content/full/350/3/2.

34. Steven W. Kopp and Mary Jane Sheffet, "The Effect of Direct-to-Consumer Advertising of Prescription Drugs on Retail Gross Margins:

Empirical Evidence and Public Policy Implications," *Journal of Public Policy & Marketing* 16, no. 2 (Fall 1997): p. 274.

35. Brian Steinberg, "Food Makes Playing Up Nutrition," *Wall Street Journal*, March 26, 2004, p. B3.

36. John Calfee, *Fear of Persuasion: A New Perspective on Advertising and Regulation* (Monnaz, Switzerland: Agora Association, 1997), pp. 28–29.

37. Janis Kohanski Pappalardo and Debra Jones Ringold, "Regulating Commercial Speech in a Dynamic Environment: Forty Years of Margarine and Oil Advertising before the NLEA," *Journal of Public Policy & Marketing* 19, no. 1 (Spring 2000): pp. 74–92.

38. Seavey, www.reason.com/0404/cr.ts.regulation.shtml.

39. James Plummer, a policy analyst at Consumer Alert, has proposed such an approach. See Plummer, "Label Wars," *Consumers' Research*, February 2004, p. 34.

40. Donald J. Boudreaux, "'Puffery' in Advertising," *Free Market*, September 1995, pp. 6–7.

41. John Carey, "Drug Ads Need Stronger Medicine" (commentary), *Business Week*, February 9, 2004, pp. 84–85.

42. Eli P. Cox, III, Michael S. Wogalter, Sara L. Stokes, and Elizabeth J. Tipton Muff, "Do Product Warnings Increase Safe Behavior? A Meta-Analysis," *Journal of Public Policy & Marketing* 16, no. 2 (Fall 1997): pp. 195–204.

43. For a discussion, see Sandra J. Burke, Sandra J. Milberg, and Wendy W. Moe, "Displaying Common but Previously Neglected Health Claims on Product Labels: Understanding Competitive Advantages, Deception, and Education," *Journal of Public Policy & Marketing* 16, no. 2 (Fall 1997): pp. 242–255.

44. Jonathan W. Emord, "Pearson v. Shalala: The Beginning of the End for FDA Speech Suppression," *Journal of Public Policy & Marketing* 19, no. 1 (Spring 2000): p. 140.

45. Wroe Anderson, "The American Economy and Christian Ethics," in John Sherman Wright and John E. Mertes, eds., *Advertising's Role in Society* (New York: West Publishing, 1974), p. 258.

46. Anthony Giorgianni, "Challengers Put Ads on the Spot," *(Raleigh, NC) News & Observer*, September 18, 1996, p. 2E.

47. Suzanne Vranica, "Pharmaceuticals Try Bolder Tactics," *Wall Street Journal*, April 5, 2004, p. B3.

# CHAPTER 7

1. James U. McNeal, *Children as Consumers: Insights and Implications* (Lexington, MA: Lexington Books, 1987), p. 86.

2. "Little Spenders" (interview with Juliet Schor), *People*, October 4, 2004, p. 85.

3. John Calfee, *Fear of Persuasion: A New Perspective on Advertising and Regulation* (Monnaz, Switzerland: Agora Association, 1997), p. 64.

4. "Swedes Toy with Advertising Ban," BBC News Online, December 20, 1999, http://news.bbc.co.uk/1/hi/world/europe/572538.stm.

5. James Lyons, "Junk Food Adverts Banished during Children's TV," *The Scotsman (UK)*, November 13, 2004.

6. Mary Story and Simone French, "Food Advertising and Marketing Directed at Children and Adolescents in the U.S.," *International Journal of Behavioral Nutrition and Physical Activity* 1, no. 3 (2004): www.ijbnpa.org/content/1/1/3.

7. Ibid.

8. Joseph Pereira and Audrey Warren, "Coming Up Next . . . ," *Wall Street Journal*, March 15, 2004, p. B1.

9. Andy Levinsky, "Unintended Consequences: Children's Television Act Has Unintended Side Effects," *Humanist*, November 1999, www.findarticles.com/p/articles/mi_m1374/is_6_59/ai_57800239.

10. Jennifer Wolcott, "Hey Kid—You Wanna Buy a . . ." *Christian Science Monitor*, April 28, 2004, pp. 11–12.

11. Katy Kelly and Linda Kulman, "Kid Power," *U.S. News & World Report*, September 13, 2004, p. 50.

12. Michelle Conlin, "The Stepford Kids," *Business Week*, September 27, 2004, p. 27.

13. Kelly and Kulman, p. 49.

14. Gary Cross, *Kids' Stuff: Toys and the Changing World of American Childhood* (Cambridge, MA: Harvard University Press, 1997), pp. 14–16.

15. John Locke, *Some Thoughts concerning Education*, in *John Locke on Politics and Education* (Roslyn, NY: Walter J. Black, 1947), p. 292.

16. National Confectioners Association, "Candy Classroom: Facts: History," 2004, www.candyusa.org/Classroom/Facts/default.asp?Fact=History.

17. Cross, p. 23.

18. Stephen Kline, "Toys, Socialization, and the Commodification of Play," in Susan Strasser and Charles McGovern, eds., *Getting and Spending:*

*American and European Consumer Society in the Twentieth Century* (Cambridge: Cambridge University Press, 1998), pp. 345–346.

19. Cross, p. 31.

20. Kline, p. 347.

21. Paul Lukas, "Toy Story," *Fortune*, March 19, 2003, www.fortune.com/smallbusiness/articles/0,15114,433766,00.html.

22. Robert L. Steiner, "Does Advertising Lower Consumer Prices?" *Journal of Marketing* 37, no. 4 (October 1973): pp. 216–217.

23. Ibid., p. 224.

24. Marshall Fishwick, "Ray and Ronald Girdle the Globe," *National Forum* 74 (Fall 1994): pp. 22–26.

25. Pereira and Warren, p. B3.

26. Quoted in "Food Advertising to Children," (UK) Advertising Association, November 24, 1997, http://www.adassoc.org.uk/position/food kids/html.

27. Pereira and Warren, p. B3.

28. Marguerite Higgins, "FTC Sees No Need to Ban Ads on Junk Food," *Washington Times*, June 8, 2004, http://washingtontimes.com/business/200 40607-100647-5002r.htm.

29. Wendy Tanson, "Adolescent Obesity Largely Caused by a Lack of Physical Activity, Study Finds," Carolina News Service #220, University of North Carolina at Chapel Hill, April 14, 2003, www.unc.edu/news/archives/apr03/sutherland040903.html.

30. Timothy J. Muris, "Don't Blame TV," *Wall Street Journal*, June 25, 2004, p. A16.

31. Ray Dunne, "Should Junk Food Ads Be Banned?" BBC News Online, April 7, 2004, http://news.bbc.co.uk/2/hi/health/3586585.stm.

32. See, for example, "Child Deaths by Injury in Rich Nations," Innocenti Report Card, no. 2. (Florence, Italy: United Nations Children's Fund, February 2001).

33. Pat Mikelson, "How Do I Choose the Best Toy for My Child?" *Highlights-Jigsaw*, 2003, www.highlightsjigsaw.com/howdoichose.cfm.

34. Kline, pp. 350–351.

35. Cross, p. 235.

36. Juliet Schor, "Those Ads Are Enough to Make Your Kids Sick," *Washington Post*, September 12, 2004, p. B04.

37. "Pester Power: A Report on Attitudes in Spain and Sweden," research by NOP Solutions for the Children's Programme, European Union, December 20, 1999, www.adassoc.org.uk/pressoffice/newsreleases/nr65_pester.html.

38. Jeffrey Goldstein, "Children and Advertising—the Research," *Commercial Communications*, July 1998, pp. 1–4.

39. "Outgoing Commission Drops Case against Greek Toy Ad Ban," press release, Advertising Association, July 30, 1999, www.adassoc.org.uk/press office/newsreleases/nr61.html.

40. Darrel D. Muehling, Les Carlson, and Russell N. Laczniak, "Parental Perceptions of Toy-based Programs: An Exploratory Analysis," *Journal of Public Policy and Marketing* 11, no. 1 (Spring 1992): p. 70.

41. Mary C. Martin, "Children's Understanding of the Intent of Advertising: A Meta-Analysis," *Journal of Public Policy and Marketing* 16, no. 2 (Fall 1997): pp. 205–216.

42. Calfee, pp. 59–60.

43. McNeal, p. 185.

44. Guy Abrahams, "Merchandising Means More to Kids than TV Ads," *Marketing*, December 20, 2001, p. 18.

45. "Hey Mom and Dad, Is It OK with You if I Buy This DVD?" *Christian Science Monitor*, September 16, 2004, p. 20.

46. Goldstein, p. 3.

47. For example, see "Real-Life Results of TV Sex," *American Enterprise*, December 2004, p. 15.

# CHAPTER 8

1. Tom Reichert, *The Erotic History of Advertising* (New York: Prometheus Books, 2003), p. 24.

2. Fred L. Israel, "1897 Sears Roebuck Catalogue," 20th-Century-History-Books.com, http://20th-century-history-books.com/0877540454.html.

3. Jan Kurtz, "Dream Girls: Women in Advertising," *USA Today* magazine 125, no. 2620 (January 1997): pp. 70–80.

4. King James I, "A Counterblaste to Tobacco," 1604, www.la.utexas.edu/research/poltheory/james/blaste/blaste.html.

5. Robert B. Ekelund, Jr., and David S. Saurman, *Advertising and the Market Process: A Modern Economic View* (San Francisco: Pacific Research Institute for Public Policy, 1988), p. 94.

6. See, for example, Carol Horton Tremblay, and Victor J. Tremblay, "Reinterpreting the Effect of an Advertising Ban on Cigarette Smoking," *International Journal of Advertising* 18, no. 1 (February 1999): p. 41.

7. Richard W. Pollay, "Propaganda, Puffing and the Public Interest," *Public Relations Review* 16, no. 3 (Fall 1990): p. 40.

8. Carl Scheraga and John Calfee, "The Industry Effects of Information and Regulation in the Cigarette Market: 1950–1965," *Journal of Public Policy & Marketing* 15, no. 2 (Fall 1996): pp. 216–226.

9. Ibid.

10. A good summary can be found in John Calfee, "The Ghost of Cigarette Advertising Past," *Regulation* 20, no. 3 (1997): www.cato.org/pubs/regulation/reg20n3d.html.

11. John Calfee, *Fear of Persuasion: A New Perspective on Advertising and Regulation* (Monnaz, Switzerland: Agora Association, 1997), pp. 73–74.

12. Ibid., p. 75.

13. See, for example, Lori Dorfman, "Advertising Health: The Case for Counter-ads," *Public Health Reports* 108, no. 6 (November–December 1993): www.findarticles.com/p/articles/mi_m0835/is_n6_v108/ai_14752040.

14. William Beaver, "What to Do about Alcohol Advertising," *Business Horizons* 40, no. 4 (July–August 1997): www.findarticles.com/p/articles/mi_m1038/is_n4_v40/ai_20141970.

15. "Liquor Companies Continue to Pursue Television Ads," *Alcoholism & Drug Abuse Weekly* 14, no. 18 (May 6, 2002): p. 8.

16. John Doyle, "Even in a Modern Era, the Possibility of Prohibiting Alcohol Consumption Still Whets Activists' Appetites," *Nation's Restaurant News*, April 5, 2004.

17. Previous pledges by alcohol companies to stay away from teen-oriented media have foundered on the definition. See Craig F. Garfield, Paul J. Chung, and Paul J. Rathouz, "Alcohol Advertising in Magazines and Adolescent Readership," *Journal of the American Medical Association* 289, no. 18 (May 14, 2003): pp. 242–250.

18. Ben Lieberman, "Free Speech and Alcohol: How Much Is Too Much?" Competitive Enterprise Institute, April 8, 1999, www.cei.org/gencon/004,01588.cfm; see also Catherine Clabby, "Wine That Maketh Glad the Brain," (Raleigh, NC) *News & Observer*, January 29, 2005, www.newsobserver.com/news/story/2065468p-8449900c.html.

19. Morris E. Chafetz, "Alcohol Ads and Adolescent Behavior: What Does Science Have to Say?" (Greensboro, NC) *News & Record*, December 17, 1996.

20. Beaver. See also A. Lipsitz, G. Brake, E. J. Vincent, and M. Winters, "Another Round for the Brewers: Television Ads and Children's Alcohol Expectancies," *Journal of Applied Social Psychology* 23, no. 6 (1993): pp. 439–450; and Gerald Wilde, "Effects of Mass Media Communications on Health and Safety Habits: An Overview of Issues and Evidence," *Addiction* 88 (1993): pp. 983–996.

21. Craig Smith, "The Figures Don't Add Up for Alcohol Advertising Critics," *Marketing*, December 20, 2001, p. 17.

22. Henry Saffer, "Alcohol Advertising and Youth," *Journal of Studies on Alcohol* 63, no. 2 (March 2002): pp. 173–182.

23. Ekelund and Saurman, p. 150.

24. Lawrence Soley and Len Reid, "Taking It Off: Are Models in Magazine Ads Wearing Less?" *Journalism Quarterly* 65 (1988): pp. 960–966.

25. Richard W. Pollay, "The Subsiding Sizzle: A Descriptive History of Print Advertising, 1900–1980," *Journal of Marketing* 49 (Summer 1985): pp. 24–37.

26. Carolyn A. Lin, "Uses of Sexual Appeals in Prime-Time Television Commercials," *Sex Roles* 38 (March 1998): pp. 461–475.

27. Cited in Tom Reichert, "The Prevalence of Sexual Imagery in Ads Targeted to Young Adults," *Journal of Consumer Affairs* 37, no. 2 (Winter 2003): pp. 403–413.

28. See, for example, Mary C. Gilly, "Sex Roles in Advertising: A Comparison of Television Advertisements in Australia, Mexico, and the United States," *Journal of Marketing* 52, no. 2 (April 1998): pp. 75–86.

29. Reichert, "The Prevalence of Sexual Imagery," pp. 403–413.

30. Tom Reichert and Jacqueline Lambiase, "How to Get 'Kissably Close': Examining How Advertisers Appeal to Consumer's Sexual Needs and Desires," *Sexuality & Culture* 7, no. 3 (Summer 2003): pp. 120–137.

31. Jill Hicks Ferguson, Peggy J. Kreshel, and Spencer F. Tinkham, "In the Pages of *Ms.*: Sex Role Portrayals of Women in Advertising," *Journal of Advertising* 19, no. 1 (Winter 1990): pp. 40–52.

32. Lawrence Soley and Gary Kurzbard, "Sex in Advertising: A Comparison of 1964 and 1984 Magazine Advertisements," *Journal of Advertising* 15, no. 3 (Summer 1986): pp. 46–56.

33. Anne Morse, "'Field Guide' Bye-Bye," *National Review* Online, December 1, 2003, www.nationalreview.com/comment/morse200312010917.asp.

34. Reichert, "Sexy Ads Target Young Adults," *USA Today* magazine 129, no. 2672 (May 2001): p. 50.

35. Seth Stevenson, "Porn, Again: Another Lewd, Suggestive Ad for Meat," Slate.com, January 10, 2005, www.slate.com/id/2111999/.

36. Suzanne Vranica, "Sirius Ad Is Best Bet for Most Sexist," *Wall Street Journal*, April 1, 2004, p. B6.

37. Linda J. Waite and Kara Joyner, "Emotional and Physical Satisfaction with Sex in Married, Cohabiting, and Dating Sexual Unions: Do Men and Women Differ?" in Edward. O. Laumann and R. T. Michael, ed., *Sex, Love,*

*and Health in America* (Chicago: University of Chicago Press, 2001), pp. 239–269.

38. Steven E. Stern and Alysia D. Handel, "Sexuality and Mass Media: The History Context of Psychology's Reaction to Sexuality on the Internet," *Journal of Sex Research*, November 2001, www.findarticles.com/p/articles/mi_m2372/is_4_38/ai_84866946.

39. Maggie Gallagher, "Defending Pornography: Free Speech, Sex, and the Fight for Women's Rights" (book review), *National Review* Online, May 15, 1995, www.findarticles.com/p/articles/mi_m1282/is_n9_v47/ai_16920449.

40. Vranica, p. B6.

41. M. Wayne Alexander and Ben Judd, Jr., "Do Nudes in Ads Enhance Brand Recall?" *Journal of Advertising Research* 18, (1978): pp. 47–50.

42. For a good general discussion of the relevant research, see Thomas W. Whipple, "The Existence and Effectiveness of Sexual Content in Advertising," in Sammy R. Danna, ed., *Advertising and Popular Culture* (Bowling Green, OH: Bowling Green State University Popular Press, 1992), pp. 134–139.

43. Marilyn Y. Jones, Andrea J. S. Stanaland, and Betsy D. Gelb, "Beefcake and Cheesecake: Insights for Advertisers," *Journal of Advertising* 27, no. 2 (Summer 1998): pp. 33–52.

44. Whipple, p. 139.

45. Ibid., p. 135.

46. Jack Reitman, "Sex Sells Pool Products That Women Buy," *Wall Street Journal*, August 16, 1993, p. B6.

47. Morse.

# CHAPTER 9

1. Kevin J. Delaney, "Ads in Videogames Pose a New Threat to Media Industry," *Wall Street Journal*, July 28, 2004, p. A1.

2. Dean Foust, "Coke: Wooing the TiVo Generation," *Business Week*, March 1, 2004, p. 77.

3. Brian Steinberg and Suzanne Vranica, "Five Key Issues Could Alter the Ad Industry," *Wall Street Journal*, January 5, 2005, p. B1.

4. Suzanne Vranica, "Aflac Duck's Paddle to Stardom: Creativity on the Cheap," *Wall Street Journal*, July 30, 2004, p. B1.

5. Sholnn Freeman, "Oprah's GM Giveaway Was Stroke of Luck for Agency, Audience," *Wall Street Journal*, September 14, 2004, p. B14.

6. Anthony Biaco, "The Vanishing Mass Market," *Business Week*, July 12, 2004, pp. 61–68.

7. Betsy Streisand, "Tuning Out TV," *U.S. News & World Report*, May 24, 2004, pp. 46–47.

8. Clayton Collins, "Lines Blur between Ads and Articles," *Christian Science Monitor*, May 27, 2004, pp. 11–12.

9. Brooks Barnes, "A Good Soap Script Includes Love, Tears, and Frosted Flakes," *Wall Street Journal*, January 17, 2005, p. A1.

10. Suzanne Vranica, "The Advertising Report: Questions for Marc Goldstein," *Wall Street Journal*, September 1, 2004, p. B2A.

11. Clayton Collins, "Billboards That Walk, Talk, and Even Flirt a Little," *Christian Science Monitor*, July 8, 2004, p. 11.

12. Clayton Collins, "Not Ready for a Super Bowl Spot: Rise of Amateur Ads," *Christian Science Monitor*, February 7, 2005, p. 1.

13. Cynthia H. Cho, "For More Advertisers, the Medium Is the Text Message," *Wall Street Journal*, August 2, 2004, p. B1.

14. Collins, "Lines Blur," p. 12.

15. Brian Steinburg, "Ad Notes," *Wall Street Journal*, February 11, 2005, p. B5.

16. For a discussion, see Israel D. Nebenzahl and Eugene D. Jaffe, "Ethical Dimensions of Advertising Executions," *Journal of Business Ethics* 17 (1998): pp. 805–815.

17. Ronald Grover, "Can Mad. Ave. Make Zap-proof Ads?" *Business Week*, February 2, 2004, p. 36.

18. Nebenzahl and Jaffe, p. 812.

19. "Spider-Man on Bases Shot Down," *USA Today*, May 8, 2004.

20. Mark D. Harmon, "Affluenza: Television Use and Cultivation of Materialism," *Mass Communication & Society* 4, no. 4 (Fall 2001): pp. 405–418.

21. George Katona, "Artificially Created Wants," in John Sherman Wright and John E. Mertes, eds., *Advertising's Role in Society* (New York: West Publishing, 1974), pp. 126–127.

# Index

ABC, 80, 181, 217–18

Abercrombie and Fitch Inc., 209, 213

Acheson, Dean, 3

*Acta Diurna*, 15

Action for Children's Television, 174–75

Adams, Charles, 120

Advertising: aesthetics of, 6–8, 42–43, 116–17, 124–45, 211–12, 222–23; agencies, 3, 22–23, 33, 66, 84–86; ancient and medieval history of, 9–15; carnival culture in, 51–53, 128, 163; celebrity endorsements in, 13–14, 39, 116, 200; children and, 6, 117, 171–94, 200–205, 210, 222; consumer prices and, 6, 95–100, 104, 112, 163–66, 182–83, 200–201, 220; daily exposure to, 119–21; direct and indirect uses of, 96, 114; ethics and morality of, 2–6, 42–54, 127–35, 144–47, 160–70, 195–214; expenditures on, 35–36, 65, 73–74, 84, 103–4, 180–82, 220; freedom theme in, 39–40, 141–42, 144–46, 200, 221; health claims in, 165–67, 200–203, 205; Hollywood films about, 1–2, 4–5, 87; novels about, 5–6; product quality and, 105–7; public opinion about, 121–23, 148–49, 191, 221; regulation of, 63, 74–75, 78, 82–83, 104–13, 153–77, 183–93, 199–214; sex and, 10, 142–43, 193–99, 206–14; sports and, 39, 69, 83, 116, 139; truth in, 74–75, 82, 105, 111, 152–58, 161, 167–70; used as complementary good, 124–26; used to convey information, 98–104, 108–9, 112, 117, 124, 165, 170, 211; used to invest

**About the Author**

JOHN HOOD is President of the John Locke Foundation, a public policy think tank based in Raleigh, North Carolina, where he also serves as publisher of the foundation's monthly newspaper, the *Carolina Journal*. A professional writer whose articles have appeared in such publications as *The New Republic*, *National Review*, *Reason*, *The Wall Street Journal*, and the *New York Times*, he is the author of *Investor Politics* and *The Heroic Enterprise*.